Frank Mugisha

Advocating for LGBTQ Rights in Uganda – Unauthorized

Omar Salim

ISBN: 9781779695925
Imprint: Telephasic Workshop
Copyright © 2024 Omar Salim.
All Rights Reserved.

Contents

The Early Years   **1**
Growing up in Uganda   1
Coming to Terms with Identity   10
Facing Discrimination   22
Seeking Support and Community   34

Bibliography   **37**

Bibliography   **41**
Education and Activism   48

The Fight for LGBTQ Rights   **61**
Legal Recognition and Equality   61
Mobilizing the LGBTQ Community   72

Bibliography   **77**
Political Engagement and Advocacy   84
Raising Public Awareness   96
International Support and Pressure   108

Bibliography   **119**

Personal and Professional Challenges   **123**
Facing Adversity and Threats   123
Balancing Personal Life and Activism   135
Professional Opportunities and Recognition   147

Bibliography   **151**
Supporting Younger LGBTQ Activists   161

Overcoming Burnout and Sustaining Momentum   173

Bibliography   177

The International Impact   187
Speaking at International Conferences and Events   187

Bibliography   195

Bibliography   199
Collaborating with Global LGBTQ Organizations   201

Bibliography   213
Advocacy on the World Stage   213
Collaboration with Celebrities and Influential Voices   225
The Role of Social Media in Amplifying the Movement   237

The Future of LGBTQ Rights in Uganda   251
Recent Developments and Changes   251
The Shifting Political and Social Landscape   262
Challenges and Opportunities Ahead   274
Strategies for Continued Advocacy and Change   286
A Hopeful Vision for the Future   298

Bibliography   307

Bibliography   309

Index   311

The Early Years

Growing up in Uganda

Family and cultural background

The family and cultural background of Frank Mugisha is pivotal in understanding his journey as an LGBTQ activist in Uganda. Born into a society where traditional norms and values dominate, Frank's upbringing was steeped in the rich tapestry of Ugandan culture, which is often characterized by its communal values, strong ties to family, and deep-rooted religious beliefs.

In Uganda, the family unit is traditionally viewed as the cornerstone of society. Families are often large and extended, encompassing not just immediate relatives but also distant kin. This communal structure can provide a sense of belonging and support; however, it can also impose significant pressures on individuals, particularly those who deviate from societal norms. For Frank, growing up in such an environment meant navigating the complexities of familial expectations while grappling with his emerging identity as a member of the LGBTQ community.

Culturally, Uganda is known for its diverse ethnic groups, each with its own unique traditions and customs. The Baganda, one of the largest ethnic groups, have a rich history of kingship and governance that influences societal norms. Within this context, the expectations placed on individuals regarding marriage, procreation, and gender roles are pronounced. Frank's family, like many others, adhered to these traditional values, which often left little room for discussions around sexual orientation and gender identity.

Furthermore, the influence of religion in Uganda cannot be overstated. The country is predominantly Christian, with a significant presence of both Catholic and Protestant denominations. Religious teachings often reinforce conservative views on sexuality, leading to widespread stigmatization of LGBTQ individuals. For Frank, growing up in a religious household meant that any deviation from the heterosexual norm was met with disapproval and condemnation. This environment created a dichotomy between his personal identity and the values instilled in him by his family and society.

The intersection of culture and family dynamics in Uganda presents a complex landscape for LGBTQ individuals. For instance, many LGBTQ individuals face the threat of ostracization from their families if they come out. This is particularly evident in the case of Frank, who, during his formative years, experienced the tension between his authentic self and the expectations of his family and community. The fear of rejection often leads individuals to suppress their identities, resulting in internalized homophobia and mental health struggles.

As Frank navigated his childhood, he encountered various cultural narratives that reinforced the idea that being LGBTQ was not only unacceptable but also a source of shame. These narratives were often perpetuated through media, religious sermons, and community dialogues. The impact of these cultural beliefs on Frank's development was profound, shaping his understanding of love, acceptance, and self-worth.

To illustrate this point, consider the concept of *cultural hegemony*, as articulated by Antonio Gramsci. This theory posits that dominant cultural norms and values are maintained through social institutions, including family and religion. In Uganda, the hegemonic narrative surrounding sexuality is one that privileges heterosexuality and marginalizes LGBTQ identities. Frank's family, influenced by these dominant cultural narratives, inadvertently contributed to his struggles with self-acceptance.

Despite these challenges, Frank's family background also provided him with resilience and a strong sense of community. The values of solidarity and support that are inherent in Ugandan culture would later become crucial in his advocacy work. As he grew older, Frank began to realize that while his family's cultural beliefs posed significant obstacles, they also offered a foundation upon which he could build his activism.

In summary, Frank Mugisha's family and cultural background played a critical role in shaping his identity and activism. The interplay of traditional values, religious beliefs, and societal expectations created a challenging environment for LGBTQ individuals in Uganda. However, it also instilled in Frank a sense of resilience and a commitment to advocating for change. Understanding this background is essential for comprehending the complexities of his journey and the broader struggle for LGBTQ rights in Uganda.

Childhood experiences and influences

Frank Mugisha's childhood in Uganda was marked by a tapestry of experiences that shaped his identity and laid the groundwork for his future activism. Growing up in a society steeped in traditional values and cultural expectations, Frank navigated a world where conformity was often prioritized over individuality. The influences of his environment were profound, and they played a pivotal role in his understanding of self and his eventual journey towards advocacy for LGBTQ rights.

From an early age, Frank was exposed to the complexities of societal norms. In Uganda, cultural narratives often dictate the roles individuals are expected to play based on their gender and sexuality. Research suggests that such societal frameworks can create a restrictive environment for self-expression (Connell, 2005). Frank's family, while loving, adhered to many of these traditional beliefs, often reinforcing the notion that deviation from the norm was unacceptable. This environment fostered a sense of internal conflict within Frank as he grappled with his emerging identity.

One significant influence in Frank's childhood was his education. Schools, often seen as microcosms of society, mirrored the broader cultural attitudes towards LGBTQ individuals. Frank encountered a duality in his educational experiences; while he was encouraged to excel academically, he was also subjected to the pervasive homophobia that permeated Ugandan educational institutions. Bullying and ostracism were common among students who were perceived as different. According to a study by the International Lesbian, Gay, Bisexual, Trans and Intersex Association (ILGA, 2019), such experiences can lead to lasting psychological effects, including anxiety and depression, which Frank would later confront in his advocacy work.

Frank's friendships during childhood were another critical aspect of his formative years. As he began to understand his sexual orientation, he sought solace in friendships with peers who shared similar feelings of isolation. These connections provided a sense of belonging, albeit fraught with the fear of discovery and societal backlash. The concept of "chosen family" became particularly relevant; many LGBTQ individuals find strength and support outside of their biological families, creating networks that affirm their identities (Weston, 1997). Frank's early friendships were a lifeline, allowing him to explore his identity in a safer context, even as the threat of societal rejection loomed.

The influence of media and popular culture also played a role in shaping Frank's understanding of himself. Growing up, he was exposed to various forms of media that often portrayed LGBTQ individuals in negative or stereotypical ways. This representation—or lack thereof—impacted his self-perception and contributed to feelings of shame and confusion. As noted by scholars such as Benshoff and Griffin (2004), media representation can significantly influence societal attitudes toward marginalized groups. Frank's early experiences with media highlighted the urgent need for more positive representations of LGBTQ individuals, a realization that would fuel his later activism.

Moreover, Frank's childhood was punctuated by moments of resilience. Despite the challenges he faced, he found inspiration in stories of individuals who defied societal norms and lived authentically. These narratives, whether from literature, folklore, or the lives of local activists, instilled in him a sense of hope and possibility. The power of storytelling cannot be overstated; it serves as a catalyst for change and a means of fostering empathy (Bruner, 2002). Frank learned that through sharing his own story, he could challenge the prevailing narratives that sought to silence him.

As Frank navigated the complexities of his childhood, he began to understand the importance of advocacy. Witnessing the struggles of those around him, he felt a growing sense of responsibility to speak out against injustice. The early experiences of feeling marginalized and witnessing discrimination laid the foundation for his future work in LGBTQ activism. He recognized that the fight for acceptance and equality was not just a personal journey but a collective struggle that required solidarity and action.

In conclusion, Frank Mugisha's childhood experiences were a crucible of influences that shaped his identity and fueled his passion for activism. The interplay of cultural norms, educational challenges, friendships, media representation, and moments of resilience created a complex landscape that he navigated with courage. These formative years were not merely a backdrop to his later work; they were instrumental in forging the advocate he would become. As he reflects on his journey, Frank understands that the struggles of his youth were not in vain; they were the seeds of a powerful movement for change that continues to grow and inspire others.

Education and early aspirations

Frank Mugisha's early education played a pivotal role in shaping his identity and aspirations. Growing up in Uganda, a country where educational access can be uneven, Frank was fortunate to attend schools that provided not only academic knowledge but also a space for personal growth and self-discovery. Education, often seen as a tool for empowerment, became a double-edged sword for Frank, as it exposed him to both progressive ideas and the harsh realities of societal norms regarding sexuality.

The Role of Education

Education in Uganda is often influenced by a myriad of factors, including socio-economic status, geographical location, and cultural beliefs. For Frank, the initial years of schooling were marked by a thirst for knowledge and a desire to excel. This aspiration was fueled by his family's emphasis on education as a pathway to a better life. His parents, despite their traditional views, recognized the importance of schooling in shaping Frank's future.

As Frank advanced through his education, he encountered a curriculum that often sidelined LGBTQ issues. This absence left a void in understanding and acceptance, which he would later confront during his activism. The lack of representation in educational materials not only perpetuated ignorance but also contributed to the stigma surrounding LGBTQ identities. Frank's experiences highlighted the need for inclusive education that addresses the realities of all students, particularly those from marginalized communities.

Early Aspirations and Influences

From a young age, Frank aspired to be a leader and advocate for change. Influenced by teachers who encouraged critical thinking and open dialogue, he began to envision a future where he could impact societal norms. His early aspirations were not merely about personal success; they were deeply intertwined with a desire to uplift others who faced discrimination and marginalization.

During his secondary education, Frank became involved in student organizations that championed various social issues, including human rights. This engagement not only honed his leadership skills but also provided a platform for him to voice concerns about the treatment of LGBTQ individuals in Uganda. The discussions he participated in often centered around equality, justice, and the importance of standing up against oppression, themes that resonated with his personal experiences.

Challenges in Education

Despite his aspirations, Frank faced significant challenges within the educational system. The pervasive homophobia in Ugandan society often seeped into schools, creating an environment where LGBTQ students were marginalized. Frank experienced bullying and discrimination from peers, which not only affected his academic performance but also took a toll on his mental health.

The internal struggle between his identity and the societal expectations imposed on him was exacerbated by the fear of being outed. This fear was not unfounded; many LGBTQ individuals in Uganda faced severe repercussions for their identities, including expulsion from educational institutions. The tension between his aspirations and the reality of his environment created a profound sense of isolation.

Supportive Figures and Mentorship

Amidst these challenges, Frank found solace in supportive teachers and mentors who recognized his potential. These individuals played a crucial role in nurturing his aspirations and encouraging him to pursue higher education. They provided guidance on navigating the complexities of identity and activism within the educational landscape.

One particular teacher, who had a background in social justice, became a mentor to Frank. This relationship was instrumental in shaping his understanding of advocacy and the importance of education in driving social change. Through discussions about global human rights movements and the role of youth in activism, Frank's aspirations began to crystallize into a clear vision: to become an advocate for LGBTQ rights in Uganda.

The Intersection of Education and Activism

As Frank transitioned into higher education, he became increasingly aware of the intersection between education and activism. He sought out programs that aligned with his passion for social justice and human rights. This pursuit led him to engage with organizations that focused on LGBTQ issues, allowing him to combine his academic interests with his advocacy work.

In university, Frank encountered a diverse array of perspectives that challenged his understanding of identity and activism. He participated in workshops and seminars that addressed the importance of inclusive education, which further fueled his desire to advocate for systemic change within the Ugandan education system. His early aspirations evolved into a commitment to ensure that future generations of LGBTQ students could access an education that affirmed their identities rather than suppressed them.

Conclusion

Frank Mugisha's educational journey was marked by both aspirations and challenges. His experiences highlight the critical role that education plays in shaping identities and fostering advocacy. As he navigated the complexities of being an LGBTQ individual in Uganda, Frank's early aspirations laid the groundwork for his future as a prominent activist. The intersection of education and activism became a cornerstone of his work, demonstrating that education is not merely a pathway to personal success but a powerful tool for societal transformation. Through his story, we see the potential for education to empower individuals to challenge oppressive systems and advocate for a more inclusive society.

Initial encounters with LGBTQ issues

In the context of Uganda, where traditional norms and cultural values often clash with the realities of sexual diversity, Frank Mugisha's early encounters with LGBTQ issues were both illuminating and challenging. Growing up in a society where homosexuality was not only stigmatized but criminalized, these initial experiences shaped his understanding of identity and belonging.

Frank's first brush with LGBTQ issues came during his adolescence, a time when the quest for self-identity is particularly poignant. As he navigated the complexities of teenage life, he began to notice the subtle yet pervasive undercurrents of homophobia in his surroundings. This societal conditioning manifested itself in various forms, from derogatory jokes about gay individuals to overt hostility towards those perceived as different. Such encounters left a profound impact on Frank, instilling in him a sense of confusion and fear.

One of the critical theories that underpin the understanding of LGBTQ issues in Uganda is the concept of *internalized homophobia*. This psychological phenomenon occurs when individuals internalize societal prejudices against their sexual orientation, leading to self-hatred and denial. For Frank, the pervasive negative attitudes towards homosexuality created an internal conflict that was difficult to reconcile. He grappled with the fear of being ostracized by his peers and family, which made it challenging to embrace his true self.

An illustrative example of this internalized struggle occurred during a school event where a guest speaker, a well-known local figure, made inflammatory remarks about LGBTQ individuals. Frank felt a wave of shame wash over him as he listened to the crowd's laughter and agreement, reinforcing the idea that being different was something to be ridiculed. In that moment, he realized that his identity was at odds with the societal narrative, a realization that would fuel his later activism.

Moreover, Frank's initial encounters with LGBTQ issues were not solely personal; they were also shaped by the political landscape of Uganda. The infamous Anti-Homosexuality Bill, which sought to impose severe penalties on homosexuality, was a looming threat during his formative years. This legislation not only criminalized same-sex relationships but also legitimized discrimination and violence against LGBTQ individuals. Frank's awareness of this political climate heightened his sense of urgency to understand the implications of being part of the LGBTQ community in Uganda.

In seeking solace and understanding, Frank began to explore LGBTQ literature and media, which provided him with a broader perspective on issues of identity and rights. Works by authors such as Audre Lorde and James Baldwin resonated with him, offering narratives that celebrated diversity and challenged societal norms. These texts became a refuge, illuminating the struggles and triumphs of LGBTQ individuals around the world and allowing Frank to envision a future where he could live authentically.

Despite the challenges he faced, Frank's initial encounters with LGBTQ issues ultimately laid the groundwork for his advocacy. They ignited a passion for justice and equality, propelling him towards a path of activism that would define his life. By confronting the harsh realities of discrimination and violence, he began to understand the importance of community and support in the fight for LGBTQ rights.

In conclusion, Frank Mugisha's early experiences with LGBTQ issues were marked by a complex interplay of societal norms, internalized prejudices, and a burgeoning awareness of his identity. These encounters not only shaped his understanding of the LGBTQ landscape in Uganda but also set the stage for his future endeavors as a prominent advocate. As he continued to navigate the challenges of growing up in a hostile environment, Frank's resolve to champion LGBTQ rights only grew stronger, laying the foundation for the impactful work he would undertake in the years to come.

Discovering personal identity

The journey of discovering one's personal identity, particularly within the LGBTQ context in Uganda, is often fraught with complexities, societal pressures, and deep introspection. For Frank Mugisha, this journey began in the vibrant landscapes of Uganda, where the interplay of culture, family, and societal norms shaped his understanding of self.

Identity formation is a multifaceted process influenced by various factors, including societal expectations, cultural norms, and personal experiences. According to Erik Erikson's theory of psychosocial development, identity versus role confusion is a critical stage during adolescence, where individuals explore their sense of self and personal values. In Uganda, where prevailing cultural attitudes often stigmatize LGBTQ identities, this exploration can be particularly challenging.

$$I = f(S, C, E) \qquad (1)$$

Where I represents personal identity, S signifies societal influences, C denotes cultural factors, and E embodies personal experiences. Each component contributes uniquely to shaping an individual's identity.

Frank's early encounters with LGBTQ issues were not just intellectual but deeply emotional. Growing up in a society that often conflated homosexuality with immorality, he faced the daunting task of reconciling his feelings with the expectations of those around him. The internal conflict was palpable; he found himself grappling with the fear of rejection from family and friends while simultaneously yearning for authenticity.

In his teenage years, Frank began to recognize the discrepancies between societal narratives and his lived reality. The societal narrative, often steeped in homophobia and discrimination, painted a picture of LGBTQ individuals as deviant or abnormal. This narrative was reinforced by religious teachings and cultural norms that positioned heterosexuality as the only acceptable orientation. As a result, he experienced moments of profound isolation, feeling as though he was trapped in a world that did not accept him.

The moment of self-discovery often comes with a catalyst—an event or realization that propels individuals toward acceptance. For Frank, this moment was sparked by a combination of peer influence and exposure to LGBTQ literature and media. He found solace in stories of others who had navigated similar paths, which provided a framework for understanding his own feelings. The visibility of LGBTQ figures in media, though limited in Uganda, offered him a glimpse of possibility, a narrative that countered the dominant discourse of shame.

Navigating this journey was not without its pitfalls. The fear of being outed loomed large, as societal repercussions could lead to harassment or violence. In Uganda, where the Anti-Homosexuality Act has led to increased persecution of LGBTQ individuals, the stakes were high. Frank's realization that his identity was not a flaw but a fundamental aspect of who he was marked a significant turning point. This realization was both liberating and terrifying, as it meant embracing a truth that society vehemently rejected.

Frank also faced the challenge of familial acceptance. Disclosing his identity to family members was a moment filled with trepidation. In many cases, LGBTQ individuals in Uganda encounter rejection or hostility from their families, which can exacerbate feelings of loneliness and despair. Frank's experience was no different; he had to navigate the delicate balance between honesty and self-preservation.

The process of self-acceptance involved not only acknowledging his identity but also actively seeking out LGBTQ spaces where he could connect with others who shared similar experiences. These spaces became vital for his emotional well-being and provided a sense of community that was often missing in his everyday life. Through interactions with fellow LGBTQ individuals, Frank learned that he was not alone in his struggles; others had faced similar challenges and had emerged stronger.

In Uganda, where the law and societal attitudes often clash with the realities of LGBTQ existence, the discovery of personal identity is intertwined with activism. Frank recognized that his journey was not just about self-acceptance but also about advocating for the rights of others who faced similar challenges. The intersection of personal identity and activism became a driving force in his life, propelling him to fight for a society that embraces diversity.

The journey of discovering personal identity is ongoing; it evolves as individuals encounter new experiences and challenges. For Frank Mugisha, the path of self-discovery was marked by resilience, courage, and a commitment to authenticity. He learned that identity is not a static concept but a dynamic interplay of self-perception, societal influence, and personal growth.

In conclusion, the process of discovering personal identity, particularly within the LGBTQ context in Uganda, is a complex journey filled with both challenges and triumphs. Frank's story exemplifies the struggle for self-acceptance in a society that often marginalizes LGBTQ individuals. His journey underscores the importance of community, visibility, and advocacy in shaping a more inclusive narrative for future generations. As he continues to navigate his identity, Frank remains a beacon of hope for those seeking to embrace their true selves in the face of adversity.

Coming to Terms with Identity

Internal struggles and self-acceptance

The journey of self-acceptance for many LGBTQ individuals is often fraught with internal conflicts and emotional turmoil. For Frank Mugisha, growing up in Uganda, a country notorious for its harsh stance against homosexuality, the path to self-acceptance was riddled with challenges that tested his resilience and sense of identity.

Understanding Internal Struggles

Internal struggles refer to the psychological conflict that arises when an individual's personal identity clashes with societal expectations and norms. This phenomenon is particularly pronounced in cultures where LGBTQ identities are stigmatized. The concept of *cognitive dissonance* (Festinger, 1957) plays a pivotal role here, as individuals experience discomfort stemming from the conflict between their feelings of attraction and the negative societal messages they receive.

Mugisha faced a profound sense of dissonance as he grappled with his sexual orientation. Growing up, he was inundated with cultural narratives that equated homosexuality with immorality and deviance. The pervasive homophobia in Ugandan society not only instilled fear but also led to feelings of shame and isolation. This internal conflict often manifests in a cycle of self-denial, where individuals suppress their true selves to conform to societal expectations.

The Role of Family and Community

Family and community expectations are critical factors that influence self-acceptance. In many cultures, including Ugandan society, family structures are built on traditional values that often reject non-heteronormative identities. Mugisha's initial reluctance to accept his identity was compounded by the fear of disappointing his family and facing rejection from his community. The expectations placed upon him created a barrier to self-acceptance, as he feared the consequences of living authentically.

Research has shown that familial acceptance is a significant predictor of positive mental health outcomes for LGBTQ youth (Ryan et al., 2009). In contrast, rejection can lead to a myriad of negative outcomes, including depression, anxiety, and suicidal ideation. For Mugisha, the fear of rejection from his family was a powerful deterrent that delayed his journey towards self-acceptance.

Cultural and Societal Pressures

The societal pressures in Uganda further exacerbated Mugisha's internal struggles. The legal framework surrounding LGBTQ rights in Uganda is characterized by severe penalties for homosexual acts, including imprisonment and societal ostracism. This hostile environment fosters a culture of silence and fear, making it difficult for individuals to embrace their identities openly.

The concept of *minority stress* (Meyer, 2003) elucidates how the chronic stress faced by marginalized groups leads to negative mental health outcomes. Mugisha experienced this stress firsthand, as societal hostility and discrimination weighed heavily on his self-perception and mental well-being. The constant threat of violence and persecution created an atmosphere where self-acceptance felt like a distant dream.

The Path to Self-Acceptance

Despite these formidable challenges, Mugisha's journey towards self-acceptance began with small, yet significant steps. Engaging with supportive friends who understood his struggles provided him with a safe space to explore his identity. This sense of belonging was crucial in counteracting the isolation imposed by societal rejection.

Moreover, Mugisha sought solace in literature and media that depicted LGBTQ experiences. Representation plays a vital role in fostering self-acceptance; seeing individuals like oneself in positive narratives can validate one's identity and inspire courage. This exposure helped Mugisha reframe his understanding of what it meant to be LGBTQ in a society that often vilified such identities.

The Importance of Self-Reflection

Self-reflection emerged as a critical tool in Mugisha's journey. Engaging in introspective practices allowed him to confront his fears and insecurities. The act of journaling, for instance, became a therapeutic outlet where he could articulate his thoughts and emotions without judgment. This process of self-exploration is essential in the journey towards self-acceptance, as it encourages individuals to embrace their authentic selves.

Psychological theories such as *self-affirmation theory* (Steele, 1988) suggest that individuals can bolster their self-worth by affirming their values and identities. Mugisha's commitment to LGBTQ advocacy became a powerful affirmation of his identity, transforming his struggles into a source of strength and purpose.

Conclusion

The internal struggles faced by Frank Mugisha on his path to self-acceptance exemplify the complex interplay between identity, societal norms, and personal resilience. While the journey is often fraught with challenges, it is also marked by moments of empowerment and growth. Through self-reflection, supportive relationships, and a commitment to advocacy, Mugisha not only embraced his identity but also became a beacon of hope for others navigating similar struggles in Uganda and beyond.

As he continues to advocate for LGBTQ rights, Mugisha's story serves as a reminder of the importance of self-acceptance in the broader fight for equality and justice. In a world that often seeks to marginalize, the journey towards embracing one's true self remains a powerful act of defiance and resilience.

Disclosing sexuality to close friends

Disclosing one's sexuality to close friends is a significant and often daunting step in the journey of self-acceptance and identity affirmation. This process, known in psychological terms as "coming out," involves revealing one's sexual orientation to others, which can have profound implications for both the individual and their relationships. This subsection will explore the complexities of this disclosure process, the emotional and social challenges it presents, and the potential outcomes that may arise.

The Importance of Disclosure

The act of disclosing one's sexuality can serve multiple purposes. According to [2], coming out can be a liberating experience that fosters authenticity and self-acceptance. It allows individuals to live openly and honestly, which can lead to a greater sense of well-being and psychological health. The process is not merely a personal one; it often involves navigating social dynamics and the perceptions of those within one's immediate circle.

Challenges of Disclosure

Despite its potential benefits, the disclosure process is fraught with challenges. Individuals may grapple with fears of rejection, judgment, or misunderstanding from their friends. Research indicates that fear of negative reactions is a significant barrier to coming out, as noted by [?]. This fear can be compounded in cultures where LGBTQ identities are stigmatized or criminalized, such as in Uganda, where societal norms strongly dictate heteronormativity.

The emotional toll of this fear can manifest in various ways, leading to anxiety and stress. For instance, [?] emphasizes that individuals often experience a heightened sense of vulnerability when sharing such personal information, which can result in internal conflict and hesitation. This internal struggle may be exacerbated by the societal pressures and expectations surrounding gender and sexuality.

Strategies for Disclosure

When preparing to disclose their sexuality, individuals may adopt various strategies to facilitate a positive conversation. One effective approach is to choose a supportive environment, as highlighted by [?]. Creating a safe space can mitigate anxiety and encourage open dialogue. Additionally, individuals may consider timing their disclosure during moments of shared intimacy or trust, which can help strengthen the bond between friends.

Another strategy involves using indirect methods of communication, such as discussing LGBTQ topics in general before revealing one's orientation. This can serve as a gauge for friends' reactions and beliefs, allowing the individual to assess the potential risks involved in disclosing their own identity.

Reactions from Friends

The reactions of friends can vary widely and may include support, confusion, or even hostility. Positive responses can reinforce the individual's sense of self and provide crucial emotional support. For example, [?] found that supportive friends often play a pivotal role in the coming-out process, helping individuals navigate their new identities and the challenges that accompany them.

Conversely, negative reactions can lead to feelings of isolation and distress. Friends may express disbelief, discomfort, or even rejection, which can profoundly impact the individual's mental health. Such experiences are not uncommon, especially in conservative environments where LGBTQ identities are less accepted.

The Role of Support Networks

In the face of potential negative reactions, having a robust support network can be invaluable. Individuals may seek guidance from LGBTQ organizations, support groups, or online communities that provide resources and encouragement. These networks can offer strategies for coping with rejection and foster resilience in the face of adversity.

Moreover, the involvement of allies—friends and family members who support LGBTQ rights—can significantly influence the outcomes of disclosure. Allies can help advocate for acceptance and understanding within the broader community, creating a more inclusive environment for all.

Conclusion

Disclosing one's sexuality to close friends is a critical milestone in the journey of self-acceptance. While it presents a host of challenges, including fear of rejection and the potential for negative reactions, it can also lead to greater authenticity and emotional support. By employing effective strategies for disclosure and fostering supportive networks, individuals can navigate this complex process with resilience and hope. Ultimately, the act of coming out is not just about revealing one's identity; it is about embracing the freedom to live one's truth and inspiring others to do the same.

Cultural and societal expectations

Cultural and societal expectations in Uganda significantly influence the lives of LGBTQ individuals, often creating a complex web of challenges that intertwine with their personal identities. In a society where traditional norms and values are deeply entrenched, the expectations surrounding gender roles, sexuality, and relationships can be particularly oppressive. This section delves into the various dimensions of these expectations, examining their impact on LGBTQ individuals and the broader implications for society.

1. Traditional Gender Roles

In Uganda, traditional gender roles are rigidly defined, with distinct expectations for men and women. Men are often seen as the breadwinners and protectors, while women are expected to be nurturing homemakers. This binary understanding of gender creates a challenging environment for those who do not conform to these roles. For instance, male individuals who identify as gay may face severe backlash not only from their families but also from their communities for deviating from the expected masculine behavior. This pressure can lead to internalized homophobia, where individuals struggle to accept their identities due to societal condemnation.

2. The Influence of Religion

Religion plays a pivotal role in shaping societal attitudes towards LGBTQ individuals in Uganda. Predominantly Christian and Muslim communities often view homosexuality as sinful, reinforcing negative stereotypes and fostering discrimination. Religious leaders frequently use their platforms to propagate anti-LGBTQ rhetoric, which further entrenches cultural expectations. For example, sermons that depict LGBTQ individuals as morally corrupt can lead to societal ostracism, making it exceedingly difficult for individuals to live openly. The intersection of faith and societal norms creates an environment where LGBTQ individuals are compelled to hide their identities, leading to a dissonance between their true selves and the personas they present to the world.

3. The Role of Family

Family expectations are another significant factor that shapes the experiences of LGBTQ individuals in Uganda. Families often prioritize societal acceptance and reputation over the well-being of their LGBTQ members. The pressure to marry and produce children can be overwhelming, creating a sense of urgency for individuals to conform to heterosexual norms. This expectation is particularly evident in the context of arranged marriages, where LGBTQ individuals may be coerced into relationships that deny them the opportunity to express their authentic selves. The fear of familial rejection can lead to profound mental health issues, including anxiety and depression, as individuals grapple with their identities in secret.

4. Societal Norms and Peer Pressure

Societal norms dictate that any deviation from heterosexuality is met with hostility. This hostility often manifests in bullying, harassment, and violence against LGBTQ individuals. Peer pressure can exacerbate these challenges, as individuals may feel compelled to conform to heteronormative behaviors to avoid being ostracized. The fear of social exclusion can lead to a phenomenon known as "passing," where LGBTQ individuals attempt to blend into heterosexual society by suppressing their identities. This suppression can have detrimental effects on their mental health, leading to feelings of isolation and despair.

5. Media Representation

The representation of LGBTQ individuals in Ugandan media is largely negative, further entrenching societal expectations. Media portrayals often depict LGBTQ individuals as deviant or immoral, which reinforces public perceptions and contributes to widespread discrimination. This negative representation creates a feedback loop where societal expectations shape media narratives, which in turn influence public attitudes. The lack of positive representation means that LGBTQ individuals often lack role models, making it more challenging to envision a future where they can live openly and authentically.

6. Intersectionality and Multiple Identities

Cultural and societal expectations do not exist in a vacuum; they intersect with other identities such as race, class, and religion. For example, an LGBTQ individual from a lower socioeconomic background may face compounded discrimination, as their financial status can limit access to resources and support networks. Intersectionality theory posits that individuals experience overlapping systems of oppression, which can exacerbate the challenges faced by LGBTQ individuals in Uganda. Understanding these intersections is crucial for developing effective advocacy strategies that address the unique experiences of marginalized groups within the LGBTQ community.

7. Conclusion

The cultural and societal expectations in Uganda create a challenging landscape for LGBTQ individuals, who must navigate a myriad of pressures while seeking to live authentically. Traditional gender roles, religious influences, family expectations, societal norms, and negative media representations all contribute to a climate of discrimination and fear. To foster a more inclusive society, it is essential to challenge these expectations through education, advocacy, and the promotion of positive representation. Only by addressing the root causes of discrimination can we hope to create a future where all individuals, regardless of their sexual orientation, can live freely and authentically in Uganda.

$$\text{Mental Health Impact} = f(\text{Cultural Expectations, Family Reactions, Societal Norms}) \tag{2}$$

This equation illustrates the complex relationship between cultural expectations, family reactions, and societal norms, and their collective impact on the mental health of LGBTQ individuals. The function f represents the multifaceted nature of these interactions, highlighting the need for comprehensive approaches to support LGBTQ individuals in Uganda.

Reactions of family and community

The journey of self-discovery and acceptance is often intertwined with the reactions of family and community. In the context of LGBTQ individuals in Uganda, these reactions can significantly influence personal identity formation and the overall well-being of individuals. This section explores the spectrum of responses encountered by Frank Mugisha as he navigated his identity, highlighting the complexities of familial and communal dynamics.

Family Reactions

Family reactions to an individual's coming out can vary widely, ranging from acceptance and support to rejection and hostility. For many LGBTQ individuals, the family represents a critical source of support, yet it can also become a battleground of conflicting values.

In Frank's case, the initial reaction from his family was one of confusion and denial. His parents, steeped in traditional beliefs, struggled to reconcile their expectations with Frank's identity. This reaction is not uncommon in Ugandan society, where cultural norms and religious beliefs often dictate perceptions of sexuality. The clash between personal identity and familial expectations can lead to emotional turmoil, as individuals grapple with the fear of losing familial bonds.

$$\text{Acceptance} = f(\text{Cultural beliefs, Religious values, Family dynamics}) \quad (3)$$

This equation illustrates that acceptance is a function of various factors, including cultural beliefs, religious values, and the dynamics within the family unit. For instance, families with strong religious affiliations may be less likely to accept LGBTQ identities due to doctrinal teachings that condemn homosexuality. Conversely, families that prioritize love and support may exhibit more acceptance, creating a nurturing environment for their LGBTQ members.

Community Reactions

The reactions of the broader community can further complicate the experiences of LGBTQ individuals. In Uganda, where societal attitudes towards homosexuality are predominantly negative, the community often mirrors the sentiments of religious and cultural institutions. The fear of ostracism and discrimination looms large, compelling many individuals to remain silent about their identities.

Frank's experiences within his community were marked by both solidarity and hostility. While he found pockets of acceptance among progressive allies and LGBTQ organizations, he also faced backlash from more conservative factions. This duality of community response underscores the importance of safe spaces where LGBTQ individuals can express themselves without fear of retribution.

$$\text{Community Support} = g(\text{Visibility, Advocacy, Cultural change}) \quad (4)$$

Here, community support is expressed as a function of visibility, advocacy efforts, and cultural change. Increased visibility of LGBTQ issues through activism and media representation can foster a more accepting environment. For example, public demonstrations and awareness campaigns have played a pivotal role in shifting perceptions, challenging stereotypes, and fostering dialogue within communities.

The Impact of Reactions on Identity Formation

The reactions of family and community significantly impact the identity formation process. Positive reinforcement from family and community can bolster an individual's self-esteem and facilitate a journey towards self-acceptance. In contrast, negative reactions can lead to internalized homophobia, mental health challenges, and feelings of isolation.

Frank's narrative illustrates the profound effects of familial and communal reactions. While he experienced moments of rejection, he also found strength in the support of chosen family and allies. This concept of chosen family is particularly vital for LGBTQ individuals, providing a sense of belonging and acceptance that may be absent in their biological families.

Examples of Support and Rejection

To illustrate the spectrum of reactions, consider the following examples:

1. **Supportive Family**: A family that embraces their child's identity may engage in open dialogues, educate themselves about LGBTQ issues, and actively support their child's advocacy efforts. This support can create a foundation for resilience and empowerment.

2. **Rejecting Family**: Conversely, a family that reacts with hostility may resort to shaming, disownment, or even violence. Such reactions can lead to significant emotional distress and may push individuals to seek refuge in LGBTQ communities, fostering resilience through solidarity.

3. **Community Allies**: Community members who stand in solidarity with LGBTQ individuals can amplify their voices and provide crucial support. These allies often participate in advocacy, challenging discriminatory practices and promoting inclusivity.

4. **Community Hostility**: On the other hand, community hostility can manifest in various forms, including harassment, exclusion from social events, and even threats to personal safety. This environment can create a climate of fear, stifling the expression of one's identity.

In conclusion, the reactions of family and community play a pivotal role in shaping the experiences of LGBTQ individuals like Frank Mugisha. Navigating these complex dynamics requires resilience, support, and a commitment to advocacy. As societal attitudes continue to evolve, the hope remains that more families and communities will embrace diversity and foster acceptance, paving the way for a more inclusive future.

Navigating LGBTQ spaces in Uganda

Navigating LGBTQ spaces in Uganda is a complex and often perilous journey, marked by a blend of resilience, community, and the ever-present threat of discrimination. The LGBTQ community in Uganda faces numerous challenges in carving out safe spaces where individuals can express their identities freely and authentically. This subsection explores the dynamics of these spaces, the theoretical frameworks that inform our understanding of them, the problems faced by LGBTQ individuals, and real-life examples that illustrate the struggle for visibility and acceptance.

Theoretical Frameworks

To understand the navigation of LGBTQ spaces in Uganda, it is essential to apply intersectionality theory, which posits that individuals experience overlapping systems of oppression based on their identities, such as sexual orientation, gender identity, ethnicity, and socio-economic status. According to Crenshaw (1989), intersectionality allows us to see how various forms of discrimination interconnect, creating unique experiences for individuals within marginalized communities. In Uganda, the intersection of colonial legacies, religious conservatism, and cultural norms significantly shapes the experiences of LGBTQ individuals.

Additionally, the concept of safe spaces is crucial in this context. Safe spaces are environments where individuals can express themselves without fear of judgment or harm. For LGBTQ individuals in Uganda, these spaces often manifest in clandestine gatherings, private homes, or online forums, where they can find solace and support. However, the precarious nature of these spaces means that they are constantly under threat from societal pressures and legal repercussions.

Challenges Faced in LGBTQ Spaces

The challenges faced by LGBTQ individuals in Uganda are manifold. One of the most pressing issues is the pervasive climate of fear and violence. Homophobic laws, such as the Anti-Homosexuality Act, create an environment where individuals risk imprisonment or violence for simply existing as LGBTQ. This legal backdrop discourages many from seeking out LGBTQ spaces, as doing so could lead to exposure and persecution.

Moreover, societal stigma surrounding homosexuality often seeps into these spaces, making it difficult for individuals to form genuine connections. The fear of being outed can lead to a culture of mistrust, where individuals are hesitant to share their true selves, even in supposedly safe environments. This mistrust can hinder the formation of supportive networks that are vital for advocacy and community-building.

Examples of LGBTQ Spaces in Uganda

Despite these challenges, LGBTQ individuals in Uganda have found innovative ways to create and maintain spaces for connection and support. One notable example is the establishment of underground support groups, where members meet discreetly to share experiences, resources, and strategies for coping with discrimination. These groups often rely on word-of-mouth and encrypted communication to protect their members' identities.

Another example is the use of social media platforms, which have become essential tools for the LGBTQ community. Online spaces allow individuals to connect with others who share similar experiences, fostering a sense of belonging that may be difficult to find in their immediate environments. Activists have leveraged platforms like Twitter and Facebook to organize events, share stories, and raise awareness about LGBTQ issues in Uganda, effectively creating virtual safe spaces.

The Role of Activism in Shaping LGBTQ Spaces

Activism plays a crucial role in shaping the landscape of LGBTQ spaces in Uganda. Organizations such as Sexual Minorities Uganda (SMUG) and other grassroots movements work tirelessly to advocate for the rights of LGBTQ individuals. These organizations often provide safe spaces for community members to gather, access resources, and engage in activism.

For example, SMUG has been instrumental in organizing events that celebrate LGBTQ identities, such as pride marches and awareness campaigns. These events not only serve as a platform for visibility but also foster solidarity among community members, reinforcing the notion that they are not alone in their struggles.

Conclusion

Navigating LGBTQ spaces in Uganda is fraught with challenges, yet it is also a testament to the resilience and creativity of the community. By employing theoretical frameworks such as intersectionality and the concept of safe spaces, we can better understand the complexities of these environments. Despite the oppressive legal and societal barriers, LGBTQ individuals continue to forge connections and create spaces that affirm their identities. The ongoing fight for visibility and acceptance is a powerful reminder of the strength found in community and the importance of solidarity in the face of adversity.

$$\text{Safe Space} = (\text{Support} + \text{Acceptance}) - \text{Fear} \qquad (5)$$

This equation illustrates that a safe space is created when support and acceptance outweigh the fear that often permeates LGBTQ experiences in Uganda. The journey towards establishing these spaces is ongoing, but with continued advocacy and community-building efforts, the future holds promise for a more inclusive and accepting society.

Facing Discrimination

The impact of homophobia in Uganda

Homophobia in Uganda is not merely a social issue; it is a pervasive phenomenon that infiltrates various aspects of life, including legal, political, and cultural dimensions. The impact of homophobia is particularly pronounced in a country where laws and societal norms are often hostile to LGBTQ individuals. This section explores the multifaceted effects of homophobia in Uganda, highlighting its theoretical underpinnings, the problems it creates, and real-life examples that illustrate its severity.

Theoretical Framework

To understand the impact of homophobia in Uganda, it is essential to consider the socio-cultural theories that explain prejudice and discrimination. Social Identity Theory posits that individuals derive a sense of self from their group memberships, leading to in-group favoritism and out-group discrimination. In Uganda, where traditional norms emphasize heteronormativity, those who identify as LGBTQ are often marginalized and subjected to systemic discrimination.

$$S = \frac{I_{in} - I_{out}}{I_{in} + I_{out}} \qquad (6)$$

Where S represents social identity, I_{in} is the perceived value of the in-group, and I_{out} is the perceived value of the out-group. In this context, the negative valuation of LGBTQ identities contributes to a hostile environment where homophobia thrives.

Legal and Political Consequences

The legal framework in Uganda exacerbates the impact of homophobia. The infamous Anti-Homosexuality Act of 2014, though annulled on a technicality, signified a governmental endorsement of anti-LGBTQ sentiments. This legislation criminalized same-sex relationships and imposed severe penalties, including life imprisonment. The mere existence of such laws fosters an environment of fear and repression, discouraging individuals from expressing their identities.

Moreover, the political climate is characterized by leaders who openly denounce LGBTQ rights, often using homophobia as a tool for political gain. President Yoweri Museveni has been known to equate homosexuality with moral decay, further embedding homophobic attitudes within the national consciousness. This rhetoric not only legitimizes discrimination but also emboldens individuals and groups to act on their prejudices, leading to increased violence against LGBTQ individuals.

Social and Psychological Impacts

The social ramifications of homophobia in Uganda are profound. LGBTQ individuals face ostracization from their families and communities, often leading to homelessness and economic disenfranchisement. The stigma associated with being LGBTQ is so severe that many individuals are compelled to hide their identities, resulting in a pervasive culture of secrecy and fear.

Psychologically, the impact of homophobia can lead to severe mental health issues, including anxiety, depression, and suicidal ideation. A study conducted by the Uganda-based organization Sexual Minorities Uganda (SMUG) found that over 80% of LGBTQ respondents reported experiencing mental health challenges due to societal discrimination. The constant threat of violence and rejection creates a hostile environment that is detrimental to the well-being of LGBTQ individuals.

Real-Life Examples

Numerous instances highlight the devastating effects of homophobia in Uganda. In 2014, the brutal murder of LGBTQ activist David Kato sent shockwaves through the community and beyond. Kato's death was not an isolated incident; it was a reflection of the violence that LGBTQ individuals face daily. Following his murder, many activists reported heightened threats to their safety, leading to increased calls for international support and intervention.

Additionally, the case of a Ugandan gay man who was publicly outed in a tabloid newspaper illustrates the dangers of living in a homophobic society. The tabloid's sensationalist coverage led to widespread harassment and violence against the individual, showcasing how media can perpetuate homophobia and endanger lives.

Conclusion

The impact of homophobia in Uganda is a complex interplay of legal, social, and psychological factors that creates a hostile environment for LGBTQ individuals. Theoretical frameworks such as Social Identity Theory provide insight into the roots of this discrimination, while real-life examples underscore the urgent need for change. Addressing the impact of homophobia requires a multifaceted approach that includes legal reform, public education, and the promotion of acceptance and inclusivity. Only through collective efforts can Uganda hope to foster a society where all individuals, regardless of their sexual orientation, can live freely and authentically.

Experiences of harassment and violence

In Uganda, the struggle for LGBTQ rights has been marred by pervasive harassment and violence directed at individuals who identify as part of the community. This section delves into the multifaceted nature of these experiences, highlighting the psychological, social, and physical ramifications of living in an environment where one's identity is not only marginalized but often criminalized.

The Context of Harassment

The legal framework in Uganda has historically been hostile towards LGBTQ individuals. The Anti-Homosexuality Act, which was introduced in 2009 and later annulled, created an atmosphere of fear and uncertainty. Even in the absence of this specific legislation, societal attitudes have remained largely negative, often fueled by religious and cultural beliefs that demonize homosexuality. As a result, LGBTQ individuals frequently face harassment in various forms, ranging from verbal abuse to physical violence.

Types of Harassment

Harassment manifests in several ways, including:

- **Verbal Abuse:** LGBTQ individuals often encounter derogatory comments, slurs, and threats in public spaces. Such verbal harassment can occur in various settings, including schools, workplaces, and even within families. For instance, a young gay man may be subjected to ridicule and insults from classmates, leading to feelings of isolation and despair.

- **Physical Violence:** Reports of physical assaults against LGBTQ individuals are alarmingly common. These attacks can range from beatings to more severe forms of violence, including sexual assault. A notable example is the case of a transgender woman who was brutally attacked in Kampala, highlighting the extreme risks faced by those who do not conform to traditional gender norms.

- **Sexual Violence:** Sexual violence against LGBTQ individuals is often used as a tool of punishment and control. Victims may be targeted not only for their sexual orientation but also for their perceived defiance of gender roles. This form of violence reinforces the notion that LGBTQ identities are unacceptable and must be corrected through coercive means.

- **Cyber Harassment:** With the rise of social media, LGBTQ individuals also face harassment online. This can include doxxing, threats, and the dissemination of personal information without consent. The digital space, while providing some opportunities for community building, can also serve as a platform for hate speech and intimidation.

Psychological Impact

The psychological toll of harassment and violence on LGBTQ individuals is profound. Many experience anxiety, depression, and post-traumatic stress disorder (PTSD) as a direct result of their experiences. The constant threat of violence can lead to hyper-vigilance, where individuals feel perpetually unsafe, even in familiar environments.

Research has shown that the minority stress theory, proposed by Meyer (2003), elucidates how chronic stressors, such as discrimination and violence, negatively impact the mental health of marginalized communities. The model posits that the stigma associated with being LGBTQ leads to increased mental health issues due to the internalization of negative societal attitudes.

$$M = S + I + E \tag{7}$$

Where:

- M = Mental health outcomes
- S = Stigma
- I = Internalized homophobia
- E = Experiences of discrimination

This equation emphasizes that mental health outcomes are influenced by stigma, internalized negative beliefs, and direct experiences of discrimination, all of which are prevalent in the lives of LGBTQ individuals in Uganda.

Community Responses

In the face of such adversity, LGBTQ individuals in Uganda have sought to create safe spaces and support networks. Activism has often emerged as a response to violence, with organizations working to provide legal aid, psychological support, and community solidarity. For instance, organizations like Sexual Minorities Uganda (SMUG) have been pivotal in advocating for LGBTQ rights and providing resources for those affected by violence.

However, these organizations themselves face significant challenges, including legal restrictions and threats from both state and non-state actors. Activists often have to navigate a precarious landscape where their safety is constantly at risk, yet they persist, driven by the need for justice and equality.

Conclusion

Experiences of harassment and violence are not merely statistics; they are lived realities for many LGBTQ individuals in Uganda. The interplay of societal stigma, legal discrimination, and cultural hostility creates an environment where fear is a constant companion. Yet, amidst these challenges, the resilience of the LGBTQ community shines through, as individuals and organizations continue to fight for their rights, dignity, and safety. The journey toward acceptance and equality is fraught with obstacles, but the collective strength of the community offers a glimmer of hope for a more inclusive future.

Discrimination within educational institutions

Discrimination against LGBTQ individuals within educational institutions is a pervasive issue that undermines the foundational principles of equality and inclusion. In Uganda, where cultural norms often stigmatize non-heteronormative identities, educational settings can become hostile environments for LGBTQ students. This subsection explores the various forms of discrimination faced by LGBTQ individuals in schools and universities, the psychological and academic impacts of such discrimination, and the broader implications for society.

Forms of Discrimination

Discrimination in educational institutions manifests in several forms, including:

- **Bullying and Harassment:** LGBTQ students frequently experience bullying from peers, which can range from verbal abuse to physical violence. According to a study conducted by the International Lesbian, Gay, Bisexual, Trans and Intersex Association (ILGA), over 70% of LGBTQ students reported being bullied in schools. This harassment often goes unaddressed by educators, further perpetuating a culture of fear and isolation.

- **Exclusion from Activities:** LGBTQ students may be excluded from participation in school activities, clubs, or sports teams. This exclusion not only affects their social interactions but also limits their opportunities for personal growth and development. For instance, a student who identifies as gay may be barred from joining a sports team, which can lead to feelings of alienation and decreased self-esteem.

- **Hostile Curriculum:** The curriculum in many Ugandan educational institutions often fails to include LGBTQ perspectives or contributions, reinforcing the notion that LGBTQ identities are illegitimate. This lack of representation can lead to feelings of invisibility among LGBTQ students, who may struggle to see themselves reflected in their education.

- **Discriminatory Policies:** Some educational institutions have policies that explicitly discriminate against LGBTQ individuals, such as dress codes that enforce gender conformity or codes of conduct that prohibit same-sex relationships. These policies can create a climate of fear and discourage students from expressing their true identities.

Psychological and Academic Impacts

The consequences of discrimination within educational institutions extend beyond immediate harm. Research indicates that LGBTQ students who face discrimination are more likely to experience mental health issues, including depression, anxiety, and suicidal ideation. The American Psychological Association (APA) highlights that LGBTQ youth are at a significantly higher risk for mental health disorders compared to their heterosexual peers.

Academically, the impact of discrimination can be profound. Students who experience bullying and harassment often exhibit decreased academic performance, increased absenteeism, and a higher likelihood of dropping out. The stress associated with navigating a hostile educational environment can detract from a student's ability to focus on their studies. A study by the Gay, Lesbian and Straight Education Network (GLSEN) found that LGBTQ students with supportive school environments had GPAs that were, on average, 0.5 points higher than those in unsupportive environments.

Examples and Case Studies

Several cases illustrate the realities of discrimination faced by LGBTQ students in Uganda. In 2014, a prominent Ugandan university expelled a student for being openly gay, citing "moral decay" as the reason. This incident sparked outrage among human rights advocates and highlighted the urgent need for policy changes within educational institutions.

Another example is the case of a secondary school in Kampala, where a group of students organized a campaign to out LGBTQ classmates. The campaign resulted in severe bullying and harassment, leading several students to withdraw from the school. These incidents underscore the urgent need for comprehensive anti-bullying policies and LGBTQ-inclusive curricula.

The Role of Educators and Administration

Educators and administrators play a crucial role in combating discrimination within educational institutions. Training programs focused on LGBTQ awareness and inclusivity can equip teachers with the tools necessary to create supportive environments. Furthermore, establishing clear anti-discrimination policies can provide a framework for addressing incidents of bullying and harassment effectively.

Schools should also consider implementing peer support programs, where students can receive guidance and support from trained peers. Such initiatives can foster a sense of community and belonging among LGBTQ students, mitigating the effects of discrimination.

Conclusion

Discrimination within educational institutions poses significant challenges for LGBTQ students in Uganda. The negative impacts on mental health, academic performance, and overall well-being are profound and far-reaching. Addressing these issues requires a concerted effort from educators, policymakers, and society as a whole to create inclusive environments that celebrate diversity and promote acceptance. Only through comprehensive reforms and proactive measures can educational institutions become safe havens for all students, regardless of their sexual orientation or gender identity.

Employment challenges for LGBTQ individuals

The journey towards equality for LGBTQ individuals in Uganda is fraught with numerous challenges, particularly in the realm of employment. Despite the strides made in advocacy and visibility, LGBTQ individuals often find themselves navigating a landscape riddled with discrimination, stigma, and systemic barriers that hinder their professional advancement and security. This section delves into the multifaceted employment challenges faced by LGBTQ individuals in Uganda, exploring the theoretical frameworks that underpin these issues, the specific problems encountered, and illustrative examples that highlight the urgency of addressing these challenges.

Theoretical Frameworks

To understand the employment challenges faced by LGBTQ individuals, we can draw upon several theoretical frameworks, including intersectionality and social identity theory. Intersectionality, a concept coined by Kimberlé Crenshaw, posits that individuals experience overlapping identities that shape their social experiences and access to resources. For LGBTQ individuals in Uganda, factors such as gender, socio-economic status, and educational background intersect with their sexual orientation, complicating their employment prospects.

Social identity theory, developed by Henri Tajfel and John Turner, suggests that individuals derive a sense of self from their group memberships. In a society where LGBTQ identities are marginalized, individuals may internalize negative stereotypes, leading to decreased self-esteem and reluctance to disclose their sexual orientation in professional settings. This theory helps explain the reluctance of many LGBTQ individuals to seek employment in environments that may not be supportive or inclusive.

Problems Encountered

The employment challenges faced by LGBTQ individuals in Uganda can be categorized into several key areas:

- **Discrimination in Hiring Practices:** LGBTQ individuals often face overt discrimination during the hiring process. Employers may harbor biases against LGBTQ applicants, leading to unfair treatment based on sexual orientation. A study conducted by the International Labor Organization (ILO) found that LGBTQ individuals are often less likely to be hired compared to their heterosexual counterparts, regardless of qualifications.
- **Hostile Work Environments:** For those who do secure employment, the workplace can become a hostile environment. Instances of verbal harassment, bullying, and exclusion from workplace activities are common. This not only affects job performance but also contributes to mental health issues such as anxiety and depression.
- **Limited Career Advancement Opportunities:** LGBTQ individuals may find themselves sidelined in terms of promotions and career development. The fear of discrimination can lead to self-censorship, where individuals choose to hide their identities to avoid backlash, thus limiting their professional growth.
- **Lack of Legal Protections:** Uganda's legal framework does not provide adequate protections for LGBTQ individuals against workplace discrimination. The absence of anti-discrimination laws exacerbates the vulnerability of LGBTQ employees, leaving them with little recourse in cases of unfair treatment or harassment.
- **Economic Insecurity:** The cumulative effect of these challenges often results in economic insecurity for LGBTQ individuals. Many are forced to accept low-paying jobs or engage in informal employment, which lacks benefits and job security. This economic vulnerability further marginalizes LGBTQ individuals within society.

Examples and Case Studies

Several poignant examples illustrate the employment challenges faced by LGBTQ individuals in Uganda.

- **Case Study 1: The Experience of Job Seekers:** A 2020 report by the Human Rights Awareness and Promotion Forum (HRAPF) highlighted the experiences of LGBTQ job seekers who reported being denied employment based solely on their sexual orientation. One individual recounted an interview where the employer asked intrusive questions about their personal life, leading to a clear indication that their sexual orientation was a determining factor in the hiring decision.

- **Case Study 2: Workplace Harassment:** Another report documented the experiences of LGBTQ employees who faced harassment from colleagues. One subject described being subjected to derogatory remarks and exclusion from team activities, which ultimately led them to resign from a position they were otherwise qualified for. This highlights the pervasive culture of intolerance that exists in many workplaces.

- **Case Study 3: The Impact of Economic Insecurity:** A survey conducted by the Uganda LGBTQ Coalition revealed that a significant percentage of LGBTQ individuals rely on informal employment or engage in sex work as a means of survival. The lack of stable employment opportunities forces many into precarious situations, further marginalizing them and exposing them to additional risks.

Conclusion

The employment challenges faced by LGBTQ individuals in Uganda are a reflection of broader societal attitudes towards sexual orientation and gender identity. Addressing these challenges requires a multifaceted approach that includes legal reforms, awareness campaigns, and the establishment of inclusive workplace policies. Advocacy efforts must focus on creating a safe and supportive environment for LGBTQ individuals, ensuring that they have equal access to employment opportunities and the ability to thrive professionally without fear of discrimination. Only through collective action and commitment to change can we hope to dismantle the barriers that hinder the progress of LGBTQ individuals in the Ugandan workforce.

The role of religion in promoting discrimination

In Uganda, religion plays a significant role in shaping societal attitudes towards LGBTQ individuals. The intertwining of religious beliefs with cultural norms creates a complex landscape where faith often dictates moral values, leading to the promotion of discrimination against those who identify as LGBTQ. This section explores the mechanisms through which religion fosters intolerance and the implications of such attitudes on LGBTQ rights and activism in Uganda.

Theological Foundations of Discrimination

Many religious doctrines in Uganda, particularly those of Christianity and Islam, espouse traditional views on sexuality that label homosexuality as sinful. The Bible, for instance, contains verses that have been interpreted to condemn same-sex relationships. Key passages often cited include Leviticus 18:22, which states, "You shall not lie with a male as with a woman; it is an abomination," and Romans 1:26-27, which discusses the consequences of abandoning natural relations. These interpretations have been used to justify negative attitudes and actions against LGBTQ individuals.

Similarly, Islamic teachings emphasize heterosexual relationships as the norm, often condemning homosexual acts. The Qur'an, while not explicitly detailing punishments for homosexuality, contains verses that have been interpreted to support the notion that same-sex relationships are against God's design. The fusion of these religious texts with cultural beliefs creates a powerful narrative that positions LGBTQ identities as not only deviant but also as threats to societal morality.

Religious Institutions and Advocacy

Religious institutions in Uganda have been vocal opponents of LGBTQ rights, using their platforms to advocate against legal protections and promote anti-LGBTQ legislation. The most notable example is the infamous Anti-Homosexuality Bill, which sought to impose severe penalties for homosexuality, including the death penalty in some cases. Religious leaders rallied their congregations, framing the bill as a necessary defense of family values and national integrity.

Churches and mosques often host events and campaigns that propagate anti-LGBTQ sentiments. These gatherings serve not only to reinforce existing prejudices but also to mobilize community action against LGBTQ individuals. The rhetoric used during these events frequently invokes fear, suggesting that acceptance of LGBTQ rights will lead to moral decay and societal collapse. This fear-mongering is effective in galvanizing support for discriminatory policies and practices.

Psychological Impact on LGBTQ Individuals

The pervasive influence of religion on societal attitudes towards LGBTQ individuals leads to significant psychological distress among those who identify as such. Many LGBTQ individuals in Uganda experience internalized homophobia, a phenomenon where individuals adopt the negative beliefs and attitudes of their society towards their own sexual orientation. This internal conflict can lead to feelings of shame, guilt, and self-loathing, significantly impacting mental health and overall well-being.

Furthermore, the fear of rejection from religious communities can deter LGBTQ individuals from seeking support, leaving them isolated and vulnerable. The stigma attached to homosexuality, reinforced by religious teachings, creates barriers to accessing mental health resources and community support, exacerbating feelings of loneliness and despair.

Resistance and Counter-Narratives

Despite the challenges posed by religious discrimination, there is a growing movement within Uganda advocating for LGBTQ rights that seeks to challenge these narratives. Some religious leaders and organizations are beginning to embrace more inclusive interpretations of their faiths, advocating for love and acceptance over condemnation. These progressive voices often highlight the fundamental tenets of compassion and empathy found in religious teachings, arguing that true faith should promote understanding rather than hatred.

For instance, initiatives such as the "Faith and Sexuality" dialogue aim to create safe spaces for LGBTQ individuals within religious contexts, allowing for discussions that bridge the gap between faith and sexual identity. These efforts are crucial in fostering acceptance and challenging the status quo that has long marginalized LGBTQ individuals in Uganda.

Conclusion

The role of religion in promoting discrimination against LGBTQ individuals in Uganda is profound and multifaceted. While religious teachings often serve as a foundation for negative attitudes, there is also a burgeoning movement within faith communities advocating for acceptance and understanding. As the dialogue continues to evolve, it is essential to address the theological underpinnings of discrimination while amplifying the voices of those who seek to reconcile their faith with their identity. Only through such efforts can Uganda hope to foster a more inclusive society that respects the rights and dignity of all its citizens, regardless of their sexual orientation.

Seeking Support and Community

Forming connections with LGBTQ individuals

In the journey of self-discovery and acceptance, forming connections with other LGBTQ individuals can be a transformative experience. For Frank Mugisha, these connections not only provided a sense of belonging but also served as a catalyst for activism and advocacy. This section explores the significance of building relationships within the LGBTQ community, the challenges faced in Uganda, and the positive impact of these connections on personal and collective empowerment.

The Importance of Community

The LGBTQ community often serves as a refuge for individuals who may feel isolated or marginalized in their broader social environments. According to *Social Identity Theory*, individuals derive a sense of self from their group memberships, which can significantly influence their self-esteem and overall well-being [1]. For many LGBTQ individuals, connecting with others who share similar experiences can foster a sense of validation and acceptance that is often lacking in heteronormative spaces.

Frank's early experiences in Uganda highlight the critical role that community plays in the lives of LGBTQ individuals. Growing up in a society that stigmatizes homosexuality, he often felt alone in his struggles. However, upon discovering LGBTQ groups and spaces, he found a sense of camaraderie that was both empowering and affirming. These connections provided him with the courage to embrace his identity and to advocate for change.

Challenges in Forming Connections

Despite the profound benefits of community, forming connections within the LGBTQ community in Uganda is fraught with challenges. The pervasive climate of fear and discrimination often discourages individuals from openly seeking out relationships. Many LGBTQ individuals face the risk of violence, ostracism, or even legal repercussions for their sexual orientation. According to a report by the International Lesbian, Gay, Bisexual, Trans and Intersex Association (ILGA),

Uganda has some of the most stringent anti-LGBTQ laws in the world, creating an environment where many individuals are hesitant to connect with others [2].

Furthermore, the societal stigma surrounding LGBTQ identities can lead to internalized homophobia, where individuals struggle to accept themselves and, by extension, others. This internal conflict can create barriers to forming meaningful connections. Frank's journey illustrates this struggle, as he initially grappled with feelings of shame and fear before finding the strength to engage with others in the community.

Building Supportive Networks

To combat these challenges, it is essential to cultivate supportive networks that can provide safety and encouragement. Frank Mugisha's experience demonstrates the power of solidarity among LGBTQ individuals. By participating in local LGBTQ organizations, he not only formed friendships but also developed a network of activists who shared his vision for equality and justice.

Research indicates that supportive relationships can significantly enhance resilience in the face of adversity [3]. The connections formed within the LGBTQ community can provide emotional support, practical resources, and a sense of belonging that is crucial for individuals navigating a hostile environment. These networks can also facilitate the sharing of information regarding safe spaces, legal rights, and health resources.

Examples of Connection in Action

One notable example of connection within the LGBTQ community is the formation of support groups that focus on mental health and well-being. These groups often provide a safe space for individuals to share their experiences, discuss their challenges, and offer mutual support. For instance, Frank participated in a peer-led support group that focused on coping strategies for dealing with discrimination and violence. This group not only provided emotional support but also empowered members to engage in collective advocacy efforts.

Additionally, social media has emerged as a powerful tool for forming connections among LGBTQ individuals, particularly in regions where physical gatherings may be unsafe. Platforms such as Facebook and Twitter allow individuals to share their stories, seek advice, and build relationships with others who understand their experiences. Frank utilized social media to connect with activists both locally and internationally, amplifying his voice and the voices of others in the community.

Conclusion

Forming connections with LGBTQ individuals is a vital aspect of personal and collective empowerment. For Frank Mugisha, these connections were instrumental in shaping his identity and fueling his activism. Despite the challenges posed by societal stigma and discrimination, the LGBTQ community offers a sanctuary of support, resilience, and solidarity. As individuals come together to share their stories and advocate for change, they not only strengthen their own identities but also contribute to the broader movement for LGBTQ rights in Uganda and beyond.

Bibliography

[1] Tajfel, H. (1979). *Social Identity and Intergroup Relations*. Cambridge University Press.

[2] International Lesbian, Gay, Bisexual, Trans and Intersex Association. (2020). *ILGA World Annual Report 2020*. Retrieved from [ILGA](https://ilga.org).

[3] Berkman, L. F., & Glass, T. (2000). Social integration, social networks, social support, and health. In *Social Epidemiology* (pp. 137-173). Oxford University Press.

Joining LGBTQ Support Groups and Organizations

The journey towards self-acceptance and community engagement is often fraught with challenges, particularly for LGBTQ individuals in environments that may be hostile or unwelcoming. Joining LGBTQ support groups and organizations serves as a vital lifeline, providing not only a sense of belonging but also a platform for advocacy and empowerment. These groups can be instrumental in fostering resilience and solidarity among individuals facing similar struggles.

The Importance of Support Networks

Support networks play a crucial role in the lives of LGBTQ individuals, particularly in societies where discrimination and stigma are prevalent. Research indicates that social support is a protective factor against mental health issues, including anxiety and depression, which are disproportionately experienced by LGBTQ individuals (Meyer, 2003). Support groups offer a safe space where members can share their experiences, seek advice, and find comfort in the understanding of others who have faced similar challenges.

Joining a support group can also facilitate the development of coping strategies for dealing with discrimination and societal rejection. For instance, members often share personal stories of resilience, which can inspire others to confront their own challenges with courage. This communal sharing fosters a collective identity, reinforcing the notion that individuals are not alone in their struggles.

Types of Support Groups

LGBTQ support groups can vary widely in focus and structure. Some groups are centered around specific identities within the LGBTQ spectrum, such as gay, lesbian, bisexual, transgender, or non-binary individuals, while others may focus on intersectional issues, addressing the unique experiences of LGBTQ individuals of color or those with disabilities.

- **Peer Support Groups:** These are often informal gatherings where individuals share their experiences and provide emotional support to one another. They may meet regularly in community centers or online platforms, allowing for greater accessibility.

- **Advocacy Organizations:** Groups like the Human Rights Campaign (HRC) or OutRight Action International focus on broader advocacy efforts, working to influence policy and promote LGBTQ rights on a national and international scale. Joining these organizations can provide members with opportunities to engage in activism and contribute to meaningful change.

- **Educational Workshops:** Many support organizations offer workshops that educate members about their rights, health issues, and strategies for advocacy. These workshops can empower individuals with knowledge and skills necessary for navigating both personal and societal challenges.

Challenges in Joining Support Groups

While the benefits of joining LGBTQ support groups are manifold, there are also challenges that individuals may face. One significant barrier is the fear of exposure and discrimination. In many cases, individuals may hesitate to join support groups due to concerns about their privacy and the potential repercussions in their personal and professional lives. This fear is compounded in environments where being openly LGBTQ can lead to harassment or violence.

Moreover, the accessibility of support groups can be limited, especially in rural or conservative areas where such organizations may not exist. Even in urban settings, individuals may struggle to find groups that resonate with their specific identity or needs. Additionally, language barriers and socio-economic factors can further hinder participation, highlighting the need for inclusivity within LGBTQ organizations.

Examples of Successful Support Groups

Despite these challenges, numerous LGBTQ support groups have made significant impacts on their communities. For instance, the *Trevor Project* provides crisis intervention and suicide prevention services to LGBTQ youth. Their hotline and online resources have become invaluable for young people seeking immediate support.

Another example is the *LGBTQ+ National Help Center*, which offers free and confidential support through its helpline and online chat services. This organization exemplifies how technology can bridge gaps in accessibility, allowing individuals from various backgrounds to connect with supportive resources.

The Role of Online Communities

In recent years, the rise of online platforms has transformed the landscape of LGBTQ support. Social media and dedicated forums provide alternative spaces for connection, particularly for individuals who may not have access to in-person support groups. These online communities can offer anonymity, allowing members to express their identities and experiences without fear of judgment.

However, it is essential to approach online communities with caution. Issues such as cyberbullying and misinformation can pose risks, underscoring the importance of fostering positive and respectful online environments. Moreover, while online support can be beneficial, it should not replace in-person connections, which are often crucial for emotional well-being.

Conclusion

Joining LGBTQ support groups and organizations is a powerful step towards personal empowerment and community engagement. These groups not only provide essential emotional support but also create avenues for advocacy and social change. Despite the challenges that may arise, the benefits of connecting with others who share similar experiences can lead to profound personal growth and resilience. As LGBTQ individuals navigate their journeys, the solidarity found within these communities can serve as a beacon of hope and strength, illuminating the path towards acceptance and equality.

Bibliography

[1] Meyer, I. H. (2003). Prejudice, social stress, and mental health in gay men. *American Psychologist*, 58(5), 440-449.

Finding solace in LGBTQ spaces

In a world that often feels hostile and unwelcoming, LGBTQ spaces serve as vital sanctuaries where individuals can find solace, acceptance, and community. These spaces—whether they are physical locations such as bars, community centers, or online forums—provide a refuge for those who have faced discrimination, isolation, or violence due to their sexual orientation or gender identity. This subsection explores the importance of these spaces, the challenges they face, and the profound impact they have on the lives of LGBTQ individuals.

The Importance of LGBTQ Spaces

LGBTQ spaces are crucial for fostering a sense of belonging among community members. According to [?], the concept of "safe spaces" is rooted in the need for individuals to express their identities without fear of judgment or reprisal. In Uganda, where societal norms are often steeped in homophobia, these spaces become even more significant. They provide a platform for individuals to share their experiences, engage in activism, and develop supportive relationships.

The psychological benefits of finding solace in LGBTQ spaces are well-documented. Research indicates that individuals who participate in supportive communities experience lower levels of anxiety and depression, and higher levels of self-esteem [?]. For many, LGBTQ spaces represent a counter-narrative to the pervasive stigma and discrimination they encounter in broader society.

Challenges Faced by LGBTQ Spaces

Despite their importance, LGBTQ spaces in Uganda face numerous challenges. One significant issue is the threat of violence and harassment. According to a report by [?], many LGBTQ individuals have been subjected to attacks when frequenting known LGBTQ venues. This violence creates an atmosphere of fear, making it difficult for individuals to access these crucial support networks.

Moreover, the legal landscape in Uganda complicates the existence of LGBTQ spaces. The Anti-Homosexuality Act, which has been proposed and debated in various forms, creates a climate of fear that discourages both patrons and business owners from openly supporting LGBTQ spaces. This legislative environment not only threatens the physical safety of these spaces but also their financial viability.

Examples of Solace in Action

In the heart of Kampala, a local LGBTQ community center has emerged as a beacon of hope for many. This center offers a range of services, from counseling to legal support, and serves as a gathering place for social events, workshops, and advocacy training. Participants often describe the center as a "home away from home," where they can be their authentic selves without fear of repercussion.

One poignant example of the power of these spaces is the story of a young Ugandan man named David, who found refuge in a local LGBTQ support group. After experiencing rejection from his family and community, David attended a meeting at the center. There, he connected with others who shared similar experiences, which helped him navigate his identity. The support he received not only aided his self-acceptance but also inspired him to become an advocate for LGBTQ rights in Uganda.

The Role of Online Spaces

In addition to physical locations, online LGBTQ spaces have become increasingly important, especially in a country where face-to-face interactions can be dangerous. Social media platforms and online forums allow individuals to connect, share stories, and access resources safely. These digital spaces enable the formation of virtual communities that transcend geographical boundaries, fostering solidarity and support among LGBTQ individuals in Uganda and beyond.

However, online spaces are not without their challenges. Cyberbullying and online harassment are significant issues that LGBTQ individuals face, which can deter them from engaging in these communities. Additionally, the constant threat of surveillance by authorities can lead to self-censorship, limiting the openness that these spaces are meant to provide.

Conclusion

Finding solace in LGBTQ spaces is essential for the mental and emotional well-being of individuals navigating the complexities of their identities in a challenging environment. These spaces not only provide refuge and support but also foster resilience and empowerment. As LGBTQ activism continues to evolve in Uganda, the preservation and expansion of these spaces remain crucial in the fight for acceptance and equality. By nurturing these communities, activists can ensure that future generations of LGBTQ individuals have the support they need to thrive and advocate for their rights.

Networking with LGBTQ activists

Networking is an essential pillar of advocacy, particularly in the realm of LGBTQ rights, where solidarity and collaboration can amplify voices and foster change. For Frank Mugisha, building connections with other activists was not merely a strategy; it was a lifeline in a landscape fraught with discrimination and hostility. This subsection delves into the significance of networking within the LGBTQ community, the challenges faced, and the transformative power of collective action.

The Importance of Networking

Networking among LGBTQ activists serves multiple purposes. It creates a space for sharing resources, strategies, and experiences, which is vital in a context where many face isolation due to societal stigma. The relationships forged through networking can lead to collaborative initiatives that address shared challenges, enhancing the efficacy of advocacy efforts.

$$C = \frac{N(N-1)}{2} \tag{8}$$

Where C represents the total number of connections possible in a network of N activists. This equation highlights the exponential potential of networking: as more activists join the fold, the opportunities for collaboration grow significantly.

Challenges in Networking

Despite its importance, networking for LGBTQ activists in Uganda is fraught with challenges. The societal stigma surrounding LGBTQ identities often leads to a fear of exposure, making individuals hesitant to connect with others. Additionally, the legal environment in Uganda, where homosexuality is criminalized, creates a backdrop of risk that complicates networking efforts. Activists must navigate the treacherous waters of potential harassment and violence while seeking to build supportive networks.

Moreover, internal divisions within the LGBTQ community can hinder networking. Differences in sexual orientation, gender identity, and cultural backgrounds can lead to fragmentation, preventing a united front in advocacy. It is crucial for activists to recognize these differences and find common ground to foster inclusivity within their networks.

Examples of Successful Networking

Frank Mugisha's journey illustrates the power of networking. He actively sought connections with other LGBTQ activists, both locally and internationally, to share knowledge and resources. One notable example was his collaboration with organizations like Sexual Minorities Uganda (SMUG), which provided a platform for activists to unite and strategize against oppressive laws.

In 2013, Mugisha participated in a regional conference that brought together LGBTQ activists from East Africa. This gathering not only allowed for the exchange of ideas but also fostered a sense of solidarity among participants. The conference resulted in the formation of a regional coalition that advocated for LGBTQ rights, demonstrating how networking can lead to organized and impactful action.

Strategies for Effective Networking

To overcome the challenges associated with networking, LGBTQ activists can employ several strategies:

1. **Creating Safe Spaces**: It is essential to establish environments where individuals feel secure to express their identities and share experiences. This can be achieved through private meetings, online forums, or support groups that prioritize confidentiality.

2. **Utilizing Technology**: Social media platforms and online communities can serve as valuable tools for networking, especially in regions where face-to-face meetings pose risks. Activists can leverage these platforms to connect with like-minded individuals and organizations globally.

3. **Participating in Workshops and Conferences**: Engaging in events focused on LGBTQ rights can facilitate networking opportunities. These gatherings not only provide education and resources but also allow activists to meet potential allies and collaborators.

4. **Building Intergenerational Networks**: Connecting with both seasoned activists and younger advocates can enrich the movement. Experienced activists can offer mentorship, while younger individuals can bring fresh perspectives and innovative approaches to advocacy.

5. **Fostering Intersectionality**: Recognizing and addressing the diverse identities within the LGBTQ community is crucial. By promoting intersectional networking, activists can ensure that all voices are heard and represented, leading to a more robust and inclusive movement.

Conclusion

Networking among LGBTQ activists is a powerful tool for fostering solidarity and driving change. Despite the challenges posed by societal stigma and legal constraints, the connections formed through networking can lead to significant advancements in the fight for LGBTQ rights. As Frank Mugisha's experiences illustrate, building a supportive community is essential for resilience and effective advocacy. By employing strategic approaches to networking, LGBTQ activists can cultivate a united front that champions equality, acceptance, and justice for all.

Building a support system for advocacy work

In the landscape of LGBTQ activism, building a robust support system is not merely beneficial; it is essential for sustaining advocacy work. This section explores the theoretical underpinnings, challenges, and practical examples of creating a support system that empowers LGBTQ activists to navigate the complexities of their work.

Theoretical Framework

A support system can be understood through the lens of social support theory, which posits that the presence of supportive relationships can mitigate stress and enhance well-being. According to Cohen and Wills (1985), social support can be categorized into three types: emotional, informational, and instrumental. Each type plays a critical role in the lives of LGBTQ activists:

1. **Emotional Support**: This involves providing empathy, care, and love. Emotional support is crucial for individuals facing discrimination and societal rejection, as it fosters resilience and encourages perseverance.

2. **Informational Support**: This encompasses sharing knowledge, advice, and resources. For LGBTQ activists, access to information about legal rights, advocacy strategies, and mental health resources can significantly impact their effectiveness and well-being.

3. **Instrumental Support**: This refers to tangible assistance, such as financial aid, logistical support, or volunteer help. Instrumental support can enable activists to organize events, campaigns, and outreach programs more effectively.

Challenges in Building a Support System

Despite the importance of a support system, several challenges can hinder its development:

- **Stigmatization and Isolation**: Many LGBTQ individuals face stigmatization within their communities, leading to feelings of isolation. This can deter them from seeking or offering support.

- **Resource Constraints**: Activist organizations often operate with limited resources, making it challenging to establish comprehensive support systems. Financial limitations can restrict access to mental health services, training programs, and networking opportunities.

- **Burnout**: Activism can be emotionally taxing. The risk of burnout can diminish the capacity of activists to both give and receive support. This cycle can lead to a lack of engagement and participation in advocacy efforts.

Strategies for Building a Support System

To overcome these challenges, LGBTQ activists can adopt several strategies to build effective support systems:

- **Creating Safe Spaces**: Establishing safe spaces for LGBTQ individuals to gather, share experiences, and support one another is vital. These spaces can be physical, such as community centers, or virtual, like online forums and social media groups. For example, the establishment of local LGBTQ community centers in Uganda has provided safe havens for individuals to connect and share resources.

- **Peer Support Networks**: Forming peer-led support groups can foster a sense of belonging and mutual understanding. These networks can facilitate emotional support and provide a platform for sharing strategies and resources. The success of initiatives like the "LGBTQ Peer Support Program" in various African nations illustrates the effectiveness of this approach.

- **Mentorship Programs**: Connecting seasoned activists with newcomers can enhance knowledge transfer and provide emotional support. Mentorship can empower younger activists by offering guidance, encouragement, and a sense of purpose. Programs like "OutMentor" have successfully paired experienced activists with those new to advocacy, fostering a culture of support and collaboration.

- **Collaborative Partnerships**: Building partnerships with local and international organizations can enhance resource availability. Collaborating with NGOs, educational institutions, and mental health services can provide activists access to essential support services. For instance, partnerships with international LGBTQ rights organizations have facilitated training workshops and resource sharing, strengthening local advocacy efforts.

- **Utilizing Technology**: Online platforms can serve as powerful tools for building support networks. Social media can facilitate connections, share resources, and mobilize community support. Campaigns like "#LGBTQSupport" have effectively utilized hashtags to raise awareness and create virtual support communities.

Examples of Successful Support Systems

Several examples highlight the impact of effective support systems in LGBTQ activism:

- **The Rainbow Support Network**: This organization in Uganda has successfully created a comprehensive support system that includes counseling services, legal aid, and peer support groups. By addressing both emotional and instrumental needs, the network has empowered many individuals to engage in advocacy work confidently.

- **The International Gay and Lesbian Human Rights Commission (IGLHRC)**: This global organization provides resources, training, and networking opportunities for LGBTQ activists worldwide. By fostering connections among activists from different regions, IGLHRC has helped build a global support system that enhances local advocacy efforts.

- **The Trevor Project**: In the United States, this organization offers crisis intervention and suicide prevention services for LGBTQ youth. By providing emotional support and resources, The Trevor Project exemplifies how a well-structured support system can save lives and empower young activists.

Conclusion

Building a support system for LGBTQ advocacy work is a multifaceted endeavor that requires intentionality, collaboration, and resilience. By understanding the theoretical foundations of social support, recognizing the challenges faced, and implementing effective strategies, activists can create an environment that nurtures their well-being and amplifies their impact. As Frank Mugisha's journey illustrates, a strong support system not only enhances personal resilience but also strengthens the collective fight for LGBTQ rights in Uganda and beyond. The ongoing commitment to fostering these networks will be crucial for sustaining momentum in the ever-evolving landscape of LGBTQ activism.

Education and Activism

Pursuing higher education opportunities

The pursuit of higher education is often seen as a pathway to personal and professional growth. For Frank Mugisha, navigating this journey as an LGBTQ activist in Uganda presented unique challenges and opportunities that shaped his identity and advocacy work. Education is not merely a means to acquire knowledge; it is also a powerful tool for empowerment and social change, particularly in contexts where marginalized communities face systemic discrimination.

The Importance of Education in Activism

Higher education plays a critical role in equipping individuals with the skills and knowledge necessary to engage in effective advocacy. Theoretical frameworks, such as Paulo Freire's concept of critical pedagogy, emphasize the importance of education as a means of liberation. Freire argues that education should be a dialogical process that encourages critical thinking and consciousness-raising among learners. This approach is particularly relevant for LGBTQ individuals in Uganda, where societal norms often suppress their identities and voices.

$$\text{Critical Consciousness} = \text{Awareness} + \text{Action} \qquad (9)$$

In this equation, critical consciousness emerges from the combination of awareness of one's social reality and the action taken to change that reality. For Frank, pursuing higher education provided him with the tools to analyze the injustices faced by the LGBTQ community and to advocate for change.

Barriers to Higher Education

Despite the potential benefits, many LGBTQ individuals in Uganda encounter significant barriers to accessing higher education. These barriers include:

- **Discrimination and Harassment:** LGBTQ students often face hostility from peers and faculty, which can lead to a hostile learning environment. This discrimination can manifest in various forms, including verbal abuse, exclusion from social groups, and even physical violence.

- **Economic Constraints:** Many LGBTQ individuals come from marginalized backgrounds, which may limit their financial resources to pursue higher education. Economic instability can lead to difficult choices, such as prioritizing immediate survival over long-term educational goals.

- **Lack of Support Systems:** The absence of supportive networks can hinder LGBTQ students from seeking higher education. Many may feel isolated and lack mentorship or guidance from individuals who understand their unique challenges.

These barriers underscore the need for targeted interventions and supportive policies that promote inclusivity within educational institutions.

Examples of Overcoming Challenges

Despite these obstacles, Frank Mugisha's journey illustrates how determination and resilience can lead to success. He sought out scholarships and financial aid programs specifically designed for marginalized communities, which alleviated some of the economic pressures he faced. Additionally, Frank actively engaged with LGBTQ organizations that provided mentorship and resources, creating a network of support that bolstered his educational pursuits.

For instance, the support group he joined not only offered emotional support but also organized workshops on academic writing and research skills. This collaborative environment fostered a sense of belonging and encouraged members to share their experiences and strategies for navigating the academic landscape.

The Role of Advocacy in Education

Frank's experiences highlight the intersection of education and activism. By pursuing higher education, he not only advanced his personal goals but also became a voice for others facing similar challenges. His involvement in student organizations and advocacy groups allowed him to address issues of discrimination within educational settings.

In one notable instance, Frank organized a campus-wide seminar on LGBTQ rights, inviting speakers from various backgrounds to discuss the importance of inclusivity in education. This event not only raised awareness among students and faculty but also fostered dialogue about the need for institutional reforms to support LGBTQ students.

Conclusion: A Path Forward

The pursuit of higher education is a vital component of Frank Mugisha's advocacy journey. It serves as a means of empowerment, allowing individuals to challenge societal norms and advocate for their rights. As LGBTQ individuals continue to face barriers in education, it is crucial to implement policies that promote inclusivity and support.

By prioritizing higher education opportunities for marginalized communities, society can foster a generation of activists equipped to challenge injustice and advocate for change. Frank's story exemplifies the transformative power of education in the fight for LGBTQ rights, inspiring others to pursue their aspirations despite the challenges they may face.

In summary, the journey toward higher education is fraught with challenges, but it is also filled with opportunities for growth and advocacy. As Frank Mugisha's life illustrates, education can be a catalyst for change, enabling individuals to not only uplift themselves but also their communities.

Exploring activism and advocacy

In the journey of advocating for LGBTQ rights, exploring activism and advocacy becomes a pivotal chapter, not only in the life of Frank Mugisha but also in the broader narrative of social justice in Uganda. This exploration is rooted in the understanding that activism is more than just a reaction to oppression; it is a proactive approach to shaping societal norms, policies, and perceptions.

At its core, activism is defined by *social movements* that aim to challenge and change the status quo. According to Tilly and Tarrow (2015), social movements are "collective challenges by people with common purposes and solidarity in sustained interaction with elites, opponents, and authorities." In the context of LGBTQ advocacy, this definition underscores the importance of collective action, shared goals, and the engagement of various stakeholders, including marginalized communities, allies, and policymakers.

Theoretical Frameworks To effectively explore activism, we must consider several theoretical frameworks that inform and guide advocacy work. One such framework is **Intersectionality**, coined by Kimberlé Crenshaw (1989), which posits that individuals experience multiple, overlapping identities that can compound discrimination. For LGBTQ activists like Mugisha, intersectionality is crucial as it highlights how race, class, gender, and sexual orientation intersect to create unique experiences of oppression and privilege. This understanding allows activists to craft more inclusive and effective strategies that address the diverse needs of the LGBTQ community in Uganda.

Another relevant theory is **Social Change Theory**, which emphasizes the processes through which societies evolve and adapt. This theory posits that social movements can lead to significant changes in laws, policies, and cultural attitudes. For instance, Mugisha's advocacy work has contributed to raising awareness and challenging discriminatory laws in Uganda, such as the Anti-Homosexuality Act of 2014, which sought to impose severe penalties on LGBTQ individuals.

Challenges in Activism Despite the theoretical frameworks that guide activism, LGBTQ advocates in Uganda face numerous challenges. One significant issue is the **criminalization of homosexuality**. The Ugandan Penal Code, which includes laws that criminalize same-sex relationships, creates an environment of fear and repression. Activists often find themselves at risk of arrest, harassment, and violence. For example, Mugisha has faced personal threats and attacks due to his visibility as an LGBTQ advocate, highlighting the dangers that come with speaking out.

Moreover, societal stigma and discrimination pose substantial barriers to effective advocacy. The pervasive homophobia in Uganda is often fueled by cultural and religious beliefs that view LGBTQ identities as deviant. This societal backdrop can hinder efforts to mobilize support and create safe spaces for LGBTQ individuals. Activists must navigate these complex social dynamics while striving to foster acceptance and understanding.

Strategies for Effective Advocacy To overcome these challenges, LGBTQ activists have developed various strategies that focus on community engagement, education, and coalition-building. One effective approach is **Grassroots Mobilization**, which involves organizing local communities to advocate for change from the ground up. This strategy empowers individuals to share their stories and experiences, fostering a sense of solidarity and collective action. Mugisha has been instrumental in organizing local LGBTQ groups, providing a platform for individuals to connect, share resources, and advocate for their rights.

Education and Awareness Campaigns also play a crucial role in activism. By educating the public about LGBTQ issues, activists can challenge misconceptions and stereotypes that perpetuate discrimination. For instance, Mugisha has participated in various outreach programs aimed at schools and community centers, using storytelling and personal narratives to humanize LGBTQ experiences. This approach not only raises awareness but also cultivates empathy and understanding within the broader community.

Furthermore, **Coalition-Building** is essential for amplifying the voices of LGBTQ individuals. By collaborating with other marginalized groups, such as women's rights organizations and human rights defenders, LGBTQ activists can create a united front against oppression. This solidarity enhances the legitimacy of their cause and broadens the scope of their advocacy efforts. Mugisha has successfully partnered with international NGOs, leveraging their resources and networks to strengthen local advocacy initiatives.

Examples of Successful Activism The impact of activism can be seen in various successful campaigns that have emerged from Uganda. One notable example is the **Pride Uganda** event, which celebrates LGBTQ identities and promotes visibility. Despite facing significant opposition, the event has become a symbol of resilience and courage within the community. It showcases the power of collective action, as LGBTQ individuals and allies come together to assert their rights and demand equality.

Additionally, Mugisha's involvement in legal battles, such as the challenge against the Anti-Homosexuality Act, exemplifies the intersection of activism and legal advocacy. By working alongside legal experts and human rights organizations, activists have made strides in challenging discriminatory laws and advocating for legal reforms. The ongoing dialogue surrounding LGBTQ rights in Uganda is a testament to the effectiveness of sustained advocacy efforts.

Conclusion In conclusion, exploring activism and advocacy within the LGBTQ movement in Uganda reveals a complex interplay of challenges, strategies, and successes. By grounding their work in theoretical frameworks like intersectionality and social change theory, activists like Frank Mugisha navigate the tumultuous landscape of discrimination and repression. Through grassroots mobilization, education, and coalition-building, they foster resilience and hope within the community. The journey of activism is ongoing, with each step taken paving the way for future generations to advocate for a more inclusive and accepting society.

Organizing and participating in LGBTQ events

Organizing and participating in LGBTQ events is a cornerstone of activism, serving as a platform for visibility, community building, and advocacy. These events range from pride parades and festivals to workshops, seminars, and community gatherings. Each event plays a unique role in fostering solidarity and promoting awareness of LGBTQ rights and issues.

The Importance of LGBTQ Events

LGBTQ events are crucial for several reasons. They provide a safe space for individuals to express their identities, celebrate their communities, and connect with others who share similar experiences. The visibility offered by these events challenges societal norms and stereotypes, promoting acceptance and understanding.

$$V = \frac{I}{D} \tag{10}$$

Where V represents visibility, I is individual engagement, and D is societal discrimination. This equation illustrates that increased individual engagement in LGBTQ events can lead to higher visibility, which, in turn, can help reduce societal discrimination.

Challenges in Organizing Events

Despite their importance, organizing LGBTQ events often comes with significant challenges. Activists may face logistical issues such as securing funding, obtaining permits, and ensuring safety for participants. Additionally, there is the ever-present threat of backlash from conservative groups or individuals opposed to LGBTQ rights.

For instance, the planning committee for a pride parade may encounter difficulties in negotiating with local authorities for permits. In some cases, events have been canceled or disrupted due to threats of violence or harassment. Activists must navigate these challenges while remaining committed to their cause.

Strategies for Successful Event Organization

To successfully organize LGBTQ events, activists can employ several strategies:

- **Community Engagement:** Involve community members in the planning process to ensure that events reflect the needs and desires of those they aim to serve. This can include surveys, focus groups, and open forums.

- **Partnerships:** Collaborate with local businesses, nonprofits, and allies to secure resources and support. Building a coalition can enhance credibility and increase the reach of the event.

- **Safety Protocols:** Develop comprehensive safety plans that include security measures, emergency contacts, and guidelines for participants. Ensuring a safe environment is paramount for fostering participation.

- **Marketing and Outreach:** Utilize social media, flyers, and community bulletins to promote events widely. Engaging storytelling can attract diverse audiences and encourage participation.

Examples of Successful LGBTQ Events

Numerous LGBTQ events worldwide have successfully raised awareness and fostered community. For instance, the annual Pride Month celebrations in cities like San Francisco and New York City draw millions of participants, showcasing the vibrant diversity of the LGBTQ community. These events not only celebrate pride but also serve as a platform for political activism, with speakers addressing issues such as marriage equality, healthcare access, and anti-discrimination laws.

Another example is the International Day Against Homophobia, Transphobia, and Biphobia (IDAHOT), observed on May 17 each year. This day involves a variety of events, including workshops, rallies, and educational campaigns, aimed at raising awareness of the discrimination faced by LGBTQ individuals globally. The collective participation in these events amplifies the message of solidarity and the ongoing struggle for rights.

The Role of Intersectionality in Events

When organizing LGBTQ events, it is essential to consider intersectionality—the interconnected nature of social categorizations such as race, class, and gender. Events that acknowledge and celebrate this diversity are more likely to resonate with a broader audience and address the unique challenges faced by different subgroups within the LGBTQ community.

For instance, events that specifically focus on the experiences of LGBTQ people of color or transgender individuals can foster inclusion and ensure that all voices are heard. This approach not only enriches the events but also strengthens the overall movement by promoting unity and understanding among diverse populations.

Conclusion

In conclusion, organizing and participating in LGBTQ events is vital for fostering community, raising awareness, and advocating for rights. While challenges abound, the strategies outlined above can help activists create impactful events that resonate with participants and promote meaningful change. By embracing the diversity within the LGBTQ community and employing intersectional approaches, these events can serve as powerful catalysts for social transformation.

Collaborating with international organizations

In the realm of LGBTQ activism, collaboration with international organizations is not merely beneficial; it is essential. This partnership serves as a bridge, connecting local struggles with global movements, thereby amplifying the voices of marginalized communities within Uganda. The significance of these collaborations can be understood through several lenses: resource sharing, capacity building, advocacy, and visibility.

One of the primary advantages of collaborating with international organizations is the access to resources. These entities often possess financial support, educational materials, and training programs that can empower local activists. For example, organizations like *Human Rights Watch* and *Amnesty International* have provided funding for workshops aimed at educating LGBTQ individuals about their rights and how to navigate the legal landscape in Uganda. This transfer of knowledge is crucial, especially in a context where local resources may be scarce or inadequate.

Moreover, international organizations can facilitate capacity building through training and mentorship programs. By partnering with experienced activists from different parts of the world, Ugandan LGBTQ advocates can learn effective strategies for mobilizing communities and organizing campaigns. For instance, the collaboration between *OutRight Action International* and local Ugandan groups has led to the development of skills in advocacy, public speaking, and grassroots organizing. These skills are indispensable for fostering a robust and resilient LGBTQ movement in Uganda.

However, the collaboration is not without its challenges. One significant problem is the potential for cultural misunderstandings. International organizations may not fully grasp the complexities of Ugandan society, including its cultural, religious, and political nuances. This can lead to strategies that, while effective elsewhere, may not resonate with the local population. For example, a campaign that works well in a Western context may inadvertently alienate Ugandan communities if it does not take into account their unique cultural values.

Furthermore, there is often a power dynamic at play in these collaborations. International organizations, by virtue of their resources and global influence, may unintentionally overshadow local voices. This can create a situation where the narratives of Ugandan activists are filtered through a Western lens, potentially distorting the true essence of their experiences. To mitigate this, it is crucial for international organizations to prioritize local leadership and ensure that Ugandan activists are at the forefront of decision-making processes.

The role of technology in facilitating these collaborations cannot be overlooked. Digital platforms allow for real-time communication and coordination, enabling activists from different parts of the world to share experiences and strategies. For instance, social media campaigns have successfully mobilized international support for Ugandan LGBTQ rights, drawing attention to human rights abuses and fostering solidarity across borders. The #FreeUganda campaign is a testament to this, where activists utilized platforms like Twitter and Facebook to raise awareness and pressure the Ugandan government.

Moreover, international organizations can play a pivotal role in advocacy on the global stage. By leveraging their networks, they can amplify local voices in international forums, such as the United Nations. This was evident when Ugandan activists collaborated with international human rights organizations to present a unified front during the Universal Periodic Review (UPR) of Uganda's human rights record. Their testimonies highlighted the systemic discrimination faced by LGBTQ individuals in Uganda, garnering international attention and pressure on the Ugandan government to improve its human rights practices.

In conclusion, while the collaboration with international organizations presents challenges, it also offers invaluable opportunities for growth, visibility, and advocacy. The key lies in fostering equitable partnerships that respect and elevate local voices, ensuring that the fight for LGBTQ rights in Uganda is both informed by global perspectives and rooted in local realities. By building these bridges, the LGBTQ movement in Uganda can gain the strength and support necessary to challenge discrimination and advocate for equality on both local and international stages.

Establishing a platform for LGBTQ rights in Uganda

The struggle for LGBTQ rights in Uganda has been fraught with challenges, yet the establishment of a robust platform for advocacy has become a cornerstone for progress. A well-defined platform not only amplifies the voices of LGBTQ individuals but also serves as a strategic framework for addressing systemic injustices. This section will explore the theoretical underpinnings of advocacy platforms, the specific problems faced in Uganda, and successful examples of initiatives that have laid the groundwork for change.

Theoretical Framework

At the heart of advocacy work is the concept of *social justice*, which emphasizes the fair distribution of resources and opportunities. According to Rawls' Theory of Justice, a just society is one that ensures fairness and equality for all individuals, regardless of their sexual orientation or gender identity. This theoretical framework underpins the necessity of establishing a platform that advocates for LGBTQ rights in Uganda, where systemic discrimination has historically marginalized these communities.

The *Collective Impact Model* is another relevant theory, which posits that large-scale social change requires a coordinated effort across multiple sectors. This model involves five key conditions: a common agenda, shared measurement systems, mutually reinforcing activities, continuous communication, and backbone support organizations. In the context of LGBTQ rights, these principles can guide the establishment of a cohesive platform that unites various stakeholders, including NGOs, community leaders, and international allies.

Challenges in Establishing a Platform

Despite the theoretical frameworks that support advocacy, numerous challenges persist in establishing a platform for LGBTQ rights in Uganda:

- **Legal Barriers:** The Ugandan Penal Code criminalizes same-sex relationships, creating a hostile environment for advocacy. This legal framework not only deters individuals from openly identifying as LGBTQ but also hinders organizations from operating effectively.

- **Societal Stigma:** Deep-rooted cultural norms and religious beliefs contribute to widespread homophobia. This societal stigma often results in discrimination, violence, and ostracization, making it difficult for LGBTQ individuals to engage in advocacy without fear of repercussions.
- **Limited Resources:** Many LGBTQ organizations in Uganda face financial constraints, limiting their ability to implement comprehensive advocacy programs. This lack of resources hampers outreach efforts and reduces the effectiveness of campaigns aimed at raising awareness about LGBTQ rights.
- **Fragmentation of Efforts:** The LGBTQ advocacy landscape in Uganda is often fragmented, with various groups pursuing different agendas. This fragmentation can dilute the impact of advocacy efforts and create confusion among stakeholders about the common goals of the movement.

Successful Examples of LGBTQ Advocacy Platforms

Despite these challenges, several initiatives have successfully established platforms for LGBTQ rights in Uganda, demonstrating resilience and innovation:

- **Sexual Minorities Uganda (SMUG):** Founded in 2004, SMUG has played a pivotal role in advocating for the rights of LGBTQ individuals in Uganda. The organization has successfully mobilized community members, provided legal support, and raised awareness about LGBTQ issues through strategic campaigns. SMUG's collaboration with international human rights organizations has also amplified its impact, showcasing the importance of global solidarity in local advocacy efforts.
- **The Uganda Pride Movement:** The annual Pride events in Uganda, despite facing significant opposition, have served as a powerful platform for visibility and community building. These events not only celebrate LGBTQ identities but also create opportunities for dialogue and advocacy. The resilience demonstrated during these events has inspired many to join the fight for equality, fostering a sense of solidarity among LGBTQ individuals.
- **Peer Support Networks:** Establishing peer support networks has been crucial in creating safe spaces for LGBTQ individuals. These networks offer emotional support, resources, and advocacy training, empowering members

to engage in activism. By fostering a sense of community, these initiatives help combat isolation and encourage collective action.

Strategies for Establishing a Strong Platform

To further strengthen the platform for LGBTQ rights in Uganda, several strategies can be employed:

- **Building Alliances:** Forming alliances with other marginalized groups can amplify advocacy efforts. Intersectional approaches that recognize the diverse identities within the LGBTQ community can foster solidarity and broaden the reach of campaigns.

- **Utilizing Digital Platforms:** Leveraging social media and digital platforms can enhance visibility and engagement. Online campaigns can raise awareness, mobilize supporters, and create safe spaces for dialogue, particularly in a context where physical gatherings may be risky.

- **Capacity Building:** Investing in training and capacity building for LGBTQ activists is essential. Providing resources and education on advocacy strategies, legal rights, and mental health can empower individuals to become effective advocates for their communities.

- **Engaging Allies:** Encouraging allies, including straight individuals and organizations, to join the fight for LGBTQ rights can help shift societal attitudes. By amplifying the voices of LGBTQ individuals and advocating for change, allies can play a crucial role in challenging discrimination and promoting inclusivity.

- **Advocacy through Art and Culture:** Utilizing art, music, and cultural expressions can be a powerful means of advocacy. Creative outlets can challenge stereotypes, promote understanding, and foster empathy, making them effective tools for social change.

Conclusion

Establishing a platform for LGBTQ rights in Uganda is not merely an act of defiance against oppression; it is a profound statement of humanity and resilience. By utilizing theoretical frameworks, addressing challenges, and learning from successful initiatives, advocates can create a sustainable platform that champions the rights of LGBTQ individuals. As Frank Mugisha and others have demonstrated, the journey toward equality is ongoing, but through collective action and unwavering determination, the vision of a just and inclusive society can become a reality.

$$\text{Social Justice} = \frac{\text{Equity} + \text{Access} + \text{Participation}}{\text{Rights}} \tag{11}$$

The Fight for LGBTQ Rights

Legal Recognition and Equality

Challenges in advocating for legal protections

Advocating for legal protections for LGBTQ individuals in Uganda presents a complex landscape filled with formidable challenges. These challenges stem from deeply entrenched cultural, political, and legal frameworks that often marginalize and criminalize LGBTQ identities. This subsection explores the multifaceted obstacles faced by activists in their pursuit of legal recognition and protections.

Cultural Resistance

One of the most significant barriers to legal protections for LGBTQ individuals in Uganda is the pervasive cultural resistance to homosexuality. Traditional beliefs and societal norms often view LGBTQ identities as deviant, leading to widespread discrimination and stigmatization. In many Ugandan communities, homosexuality is not only taboo but is also often equated with immorality. This cultural backdrop creates an environment where advocating for legal protections can be seen as a direct challenge to societal values.

Political Climate

The political climate in Uganda exacerbates the challenges faced by LGBTQ activists. The Ugandan government, led by President Yoweri Museveni, has a history of using anti-LGBTQ rhetoric to rally support among conservative voters. Legislative efforts, such as the infamous Anti-Homosexuality Bill of 2014, reflect the political exploitation of homophobia. Although the bill was annulled on a technicality, the mere existence of such legislation highlights the precarious position of LGBTQ rights within the political discourse. Activists are often met with hostility from lawmakers who view their efforts as an affront to national values and security.

Legal Framework

The existing legal framework in Uganda further complicates the fight for LGBTQ rights. Homosexuality is criminalized under Section 145 of the Penal Code, which prohibits "carnal knowledge against the order of nature." This law not only criminalizes same-sex relationships but also provides a basis for discrimination in various sectors, including employment, healthcare, and education. The lack of legal protections against discrimination means that LGBTQ individuals are vulnerable to harassment and violence without recourse to justice.

Fear of Repercussions

The fear of repercussions is another significant challenge that LGBTQ activists face. Many individuals are reluctant to openly advocate for their rights due to the potential for backlash, including violence, social ostracism, and legal penalties. Activists often operate in secrecy, which limits their ability to mobilize and organize effectively. This climate of fear stifles open dialogue about LGBTQ issues and hinders the development of a robust advocacy movement.

Limited Resources

Activists also contend with limited resources for advocacy work. Many LGBTQ organizations in Uganda operate on tight budgets and rely heavily on international funding. However, the political climate can make it difficult to secure funding, as potential donors may be wary of the risks involved in supporting LGBTQ initiatives in a hostile environment. This financial strain can hinder the ability to conduct outreach, provide legal assistance, and engage in public awareness campaigns.

International Relations

The intersection of international relations and local advocacy presents another layer of complexity. While international human rights laws advocate for the protection of LGBTQ rights, the Ugandan government often dismisses these frameworks as neo-colonial impositions. This rejection can lead to tensions between the Ugandan government and foreign entities, complicating the work of local activists who seek to leverage international support for legal reform.

Conclusion

In summary, the challenges in advocating for legal protections for LGBTQ individuals in Uganda are deeply rooted in cultural, political, and legal contexts. The intersection of these factors creates a hostile environment for advocacy, where cultural resistance, political exploitation, legal barriers, fear of repercussions, resource limitations, and international relations all play significant roles. Overcoming these challenges requires a multifaceted approach that not only addresses legal reform but also seeks to shift cultural perceptions and engage political leaders in meaningful dialogue. As activists continue to navigate this complex landscape, their resilience and determination remain crucial in the ongoing struggle for LGBTQ rights in Uganda.

The role of international human rights law

International human rights law plays a pivotal role in the advocacy for LGBTQ rights, particularly in regions where such identities are criminalized or marginalized. This body of law encompasses various treaties, conventions, and customary international law that collectively aim to protect the fundamental rights and freedoms of all individuals, regardless of their sexual orientation or gender identity.

The Framework of International Human Rights Law

The cornerstone of international human rights law is the Universal Declaration of Human Rights (UDHR), adopted by the United Nations General Assembly in 1948. The UDHR asserts that "all human beings are born free and equal in dignity and rights" (Article 1) and emphasizes the right to life, liberty, and security (Article 3). Although the UDHR does not explicitly mention sexual orientation or gender identity, its principles have been interpreted to include these aspects of identity under the umbrella of human rights.

Key international treaties that further reinforce these principles include:

- **The International Covenant on Civil and Political Rights (ICCPR)**: This treaty obligates state parties to respect and ensure the rights of individuals, including the right to non-discrimination (Article 26) and the right to privacy (Article 17). These provisions have been invoked in cases involving LGBTQ individuals.

- **The International Covenant on Economic, Social and Cultural Rights (ICESCR)**: This covenant recognizes the right to work, education, and an adequate standard of living, which are essential for LGBTQ individuals facing discrimination in these areas.

- **The Convention on the Elimination of All Forms of Discrimination Against Women (CEDAW):** While primarily focused on women's rights, CEDAW's provisions against discrimination have been interpreted to apply to LGBTQ individuals as well.

Challenges in Enforcement and Application

Despite the existence of these international legal frameworks, the enforcement of human rights laws concerning LGBTQ rights remains fraught with challenges. Many states, particularly those with conservative or authoritarian regimes, resist international norms that conflict with local cultural or religious beliefs. This resistance can manifest in several ways:

- **Sovereignty vs. Universalism:** Many governments argue that international human rights standards impose Western values that do not align with their cultural or religious traditions. This tension raises questions about the universality of human rights and the extent to which states should adhere to international norms.

- **Lack of Political Will:** Even when international treaties are ratified, the lack of political will to implement and enforce these laws can hinder progress. In many cases, LGBTQ individuals face systemic discrimination that is perpetuated by state actors, including law enforcement and judiciary members.

- **Insufficient Legal Frameworks:** In some countries, existing legal frameworks do not adequately protect LGBTQ individuals from discrimination or violence. The absence of anti-discrimination laws or hate crime legislation leaves many vulnerable to abuse without recourse.

Case Studies and Examples

International human rights law has been instrumental in several landmark cases that have advanced LGBTQ rights:

- **Toonen v. Australia (1994):** This case marked a significant moment in the application of international human rights law to LGBTQ issues. The United Nations Human Rights Committee ruled that Tasmania's laws criminalizing homosexual conduct violated the ICCPR's provisions on privacy and non-discrimination. This ruling not only led to the decriminalization of homosexuality in Tasmania but also set a precedent for similar cases globally.

- **The Yogyakarta Principles (2007):** These principles were developed by a group of international human rights experts to address the human rights of LGBTQ individuals. They provide a framework for states to implement laws and policies that protect sexual orientation and gender identity, reinforcing the application of existing international human rights law.

- **The European Court of Human Rights (ECHR):** The ECHR has issued several rulings that affirm the rights of LGBTQ individuals, such as the case of *Schalk and Kopf v. Austria (2010)*, which recognized the right to a family life for same-sex couples. Such rulings underscore the importance of international human rights law in shaping national policies.

The Role of Advocacy and International Pressure

Advocacy groups play a crucial role in leveraging international human rights law to promote LGBTQ rights. By documenting human rights abuses and mobilizing public opinion, these organizations can apply pressure on governments to comply with their international obligations. The following strategies have proven effective:

- **Engagement with International Bodies:** Advocacy groups often engage with the United Nations and regional human rights mechanisms to highlight violations and demand accountability. This engagement can lead to recommendations for states to improve their human rights practices.

- **Coalition Building:** Collaborating with local and international NGOs enhances the visibility of LGBTQ issues and fosters solidarity among diverse groups. This coalition-building can amplify voices and create a more formidable front against discrimination.

- **Public Awareness Campaigns:** Utilizing media and social platforms, advocacy groups can raise awareness about LGBTQ rights and mobilize public support for change. Campaigns that humanize LGBTQ individuals and highlight their struggles can shift public opinion and influence policymakers.

Conclusion

The role of international human rights law in advocating for LGBTQ rights is both foundational and complex. While it provides essential protections and frameworks for action, the challenges of enforcement and cultural resistance necessitate persistent advocacy and strategic engagement. As the global landscape evolves, the continued application of these laws will be crucial in the fight for equality and justice for LGBTQ individuals, particularly in regions like Uganda, where such rights are under constant threat.

Working with lawyers and legal experts

In the quest for legal recognition and equality for LGBTQ individuals in Uganda, collaboration with lawyers and legal experts has proven to be an indispensable strategy. This partnership not only facilitates a deeper understanding of the legal landscape but also enhances the effectiveness of advocacy efforts aimed at dismantling discriminatory laws and practices.

The first challenge that activists face in this collaboration is the pervasive climate of fear among legal professionals. Many lawyers in Uganda are hesitant to engage with LGBTQ issues due to potential backlash, including professional ostracism or even threats to personal safety. This fear is compounded by the fact that Uganda has historically criminalized homosexuality, with laws that impose severe penalties on those found guilty of same-sex relationships. As a result, legal experts must navigate a treacherous environment where their commitment to human rights can put them at risk.

To combat this, LGBTQ activists have employed several strategies to foster a supportive network of legal professionals. One effective approach has been the establishment of safe spaces for dialogue and collaboration, allowing lawyers to discuss their concerns and share experiences without fear of reprisal. For instance, workshops and training sessions have been organized, focusing on human rights law and the specific challenges faced by LGBTQ individuals. These gatherings not only educate lawyers about the legal intricacies of LGBTQ rights but also build a community of allies who can work together towards common goals.

A notable example of successful collaboration between LGBTQ activists and legal experts is the case of *The Sexual Minorities Uganda (SMUG) v. Uganda*. In this landmark case, SMUG, a prominent LGBTQ advocacy group, partnered with local and international legal experts to challenge the constitutionality of anti-homosexuality laws in Uganda. The legal team, comprised of both Ugandan and international lawyers, utilized a multifaceted approach that included extensive research, legal documentation, and strategic public advocacy to bring attention to the case.

The theoretical framework underpinning this collaboration draws from the principles of **strategic litigation**, which posits that carefully selected legal cases can serve as catalysts for broader social change. This approach emphasizes the importance of not only winning individual cases but also setting legal precedents that can influence future rulings and legislative reforms. For instance, by successfully challenging the discriminatory laws in court, activists can create a ripple effect that encourages other legal professionals to engage with LGBTQ rights, ultimately fostering a more inclusive legal environment.

Moreover, the collaboration extends beyond litigation. Legal experts play a crucial role in drafting policy proposals and legal reform initiatives aimed at decriminalizing homosexuality and protecting the rights of LGBTQ individuals. This involves analyzing existing laws, identifying gaps in legal protections, and proposing amendments that align with international human rights standards.

However, the path is fraught with challenges. Activists often encounter resistance from government officials and traditional legal institutions that are deeply entrenched in conservative values. This resistance can manifest in various forms, including bureaucratic delays, hostile political rhetoric, and even attempts to intimidate legal professionals who advocate for LGBTQ rights.

To counteract these obstacles, it is essential for activists to employ a combination of legal strategies and public advocacy. Engaging in media campaigns that highlight the stories of LGBTQ individuals affected by discriminatory laws can create public pressure on legal and political institutions to reform. Additionally, forming coalitions with other human rights organizations can amplify the message and increase visibility, making it harder for authorities to ignore the demands for change.

In conclusion, the collaboration between LGBTQ activists and legal experts is a vital component in the fight for legal recognition and equality in Uganda. By working together, they can navigate the complexities of the legal system, advocate for necessary reforms, and ultimately strive for a future where LGBTQ individuals can live freely and authentically. The journey is undoubtedly challenging, but it is through these partnerships that hope for change is sustained and strengthened.

Court battles and landmark legal victories

In the pursuit of LGBTQ rights in Uganda, the courtroom has become a battleground where the fight for dignity, recognition, and justice unfolds. The legal landscape in Uganda is fraught with challenges, yet it is also marked by significant victories that inspire hope and resilience among activists and the broader LGBTQ community. This subsection delves into the complexities of court battles, the landmark legal victories achieved, and the implications of these outcomes for LGBTQ rights in Uganda.

The Legal Framework

The legal framework in Uganda is primarily influenced by colonial-era laws that criminalize homosexuality. Under Section 145 of the Penal Code Act, homosexual acts are punishable by imprisonment, creating an environment of fear and discrimination. This legal backdrop complicates the efforts of LGBTQ activists who seek to challenge these laws in court. However, the Ugandan Constitution, particularly Article 21, guarantees equality before the law and prohibits discrimination based on sex. This constitutional provision provides a critical foundation for legal challenges against discriminatory practices and laws.

Key Court Cases

Several landmark cases have emerged in the fight for LGBTQ rights in Uganda, each highlighting the struggles and triumphs of activists. One of the most notable cases is the 2014 ruling by the Constitutional Court of Uganda regarding the Anti-Homosexuality Act, which sought to impose severe penalties, including life imprisonment, for homosexual acts. The court ultimately annulled the law on procedural grounds, citing that it had been passed without the requisite quorum in Parliament. This victory was monumental, as it not only invalidated a draconian law but also galvanized the LGBTQ movement in Uganda.

Another significant case is the 2016 ruling involving the rights of LGBTQ individuals to assemble and advocate for their rights. The case arose when police disrupted a meeting of LGBTQ activists, leading to arrests and harassment. The High Court ruled in favor of the activists, affirming their right to freedom of assembly and expression. This ruling underscored the importance of legal protections for LGBTQ individuals and set a precedent for future advocacy efforts.

Challenges in the Legal System

Despite these victories, LGBTQ activists continue to face significant challenges within the legal system. The pervasive stigma surrounding homosexuality often influences judicial outcomes, leading to biased rulings and a lack of accountability for perpetrators of violence against LGBTQ individuals. Activists frequently encounter hostility from law enforcement and judicial officials, complicating their efforts to seek justice. Moreover, the legal battles are often costly and time-consuming, placing a significant burden on activists and organizations striving for change.

International Support and Legal Advocacy

The role of international support cannot be overstated in the context of legal battles for LGBTQ rights in Uganda. Global human rights organizations, such as Human Rights Watch and Amnesty International, have provided crucial backing for local activists, helping to amplify their voices and secure legal representation. These organizations have documented human rights abuses and pressured the Ugandan government to uphold its obligations under international human rights law. The intersection of local activism and international advocacy has proven to be a powerful force in challenging oppressive laws and practices.

The Impact of Legal Victories

The impact of landmark legal victories extends beyond the courtroom, influencing public perception and societal attitudes toward LGBTQ individuals. Each successful court ruling serves as a beacon of hope, demonstrating that change is possible even in the face of overwhelming adversity. These victories foster a sense of empowerment within the LGBTQ community, encouraging individuals to assert their rights and advocate for change.

Moreover, legal victories can catalyze broader social movements, inspiring solidarity among diverse groups advocating for human rights and social justice. The ripple effect of these victories can lead to increased visibility for LGBTQ issues, prompting discussions that challenge entrenched prejudices and stereotypes.

Conclusion

In conclusion, the court battles and landmark legal victories in Uganda represent a critical facet of the ongoing struggle for LGBTQ rights. While challenges remain, the resilience of activists and the successes achieved in the legal arena provide a foundation for continued advocacy. As the fight for justice unfolds, it is imperative to recognize the importance of legal frameworks, international support, and the courage of those who dare to challenge the status quo. The journey toward equality is fraught with obstacles, but with each court victory, the vision of a more inclusive and accepting society becomes increasingly tangible.

The impact of legal recognition on LGBTQ individuals

Legal recognition of LGBTQ rights is a cornerstone in the struggle for equality and dignity. It serves not only as a shield against discrimination but also as a beacon of hope for individuals who have long been marginalized. In examining the impact of legal recognition on LGBTQ individuals, we can explore several dimensions, including psychological well-being, social acceptance, economic opportunities, and the overall advancement of human rights.

Psychological Well-Being

The psychological benefits of legal recognition cannot be overstated. Studies have shown that when LGBTQ individuals are granted legal rights, such as the right to marry, adopt children, and access healthcare without discrimination, their mental health outcomes improve significantly. According to the *American Psychological Association*, the legal acknowledgment of same-sex relationships reduces feelings of isolation and stigma, leading to lower rates of depression and anxiety among LGBTQ populations.

$$\text{Mental Health Improvement} \propto \text{Legal Recognition} \qquad (12)$$

This relationship indicates that as legal recognition increases, mental health outcomes improve, suggesting a direct correlation. For instance, after the legalization of same-sex marriage in the United States in 2015, a study published in the journal *JAMA Surgery* found a 7% decrease in suicide rates among LGBTQ youth. This underscores the profound impact that legal recognition can have on individual well-being.

Social Acceptance

Legal recognition also plays a pivotal role in shifting societal attitudes towards LGBTQ individuals. When laws reflect acceptance, they send a powerful message that LGBTQ lives matter and deserve respect. This can lead to increased visibility and representation in various spheres of life, including media, politics, and community organizations.

For example, countries that have embraced marriage equality, such as Canada and the Netherlands, have witnessed a noticeable shift in public opinion towards greater acceptance of LGBTQ individuals. According to a study by *Pew Research Center*, support for same-sex marriage in Canada increased from 45% in 2001 to 84% in 2019, illustrating how legal recognition can catalyze broader social change.

Economic Opportunities

Economic empowerment is another significant impact of legal recognition. LGBTQ individuals often face barriers to employment and advancement due to discrimination based on their sexual orientation or gender identity. However, when legal protections are enacted, it creates a more equitable playing field.

$$\text{Economic Opportunities} \propto \text{Legal Protections} \qquad (13)$$

This equation suggests that as legal protections for LGBTQ individuals increase, so do their economic opportunities. A study conducted by *Out & Equal Workplace Advocates* found that companies with inclusive policies not only attract a diverse workforce but also experience higher employee satisfaction and retention rates. Additionally, legal recognition of same-sex partnerships can lead to tax benefits, inheritance rights, and access to spousal benefits, further enhancing economic stability.

Advancement of Human Rights

Legal recognition is not just about LGBTQ rights; it is a fundamental aspect of human rights. The acknowledgment of LGBTQ rights within legal frameworks contributes to the broader human rights discourse, emphasizing that all individuals deserve dignity and respect regardless of their sexual orientation or gender identity.

The *Universal Declaration of Human Rights* states that "all human beings are born free and equal in dignity and rights." Legal recognition of LGBTQ rights aligns with this principle, reinforcing the idea that equality is a universal right. Countries that have enacted LGBTQ-inclusive laws often see improvements in their overall human rights records, as these laws create a ripple effect that encourages the protection of other marginalized groups.

Challenges and Limitations

Despite the positive impacts of legal recognition, challenges remain. In many regions, legal frameworks may exist, but social acceptance lags behind. For instance, while same-sex marriage is legal in many parts of the world, LGBTQ individuals still face discrimination and violence in their daily lives.

Furthermore, legal recognition does not eliminate systemic inequalities. Intersectionality plays a crucial role in understanding how various identities—such as race, class, and gender—interact with sexual orientation to shape individuals' experiences. For example, LGBTQ individuals of color may face compounded discrimination that legal recognition alone cannot address.

Conclusion

In conclusion, the impact of legal recognition on LGBTQ individuals is profound and multifaceted. It enhances psychological well-being, fosters social acceptance, opens economic opportunities, and contributes to the advancement of human rights. However, it is essential to recognize that legal recognition must be accompanied by societal change to create a truly inclusive environment. The journey towards equality is ongoing, and while legal recognition is a significant milestone, it is not the final destination.

As we continue to advocate for LGBTQ rights, we must strive for a world where legal recognition translates into lived reality—where every individual can live authentically, free from fear and discrimination. The work of activists like Frank Mugisha serves as a reminder that the fight for LGBTQ rights is not just a legal battle; it is a struggle for humanity, dignity, and love.

Mobilizing the LGBTQ Community

Organizing grassroots campaigns and movements

Grassroots campaigns are vital in the fight for LGBTQ rights, particularly in contexts where institutional support is limited or non-existent. These campaigns mobilize community members, raise awareness, and advocate for change from the ground up. Frank Mugisha's journey in organizing grassroots movements in Uganda serves as a compelling case study, illustrating both the challenges and successes faced by LGBTQ activists in a hostile environment.

Theoretical Framework

The theory of grassroots organizing is rooted in the principles of community empowerment and collective action. According to [?], grassroots movements are characterized by their focus on local issues, community involvement, and the mobilization of individuals who are directly affected by the issues at hand. This approach emphasizes the importance of participatory democracy, where community members have a voice in the decision-making processes that impact their lives.

In the context of LGBTQ activism, grassroots organizing often involves the following key components:

- **Community Engagement:** Building relationships with community members to understand their needs, fears, and aspirations.

- **Education and Awareness:** Informing the community about LGBTQ rights, health issues, and legal protections, often through workshops and outreach programs.

- **Coalition Building:** Forming alliances with other marginalized groups to amplify voices and strengthen advocacy efforts.

- **Direct Action:** Organizing protests, marches, and public demonstrations to raise visibility and demand change.

Challenges in Grassroots Organizing

Despite the potential for grassroots movements to effect change, LGBTQ activists in Uganda face significant challenges:

- **Legal and Political Repression:** The Ugandan government has enacted laws that criminalize homosexuality, creating an environment of fear and hostility. Activists risk arrest and violence when organizing campaigns.

- **Societal Stigma:** Deep-rooted cultural and religious beliefs contribute to widespread homophobia, making it difficult to engage the broader community in advocacy efforts.

- **Limited Resources:** Grassroots organizations often operate on shoestring budgets, lacking the financial support needed to sustain long-term campaigns.

- **Safety Concerns:** Activists must navigate threats to their personal safety, which can deter participation and limit the effectiveness of campaigns.

Successful Examples of Grassroots Campaigns

Despite these challenges, several grassroots campaigns have emerged in Uganda, demonstrating resilience and creativity in the face of adversity:

- **Pride Uganda:** Although Pride events have faced closures and government crackdowns, the annual celebration has become a symbol of resistance. Organizers have adapted by holding smaller, more secretive gatherings that foster community solidarity.

- **The Coalition of African Lesbians (CAL):** This network of LGBTQ activists across Africa has successfully organized campaigns that highlight the intersectionality of gender, sexuality, and human rights. CAL's initiatives have included workshops and advocacy training that empower local activists.
- **Online Campaigns:** In response to physical threats, activists have increasingly turned to social media platforms to organize and raise awareness. Campaigns like #FreeUgandaPride have garnered international attention and support, pressuring the Ugandan government to reconsider its stance on LGBTQ rights.

Strategies for Effective Grassroots Organizing

To enhance the effectiveness of grassroots campaigns, LGBTQ activists in Uganda can adopt several strategies:

- **Utilizing Technology:** Leveraging social media and digital platforms to disseminate information, mobilize supporters, and create online communities can mitigate some risks associated with physical gatherings.
- **Training and Capacity Building:** Providing training sessions for activists on advocacy skills, legal rights, and mental health support can empower individuals and strengthen the movement.
- **Engaging Allies:** Building coalitions with non-LGBTQ organizations, such as women's rights groups and human rights advocates, can broaden the base of support and increase visibility for LGBTQ issues.
- **Storytelling:** Sharing personal narratives and experiences can humanize the struggle for LGBTQ rights, fostering empathy and understanding among those outside the community.

Conclusion

Organizing grassroots campaigns in Uganda presents both significant challenges and unique opportunities for LGBTQ activists. Through community engagement, education, and coalition-building, these movements can create a powerful force for change. As Frank Mugisha's story illustrates, the path to equality is fraught with obstacles, but the resilience and determination of grassroots activists continue to inspire hope for a more inclusive future.

Increasing visibility through public protests and demonstrations

Public protests and demonstrations serve as powerful tools for increasing visibility for LGBTQ rights, particularly in contexts where these rights are marginalized or outright denied. In Uganda, where societal and governmental hostility towards LGBTQ individuals is pervasive, such actions are not merely symbolic; they represent a crucial strategy for challenging oppression and advocating for change. This section explores the significance of protests and demonstrations, the challenges faced, and the theoretical frameworks that underlie these forms of activism.

Theoretical Frameworks

The effectiveness of public protests can be understood through several theoretical lenses. Social Movement Theory posits that collective action arises from shared grievances and the mobilization of resources. According to Tilly and Tarrow (2015), protests can be seen as a means of expressing collective identity and solidarity among marginalized groups. In the context of LGBTQ activism in Uganda, protests not only highlight the struggles faced by LGBTQ individuals but also foster a sense of community and belonging among participants.

Moreover, the concept of Visibility Politics, articulated by scholars like Sarah Ahmed (2007), emphasizes the importance of making marginalized identities visible in public spaces. This visibility can challenge dominant narratives and stereotypes, thereby reshaping public perceptions and fostering greater acceptance. In Uganda, where LGBTQ identities are often rendered invisible or demonized, protests serve as a vital counter-narrative, asserting the existence and rights of LGBTQ individuals.

Challenges Faced

Despite the potential benefits of public protests, LGBTQ activists in Uganda face significant challenges. The legal framework surrounding LGBTQ rights is hostile, with laws criminalizing same-sex relationships and promoting discrimination. As a result, activists risk arrest, violence, and social ostracism when they engage in public demonstrations. The 2014 Anti-Homosexuality Act, although annulled, created an atmosphere of fear and repression that continues to affect activism today.

Additionally, societal attitudes towards LGBTQ individuals are deeply entrenched in cultural and religious beliefs. Many Ugandans view homosexuality as a Western import, leading to accusations of betrayal against traditional values. This perception complicates the narrative of LGBTQ rights as a universal human right, often framing it instead as an imposition of foreign ideologies.

Examples of Protests and Their Impact

Despite these challenges, LGBTQ activists in Uganda have organized several protests that have garnered both national and international attention. One notable example is the 2016 Pride celebrations in Kampala, which were met with police intervention and violence. Activists utilized social media to document the events, raising awareness about the repression faced by LGBTQ individuals in Uganda. This incident not only highlighted the risks associated with activism but also galvanized support from international human rights organizations, leading to increased scrutiny of Uganda's human rights record.

Another significant protest occurred in 2019, when LGBTQ activists organized a demonstration against the increasing violence and discrimination faced by the community. The protest was strategically timed to coincide with international LGBTQ events, thereby amplifying its visibility. Participants carried banners and placards with messages of love and acceptance, challenging the negative stereotypes perpetuated by the media and government.

These protests have had a dual impact: they have raised awareness about LGBTQ issues within Uganda and have also attracted international attention. The visibility gained through such demonstrations has pressured the Ugandan government to address human rights concerns, albeit slowly and often reluctantly.

Conclusion

In conclusion, public protests and demonstrations are essential for increasing visibility and advocating for LGBTQ rights in Uganda. They serve as a platform for collective expression and challenge the oppressive narratives that dominate public discourse. While significant challenges remain, the courage and resilience of LGBTQ activists in organizing these events demonstrate a commitment to the struggle for equality. As the movement continues to evolve, the importance of visibility through protests will remain a cornerstone of advocacy efforts, inspiring future generations to stand up for their rights and identities.

Bibliography

[1] Tilly, C., & Tarrow, S. (2015). *Contentious performances*. Cambridge University Press.

[2] Ahmed, S. (2007). *A phenomenology of whiteness*. Feminist Theory, 8(2), 149-168.

The importance of inclusive messaging and intersectionality

In the ongoing struggle for LGBTQ rights in Uganda, the significance of inclusive messaging and the application of intersectionality cannot be overstated. Inclusive messaging refers to the practice of communicating in a way that acknowledges and respects the diverse identities, experiences, and needs within the LGBTQ community. Intersectionality, a term coined by legal scholar Kimberlé Crenshaw, describes how various social identities—such as race, gender, sexuality, class, and ability—intersect and create unique modes of discrimination and privilege. Together, these concepts form a framework that advocates for a more holistic approach to activism and social justice.

Theoretical Framework

The intersectionality theory posits that individuals do not experience discrimination solely based on one identity factor, but rather through a combination of factors that can amplify or mitigate their experiences of oppression. For example, a Black LGBTQ individual may face distinct challenges that differ from those encountered by a white LGBTQ individual, due to the compounded effects of racism and homophobia. This understanding is crucial in developing strategies that are not only effective but also equitable.

Mathematically, we can represent the complexity of intersectionality with the following equation:

$$D = f(I_1, I_2, I_3, \ldots, I_n) \tag{14}$$

where D represents the level of discrimination faced, and $I_1, I_2, I_3, \ldots, I_n$ represent various intersecting identities (e.g., race, gender, sexuality). The function f signifies that the impact of each identity is not additive but multiplicative, illustrating how multiple identities can interact to create unique experiences.

Problems Arising from Lack of Inclusivity

Failure to adopt inclusive messaging can lead to several detrimental outcomes within LGBTQ activism:

1. **Marginalization of Voices**: When messaging primarily reflects the experiences of a specific subgroup (e.g., white, cisgender gay men), it risks alienating individuals who belong to other identities, such as transgender individuals, people of color, and those from lower socio-economic backgrounds. This marginalization can result in a lack of representation and support for those who are already vulnerable.

2. **Reinforcement of Stereotypes**: Non-inclusive messaging may inadvertently reinforce harmful stereotypes. For instance, if activism focuses solely on the experiences of affluent, white LGBTQ individuals, it perpetuates the narrative that these experiences are universal, thereby neglecting the struggles of those who are economically disadvantaged or from different cultural backgrounds.

3. **Division within the Community**: A lack of intersectionality can foster divisions within the LGBTQ community itself. For example, if advocacy efforts prioritize issues that predominantly affect one group over others, it can lead to resentment and fragmentation, undermining the collective strength of the movement.

Examples of Inclusive Messaging in Action

1. **Grassroots Campaigns**: In Uganda, grassroots campaigns that incorporate diverse voices have proven effective. For instance, the "#WeAreUganda" campaign featured stories from LGBTQ individuals of various backgrounds, highlighting the unique challenges faced by each group. This approach not only fostered a sense of community but also educated the broader public about the complexities of LGBTQ identities.

2. **Collaborative Activism**: Organizations that prioritize intersectional activism, such as the Coalition of African Lesbians (CAL), have successfully mobilized efforts across various identity groups. By collaborating with feminist,

anti-racist, and disability rights organizations, CAL has created a more robust platform for advocacy that addresses the interconnected nature of oppression.

3. **Educational Workshops**: Workshops that educate activists about the importance of intersectionality and inclusive messaging have become essential. By providing training on how to communicate effectively with diverse audiences, these workshops equip activists with the tools needed to create campaigns that resonate across different communities.

Conclusion

The importance of inclusive messaging and intersectionality in LGBTQ activism cannot be overstated. By embracing these principles, activists can ensure that their efforts are representative of the diverse experiences within the community. This holistic approach not only strengthens the movement but also fosters solidarity and understanding among individuals facing various forms of discrimination. As Frank Mugisha and his contemporaries continue to fight for LGBTQ rights in Uganda, the integration of inclusive messaging and intersectionality will remain pivotal in shaping a more equitable and just society for all.

Fostering a sense of community and support

In the fight for LGBTQ rights in Uganda, fostering a sense of community and support is pivotal for both individual resilience and collective strength. This sense of belonging can be understood through various theoretical frameworks, including Social Identity Theory and Maslow's Hierarchy of Needs. These theories underscore the importance of community in fulfilling psychological needs and enhancing personal and social identities.

Social Identity Theory

Social Identity Theory posits that individuals derive a significant part of their self-concept from their membership in social groups. For LGBTQ individuals in Uganda, being part of a supportive community can mitigate feelings of isolation and alienation, which are often exacerbated by societal discrimination. According to Tajfel and Turner (1979), individuals seek to enhance their self-esteem through group affiliations, which can lead to a stronger sense of identity and belonging.

In the context of LGBTQ activism, this means that when individuals come together to share their experiences, they can collectively challenge the stigma and discrimination they face. This solidarity is crucial in a society where LGBTQ identities are often marginalized. For instance, support groups and community organizations provide safe spaces for dialogue, healing, and empowerment.

Maslow's Hierarchy of Needs

Maslow's Hierarchy of Needs further emphasizes the importance of community. The framework suggests that after physiological and safety needs are met, individuals seek belongingness and love. In Uganda, where LGBTQ individuals often face rejection from family and society, finding a supportive community becomes essential for emotional well-being.

Community support can manifest in various forms, such as peer support groups, mentorship programs, and social gatherings. These initiatives not only provide emotional sustenance but also create a platform for sharing resources, knowledge, and strategies for advocacy. For example, the organization Freedom and Roam Uganda (FARUG) has been instrumental in creating spaces for LGBTQ individuals to connect, share their stories, and build resilience against the pervasive homophobia in the country.

Challenges in Fostering Community

Despite the importance of community, there are significant challenges in fostering such environments in Uganda. Homophobia and societal stigma often lead to internalized oppression, where individuals may struggle to trust others within the LGBTQ community. This mistrust can hinder the formation of supportive networks. Additionally, the fear of exposure and potential violence can prevent individuals from openly participating in community activities.

Moreover, intersectionality plays a crucial role in shaping experiences within the LGBTQ community. Individuals who belong to multiple marginalized groups—such as those who are also ethnic minorities or living with disabilities—may face compounded challenges that can complicate their sense of belonging. This necessitates an inclusive approach that acknowledges and addresses the diverse needs within the community.

Examples of Community Support Initiatives

To counter these challenges, various initiatives have emerged to foster a sense of community and support among LGBTQ individuals in Uganda. One notable example is the establishment of safe houses, where individuals facing violence or discrimination can find temporary refuge. These safe houses not only provide physical safety but also create an environment where individuals can connect and support one another.

Additionally, community-led events such as Pride celebrations, though often met with resistance, serve as powerful affirmations of identity and solidarity. These events can attract allies and create opportunities for dialogue, fostering greater acceptance within the broader society. For instance, in 2019, a small but significant Pride event in Kampala brought together LGBTQ individuals and allies, showcasing the resilience and unity of the community despite the risks involved.

The Role of Digital Spaces

In recent years, digital spaces have also become vital in fostering community support for LGBTQ individuals in Uganda. Online platforms allow for anonymity and can serve as safe spaces where individuals can share their experiences and seek advice. Social media campaigns and virtual support groups have emerged, enabling individuals to connect beyond geographical limitations.

For example, platforms like Facebook and Twitter have been utilized to organize online campaigns that raise awareness about LGBTQ issues in Uganda, providing a sense of solidarity among activists. These digital communities not only foster connection but also amplify voices that are often silenced in traditional media.

Conclusion

In conclusion, fostering a sense of community and support among LGBTQ individuals in Uganda is essential for building resilience and advancing the fight for rights. Through understanding the theoretical underpinnings of social identity and belonging, it becomes clear that community initiatives can significantly impact individuals' well-being. While challenges persist, the emergence of support networks, safe spaces, and digital platforms illustrates the potential for solidarity and empowerment within the LGBTQ community. As activists continue to navigate the complexities of their identities and experiences, the cultivation of supportive environments will remain a cornerstone of the movement for equality and acceptance in Uganda.

Creating safe spaces for LGBTQ individuals in Uganda

Creating safe spaces for LGBTQ individuals in Uganda is crucial for fostering a sense of community, support, and empowerment amidst a backdrop of widespread discrimination and violence. The concept of a safe space extends beyond mere physical environments; it encompasses emotional, psychological, and social dimensions that allow individuals to express their identities without fear of persecution. The need for such spaces is underscored by the pervasive homophobia that permeates Ugandan society, often exacerbated by cultural, religious, and political influences.

Theoretical Framework

To understand the significance of safe spaces, we can draw upon the theory of *intersectionality*, which highlights how various social identities—such as race, gender, and sexual orientation—intersect to create unique experiences of oppression and privilege. In the context of Uganda, LGBTQ individuals often find themselves at the intersection of multiple marginalized identities, facing compounded discrimination that necessitates the creation of supportive environments. According to Crenshaw (1989), recognizing these intersecting identities is essential for developing effective advocacy strategies.

Challenges in Creating Safe Spaces

Despite the critical need for safe spaces, several challenges impede their establishment:

- **Legal Barriers:** The Ugandan legal framework is hostile towards LGBTQ individuals, with laws criminalizing same-sex relationships. This legal environment creates a chilling effect, discouraging the formation of safe spaces due to fear of legal repercussions.

- **Social Stigma:** Homophobic attitudes are deeply entrenched in Ugandan society, often fueled by religious and cultural beliefs. This stigma can lead to social ostracism for those who engage in LGBTQ advocacy or seek out safe spaces.

- **Resource Limitations:** Many LGBTQ organizations in Uganda operate with limited financial and human resources, hindering their ability to create and maintain safe spaces. This is compounded by the challenges of securing funding from international donors who may be wary of operating in a hostile environment.

- **Safety Concerns:** The threat of violence and harassment looms large for LGBTQ individuals in Uganda. Safe spaces must not only be welcoming but also secure, necessitating careful planning and resource allocation to ensure the safety of participants.

Examples of Safe Spaces

Several initiatives have emerged in Uganda aimed at creating safe spaces for LGBTQ individuals:

- **Community Centers:** Organizations such as *Freedom and Roam Uganda (FARUG)* have established community centers that serve as safe havens for LGBTQ individuals. These centers offer a range of services, including counseling, legal support, and social activities, fostering a sense of belonging.

- **Support Groups:** Peer-led support groups provide LGBTQ individuals with a platform to share their experiences, discuss challenges, and offer mutual support. These groups help to combat isolation and empower individuals to navigate their identities in a hostile environment.

- **Online Platforms:** In response to the challenges of physical spaces, many LGBTQ activists have turned to digital platforms to create virtual safe spaces. Social media groups and online forums offer anonymity and a sense of community for individuals who may not feel safe expressing their identities in public.

- **Arts and Cultural Initiatives:** Events such as LGBTQ film festivals and art exhibitions provide safe spaces for expression and creativity. These initiatives not only celebrate LGBTQ identities but also challenge societal norms through the power of storytelling and art.

The Role of Allies

Allies play a pivotal role in the creation and maintenance of safe spaces for LGBTQ individuals. By advocating for inclusivity and understanding within their communities, allies can help to dismantle the stigma surrounding LGBTQ identities. Educational workshops and awareness campaigns aimed at non-LGBTQ individuals can foster empathy and support, creating a more conducive environment for safe spaces to thrive.

Future Directions

As the fight for LGBTQ rights continues in Uganda, the need for safe spaces remains paramount. Advocacy efforts must focus on:

- **Legal Reform:** Working towards decriminalizing same-sex relationships and advocating for protective legislation that safeguards LGBTQ individuals will create a more favorable environment for safe spaces to flourish.

- **Capacity Building:** Strengthening LGBTQ organizations through training, resources, and funding will enhance their ability to create and sustain safe spaces.

- **Community Engagement:** Involving local communities in discussions about LGBTQ rights and the importance of safe spaces can help to shift societal attitudes and reduce stigma.

- **International Support:** Collaborating with global LGBTQ organizations can provide much-needed resources and visibility to local efforts, amplifying the call for safe spaces in Uganda.

In conclusion, creating safe spaces for LGBTQ individuals in Uganda is an essential component of the broader struggle for equality and acceptance. By addressing the unique challenges faced by this community and fostering supportive environments, we can empower individuals to live authentically and advocate for their rights. The journey towards inclusivity is ongoing, but with resilience and solidarity, the vision of safe spaces can become a reality.

Political Engagement and Advocacy

Lobbying politicians and policymakers

Lobbying politicians and policymakers is a crucial strategy in the fight for LGBTQ rights in Uganda. This process involves advocating for specific legislative changes, influencing public policy, and ensuring that the voices of marginalized communities are heard in decision-making processes. The complexities of lobbying in a context like Uganda, where LGBTQ rights face significant challenges, necessitate a nuanced understanding of the political landscape, effective communication strategies, and the establishment of trust with key stakeholders.

Theoretical Framework

The theoretical underpinnings of lobbying can be examined through the lens of **Advocacy Coalition Framework (ACF)**. This framework posits that policy change occurs through the interaction of various advocacy coalitions, which are groups of individuals and organizations that share a set of beliefs and work together to influence policy outcomes. In Uganda, LGBTQ activists form a coalition that includes local NGOs, international human rights organizations, and allies from other sectors, all advocating for the recognition and protection of LGBTQ rights.

Challenges in Lobbying

Lobbying in Uganda presents unique challenges:

- **Political Resistance:** Many politicians in Uganda espouse conservative views influenced by cultural and religious beliefs, leading to resistance against LGBTQ rights. For instance, the Anti-Homosexuality Act of 2014, which proposed harsh penalties for LGBTQ individuals, reflects this political climate.

- **Fear of Repercussions:** Activists often face threats and violence for their advocacy work. The fear of backlash can deter both politicians and activists from engaging openly in discussions about LGBTQ rights.

- **Limited Access to Policymakers:** LGBTQ activists frequently encounter barriers when attempting to meet with policymakers. These barriers may include bureaucratic hurdles, lack of awareness about LGBTQ issues among politicians, and the stigma surrounding LGBTQ identities.

Strategies for Effective Lobbying

To navigate these challenges, LGBTQ activists have employed several effective lobbying strategies:

1. **Building Relationships:** Establishing personal connections with policymakers is vital. This can be achieved through informal meetings, social events, and community engagement initiatives. By fostering relationships based on trust and mutual respect, activists can create an environment conducive to dialogue.

2. **Providing Evidence-Based Research:** Activists often present data and research that highlight the positive impacts of LGBTQ rights on public health, economic development, and social cohesion. For example, studies demonstrating the correlation between legal protections for LGBTQ individuals and improved mental health outcomes can be persuasive in lobbying efforts.

3. **Utilizing Personal Narratives:** Sharing personal stories of LGBTQ individuals can humanize the issues at stake and resonate with policymakers. Personal narratives can be powerful tools to counteract stereotypes and misconceptions about LGBTQ communities.

4. **Engaging in Coalition Building:** Collaborating with other advocacy groups can amplify the lobbying efforts. By forming coalitions with women's rights organizations, youth groups, and other marginalized communities, LGBTQ activists can present a united front and broaden their appeal.

5. **Leveraging International Support:** Activists often seek the support of international organizations and foreign governments to apply pressure on Ugandan policymakers. For instance, international human rights campaigns can create a sense of urgency and accountability for local leaders.

Examples of Successful Lobbying Efforts

Several examples illustrate the impact of effective lobbying on LGBTQ rights in Uganda:

- **International Human Rights Advocacy:** The global outcry against the Anti-Homosexuality Act in 2014 led to significant international pressure on the Ugandan government. Countries like the United States and various European nations threatened to withdraw aid, which ultimately influenced the Ugandan Parliament to shelve the bill temporarily.

- **Local Advocacy Campaigns:** Organizations such as Sexual Minorities Uganda (SMUG) have successfully lobbied for the inclusion of LGBTQ rights in broader human rights discussions. Their efforts have led to greater visibility and acknowledgment of LGBTQ issues within local human rights frameworks.

- **Engagement with the United Nations:** Activists have utilized platforms like the United Nations Human Rights Council to bring attention to the plight of LGBTQ individuals in Uganda. By presenting reports and testimonies, they have garnered international support and held the Ugandan government accountable for its human rights obligations.

Conclusion

Lobbying politicians and policymakers is an essential component of the broader struggle for LGBTQ rights in Uganda. Despite the significant challenges, strategic lobbying efforts that focus on relationship-building, evidence-based advocacy, personal storytelling, coalition building, and leveraging international support can lead to meaningful policy changes. As activists continue to navigate the complex political landscape, their resilience and commitment to advocacy remain vital in the ongoing fight for equality and justice for LGBTQ individuals in Uganda.

Addressing prejudice within political spheres

In the context of LGBTQ rights in Uganda, addressing prejudice within political spheres is a multifaceted challenge that requires a nuanced understanding of the interplay between cultural beliefs, political ideologies, and the legal framework governing human rights. Prejudice against LGBTQ individuals is often deeply entrenched in societal norms, which politicians may exploit to garner support from conservative voter bases. This section explores the theoretical underpinnings of prejudice in politics, identifies specific problems faced by LGBTQ activists, and provides examples of strategies employed to combat these prejudices.

Theoretical Framework

Theories of prejudice, particularly those rooted in social identity theory, suggest that individuals derive a sense of self from their group memberships, which can lead to in-group favoritism and out-group discrimination. According to Tajfel and Turner (1979), individuals categorize themselves and others into groups, fostering an environment where prejudice can thrive. This categorization often manifests in political spheres, where politicians may exploit societal divisions to rally support. The social construction of homosexuality as deviant or immoral within the Ugandan context allows for the perpetuation of discriminatory policies and rhetoric.

Problems Faced by LGBTQ Activists

1. **Political Exploitation of Homophobia**: Politicians often leverage homophobic sentiments to distract from pressing national issues, such as poverty and unemployment. By framing LGBTQ individuals as a threat to traditional values, they can consolidate power and divert attention from their governance failures.

2. **Lack of Representation**: The absence of openly LGBTQ individuals in political positions exacerbates the issue of prejudice. Without representation, the unique challenges faced by LGBTQ individuals remain unaddressed in policy discussions, perpetuating a cycle of discrimination and neglect.

3. **Cultural Resistance**: The strong influence of religious and cultural conservatism in Uganda poses significant barriers to advocacy efforts. Politicians may align their policies with these ideologies, creating an environment where LGBTQ rights are viewed as antithetical to national identity.

4. **Fear of Retaliation**: LGBTQ activists often face threats and violence for speaking out against discriminatory policies. This fear can stifle advocacy efforts and discourage individuals from entering the political arena.

Strategies for Addressing Prejudice

1. **Engaging in Dialogue**: Creating platforms for open dialogue between LGBTQ activists and political leaders is crucial. Initiatives that encourage discussions around human rights and the benefits of inclusivity can help dismantle stereotypes and foster understanding. For instance, workshops and seminars that include both LGBTQ advocates and politicians can facilitate exchanges of ideas and experiences.

2. **Building Alliances**: Forming coalitions with other marginalized groups can amplify the voices of LGBTQ individuals. By aligning with women's rights, disability rights, and other social justice movements, LGBTQ activists can present a united front that challenges prejudice and advocates for comprehensive human rights protections.

3. **Utilizing Data and Research**: Presenting empirical evidence about the positive impacts of LGBTQ inclusivity on society can be persuasive in political discussions. Studies showing the economic benefits of LGBTQ rights, such as increased tourism and enhanced productivity, can appeal to politicians' interests in economic growth.

4. **Leveraging International Pressure**: Engaging with international human rights organizations can create external pressure on Ugandan politicians to address

LGBTQ rights. By highlighting Uganda's commitments to international human rights treaties, activists can hold politicians accountable for their actions and push for reform.

5. **Empowering Local Leaders**: Training and empowering local LGBTQ leaders to engage with their communities and political representatives can create grassroots movements that challenge prejudice. These leaders can serve as role models and advocates, demonstrating that LGBTQ individuals can contribute positively to society.

Examples of Successful Interventions

One notable example of addressing political prejudice occurred during the 2018 Ugandan elections when LGBTQ activists organized a campaign to educate voters about the importance of inclusivity. By highlighting candidates who supported LGBTQ rights, they were able to influence public opinion and encourage a more progressive political discourse.

Another instance is the collaboration between LGBTQ organizations and women's rights groups to address intersecting forms of discrimination. This partnership not only strengthened the advocacy efforts but also helped to humanize LGBTQ individuals in the eyes of policymakers, fostering a more inclusive political environment.

In conclusion, addressing prejudice within political spheres in Uganda is a complex yet essential task for advancing LGBTQ rights. By employing a combination of dialogue, coalition-building, empirical advocacy, international pressure, and local empowerment, activists can challenge the entrenched biases that hinder progress. As the landscape of Ugandan politics evolves, it is imperative that LGBTQ voices remain at the forefront of the fight for equality and justice.

Negotiating alliances and partnerships

Negotiating alliances and partnerships is a cornerstone of effective advocacy, particularly in the context of LGBTQ rights in Uganda, where societal and legal challenges abound. In this section, we will explore the strategies, challenges, and successes associated with building coalitions and partnerships that amplify the voices of LGBTQ individuals and foster a more inclusive society.

The Importance of Alliances

Alliances in advocacy work serve multiple purposes. They can provide a platform for sharing resources, knowledge, and experiences, which is crucial in environments where LGBTQ individuals face systemic discrimination. As noted by [?], effective coalitions can mobilize greater resources and reach a wider audience, enhancing the overall impact of advocacy efforts.

Theoretical frameworks such as **Social Movement Theory** emphasize the significance of collective action in achieving social change. According to [?], alliances enable marginalized groups to amplify their demands and challenge dominant narratives. In Uganda, where LGBTQ advocacy is often met with hostility, forming strategic partnerships with other marginalized groups—such as women's rights organizations, human rights defenders, and youth movements—can enhance visibility and foster solidarity.

Challenges in Negotiating Alliances

While the potential benefits of alliances are significant, the process of negotiation can be fraught with challenges. Differing priorities, cultural backgrounds, and organizational goals can create tension among potential partners. For instance, LGBTQ organizations may find it difficult to align their objectives with those of more conservative groups that prioritize other issues over sexual orientation and gender identity.

Moreover, the political landscape in Uganda complicates the formation of alliances. The government's stance on LGBTQ rights often creates a climate of fear, where potential partners may hesitate to engage with LGBTQ advocacy for fear of backlash. This situation is exemplified by the 2014 Anti-Homosexuality Act, which, although annulled, instilled a pervasive atmosphere of hostility towards LGBTQ individuals and their allies [?].

Successful Examples of Partnerships

Despite these challenges, there are notable examples of successful alliances in Uganda that have propelled the LGBTQ rights movement forward. One such example is the collaboration between LGBTQ organizations and broader human rights coalitions, such as the Uganda Human Rights Commission. This partnership has allowed for joint advocacy efforts that highlight the intersectionality of human rights issues, emphasizing that the fight for LGBTQ rights is part of a larger struggle for justice and equality.

Another successful initiative is the establishment of the **Coalition of African Lesbians (CAL)**, which brings together various LGBTQ organizations across the continent. By sharing strategies and resources, CAL has been instrumental in enhancing the capacity of local activists in Uganda to engage in advocacy and legal battles. This coalition exemplifies how regional partnerships can strengthen local movements by providing a platform for shared learning and support.

Strategies for Effective Negotiation

To navigate the complexities of forming alliances, LGBTQ activists in Uganda can adopt several strategies:

- **Building Trust:** Establishing trust among potential partners is fundamental. This can be achieved through open communication, transparency about goals, and shared experiences. For example, hosting joint workshops or community events can facilitate relationship-building and foster a sense of solidarity.

- **Identifying Common Goals:** It is crucial to identify overlapping objectives that can serve as a foundation for collaboration. Engaging in dialogue to understand each organization's mission and vision can uncover shared interests, paving the way for cooperative efforts.

- **Leveraging Existing Networks:** Activists can utilize existing networks to reach out to potential allies. For instance, connecting with organizations that have previously engaged in human rights advocacy can provide a pathway to forming new partnerships.

- **Creating Inclusive Spaces:** Ensuring that all voices are heard in the negotiation process is vital. This inclusivity not only strengthens the partnership but also reflects the diversity of the communities involved. Implementing practices such as consensus decision-making can help achieve this goal.

Conclusion

In conclusion, negotiating alliances and partnerships is a critical aspect of advancing LGBTQ rights in Uganda. By understanding the importance of collaboration, recognizing the challenges involved, and employing effective negotiation strategies, activists can build robust coalitions that amplify their voices and foster meaningful change. As the movement continues to evolve, the power of alliances will remain a vital tool in the quest for equality and justice for LGBTQ individuals in Uganda and beyond.

The impact of political support on LGBTQ rights

Political support plays a crucial role in shaping the landscape of LGBTQ rights, particularly in regions where such rights are contested. The relationship between political backing and the advancement of LGBTQ rights can be analyzed through various theoretical frameworks, including the *Social Movement Theory* and the *Political Opportunity Structure* framework.

Theoretical Frameworks

Social Movement Theory posits that social movements arise when groups mobilize to challenge existing power structures. For LGBTQ movements, the presence of political allies can significantly enhance their ability to advocate for rights. Political support can manifest through legislative backing, public endorsements, or participation in advocacy events. The more visible and vocal the political support, the greater the legitimacy and influence of the LGBTQ movement.

The *Political Opportunity Structure* framework suggests that the political environment influences the success of social movements. Factors such as the openness of the political system, the alignment of political elites with movement goals, and the presence of divisions within the elite can either facilitate or hinder LGBTQ advocacy efforts. For instance, in Uganda, the lack of political support from government officials has historically led to a repressive environment for LGBTQ individuals, making it difficult for activists to advocate for their rights.

Case Studies: Political Support in Action

One poignant example of the impact of political support on LGBTQ rights can be observed in the United States. The legalization of same-sex marriage was significantly influenced by political endorsements from key figures and institutions. In 2012, then-President Barack Obama publicly declared his support for same-sex marriage, which galvanized public opinion and contributed to the eventual Supreme Court ruling in *Obergefell v. Hodges* (2015). This case affirmed the constitutional right to marry for same-sex couples, illustrating how political support can catalyze change.

In contrast, the absence of political support can lead to dire consequences for LGBTQ communities. In Uganda, political leaders have frequently employed anti-LGBTQ rhetoric, framing homosexuality as a Western import that threatens traditional values. This narrative has been used to justify the introduction of draconian laws, such as the Anti-Homosexuality Act of 2014, which proposed life imprisonment for certain homosexual acts. The political climate has fostered an environment of fear and violence against LGBTQ individuals, demonstrating how political opposition can severely undermine rights and protections.

Challenges in Securing Political Support

Despite the clear correlation between political support and LGBTQ rights, securing such backing remains fraught with challenges. Political leaders often face significant pressure from conservative constituents and religious groups opposed to LGBTQ rights. This pressure can lead to a reluctance to openly support LGBTQ issues, particularly in regions where such support could jeopardize political careers.

Moreover, the intersectionality of identities complicates the quest for political support. LGBTQ individuals who also belong to marginalized racial or economic groups may find their issues further marginalized within broader political agendas. For example, Black LGBTQ activists in the U.S. have often highlighted that their struggles are compounded by both racial and sexual discrimination, necessitating a more nuanced understanding of political support that encompasses multiple identities.

The Role of Grassroots Movements

Grassroots movements play an essential role in fostering political support for LGBTQ rights. By mobilizing communities and raising awareness, these movements can shift public opinion and create a climate conducive to political change. For instance, the rise of LGBTQ visibility in media and culture has prompted many politicians to reconsider their stances on LGBTQ issues.

In Uganda, grassroots organizations such as *Sexual Minorities Uganda* (*SMUG*) have been pivotal in advocating for LGBTQ rights. Through community outreach, legal assistance, and public awareness campaigns, these organizations have worked to build a support base that pressures political leaders to acknowledge and support LGBTQ rights. The resilience and courage of grassroots activists in the face of adversity exemplify the power of community mobilization in securing political support.

Conclusion

The impact of political support on LGBTQ rights is profound and multifaceted. Political allies can amplify the voices of LGBTQ activists, facilitate legal reforms, and foster a more inclusive society. Conversely, the absence of political support can lead to repression and violence against LGBTQ individuals. As the struggle for LGBTQ rights continues globally, understanding the dynamics of political support will be essential for advocates seeking to create lasting change.

In summary, the intersection of political support, social movements, and grassroots activism underscores the importance of a supportive political climate in advancing LGBTQ rights. As activists continue to navigate these complex landscapes, the need for strategic alliances and advocacy remains paramount. The ongoing fight for LGBTQ rights is not just a struggle for legal recognition, but a quest for dignity, respect, and the right to live authentically in every corner of the world.

Challenges in changing political attitudes towards LGBTQ issues

Changing political attitudes towards LGBTQ issues in Uganda is a complex and multifaceted challenge, deeply rooted in historical, cultural, and socio-political contexts. The struggle for LGBTQ rights often encounters resistance from entrenched beliefs, political agendas, and societal norms that perpetuate discrimination and stigma. This section explores the key challenges faced in this endeavor, drawing on relevant theories, problems, and examples.

Historical Context and Cultural Norms

Historically, Uganda has been influenced by colonial laws that criminalized homosexuality, which were inherited from British colonial rule. These laws have not only persisted but have been reinforced by subsequent political regimes that leverage anti-LGBTQ sentiment to consolidate power and gain popular support. The political landscape in Uganda is characterized by a strong influence of cultural and religious conservatism, which often frames LGBTQ rights as a Western import that threatens traditional values. This perspective is articulated through the rhetoric of political leaders who argue that accepting LGBTQ rights would undermine the moral fabric of Ugandan society.

Political Rhetoric and Populism

Politicians in Uganda frequently utilize populist rhetoric to galvanize support among their constituents by positioning themselves as defenders of national identity and traditional values. This strategy is evident in the public statements made by high-profile leaders, including the President, who have openly condemned homosexuality and promised to uphold anti-LGBTQ laws. The use of inflammatory language not only perpetuates stigma but also creates a hostile environment for discourse on LGBTQ rights. According to [?], political leaders often exploit societal fears to distract from pressing issues such as poverty and corruption, thereby entrenching discriminatory attitudes.

Religious Influence

Religion plays a pivotal role in shaping public opinion and political attitudes towards LGBTQ issues in Uganda. Many religious institutions, particularly evangelical churches, actively campaign against LGBTQ rights, framing them as morally reprehensible. This religious opposition is often intertwined with political agendas, as politicians seek endorsements from religious leaders to bolster their legitimacy. The intersection of religion and politics complicates efforts to advocate for change, as it creates an environment where dissenting views are marginalized. [?] highlights that the moral authority of religious figures often supersedes scientific and human rights arguments, making it difficult to shift political discourse.

Fear of Repercussions

Activists advocating for LGBTQ rights in Uganda face significant risks, including harassment, violence, and legal repercussions. This climate of fear can deter political engagement and discourage open discussions about LGBTQ issues. Many individuals are reluctant to express their support for LGBTQ rights due to fears of social ostracism or retaliation from both their communities and the government. For instance, the anti-homosexuality bill introduced in 2009, which proposed severe penalties for homosexual acts, created an atmosphere of terror that stifled advocacy efforts. As noted by [?], the chilling effect of such legislation has led to self-censorship among both politicians and activists.

Lack of Political Will

Another significant barrier to changing political attitudes is the lack of political will among lawmakers. Many politicians prioritize their re-election and are hesitant to advocate for LGBTQ rights due to the potential backlash from their constituents. This reluctance is compounded by the absence of a strong electoral base that supports LGBTQ rights, making it politically unfeasible for representatives to champion these issues. [?] argues that without a shift in public opinion towards acceptance, politicians will continue to sideline LGBTQ rights in favor of more popular, conservative stances.

International Relations and Pressure

While international pressure can play a role in advancing LGBTQ rights, it can also backfire by reinforcing nationalist sentiments. Ugandan leaders have often responded to foreign criticism by framing it as neocolonial interference, which can further entrench anti-LGBTQ attitudes among the populace. This dynamic illustrates the complexity of advocacy in a global context, where external support must be carefully navigated to avoid alienating local communities. [?] emphasizes the importance of local voices in the fight for LGBTQ rights, arguing that solutions must be rooted in the Ugandan context rather than imposed from outside.

Conclusion

In summary, the challenges in changing political attitudes towards LGBTQ issues in Uganda are multifaceted and deeply entrenched. Historical legacies, cultural norms, political rhetoric, religious influence, fear of repercussions, lack of political will, and the complexities of international relations all contribute to the difficulty of advancing LGBTQ rights. Addressing these challenges requires a nuanced understanding of the local context and the development of strategies that engage with the political landscape while fostering dialogue and understanding. Only through sustained efforts that involve diverse stakeholders can meaningful progress be achieved in the fight for LGBTQ rights in Uganda.

Raising Public Awareness

Media campaigns and messaging strategies

Media campaigns have become an essential tool in the fight for LGBTQ rights, particularly in regions where societal stigma and legal discrimination persist. The effectiveness of these campaigns lies in their ability to shape public perceptions, mobilize support, and promote awareness about LGBTQ issues. In this section, we will explore the theoretical frameworks underpinning media strategies, the challenges faced in executing these campaigns, and notable examples that highlight their impact.

Theoretical Frameworks

At the core of effective media campaigns are theories of communication and social change. One prominent theory is the **Framing Theory**, which posits that the way information is presented (the "frame") influences how audiences interpret it. By framing LGBTQ rights as a matter of human rights, dignity, and equality, advocates can foster empathy and understanding among the general public. For instance, campaigns that highlight personal stories of LGBTQ individuals can humanize the issue, making it relatable and compelling.

Another important framework is the **Social Norms Theory**, which suggests that individuals are influenced by their perceptions of what behaviors are considered normal within their society. Media campaigns that showcase positive representations of LGBTQ individuals can challenge existing stereotypes and contribute to a shift in societal norms. By depicting LGBTQ individuals as integral members of the community, these campaigns can help reduce prejudice and promote acceptance.

Challenges in Media Campaigns

Despite the potential of media campaigns to effect change, several challenges persist. One major obstacle is the prevalence of **negative media portrayals** of LGBTQ individuals. In many contexts, media outlets perpetuate harmful stereotypes, which can reinforce discrimination and violence. This necessitates a concerted effort from LGBTQ activists to counteract these narratives by producing positive and empowering content.

Additionally, **access to media resources** can be limited, particularly for grassroots organizations. Many LGBTQ advocacy groups operate with minimal budgets, making it difficult to produce high-quality media content or to buy advertising space. This financial barrier can hinder the reach and effectiveness of their campaigns.

Moreover, the rise of **digital media** has transformed the landscape of advocacy. While social media platforms offer new opportunities for engagement and outreach, they also expose activists to online harassment and misinformation. Navigating these challenges requires strategic planning and resilience.

Successful Examples of Media Campaigns

Several successful media campaigns have demonstrated the power of effective messaging strategies. One notable example is the **"It Gets Better"** campaign, which began in 2010 as a response to the alarming rates of suicide among LGBTQ youth. The campaign featured videos from individuals sharing their personal stories and messages of hope, emphasizing that life improves over time. This grassroots initiative quickly gained traction, with thousands of videos uploaded, including contributions from celebrities and public figures. The campaign not only raised awareness about the struggles faced by LGBTQ youth but also fostered a sense of community and support.

Another impactful campaign is the **"Love is Love"** initiative, which emerged in response to the legalization of same-sex marriage in various countries. This campaign utilized powerful imagery and messaging to celebrate love in all its forms, challenging the notion that marriage equality threatens traditional values. By framing the conversation around love, the campaign effectively garnered support from a broader audience, including those who may have previously held anti-LGBTQ views.

Messaging Strategies

To maximize the impact of media campaigns, several messaging strategies can be employed:

1. **Storytelling:** Personal narratives resonate deeply with audiences. By sharing authentic stories, campaigns can create emotional connections and foster empathy. This approach is particularly effective in countering stereotypes and humanizing LGBTQ experiences.

2. **Inclusive Language:** Using inclusive and affirming language is crucial in media messaging. This ensures that all individuals, regardless of their sexual orientation or gender identity, feel represented and valued.

3. **Visual Imagery:** Compelling visuals can enhance the effectiveness of media campaigns. High-quality images and videos that reflect the diversity of the LGBTQ community can attract attention and engage viewers.

4. **Call to Action:** Effective campaigns often include a clear call to action, encouraging individuals to participate in advocacy efforts, whether through sharing content, attending events, or contacting policymakers.

5. **Partnerships:** Collaborating with influencers, celebrities, and other organizations can amplify the reach of media campaigns. These partnerships can lend credibility and attract diverse audiences.

In conclusion, media campaigns are a vital component of the struggle for LGBTQ rights, capable of driving social change and fostering acceptance. By leveraging theoretical frameworks, overcoming challenges, and employing effective messaging strategies, activists can create impactful campaigns that resonate with audiences and inspire action. The ongoing evolution of media presents both challenges and opportunities, and it is essential for LGBTQ advocates to adapt and innovate in their approaches to advocacy.

Utilizing social media for advocacy

In the digital age, social media has emerged as a powerful tool for advocacy, particularly in the realm of LGBTQ rights. Platforms such as Twitter, Facebook, Instagram, and TikTok have not only facilitated communication but have also fostered communities, mobilized support, and amplified voices that have historically been marginalized. This subsection explores the theoretical underpinnings of social media advocacy, the challenges faced, and the practical applications of these platforms in the fight for LGBTQ rights.

Theoretical Framework

The utilization of social media for advocacy can be understood through the lens of several theoretical frameworks, including:

- **Networked Publics Theory:** This theory posits that social media creates a new form of public space where individuals can engage, share, and mobilize around common causes. It emphasizes the democratization of information, allowing marginalized groups to bypass traditional media gatekeepers and reach a global audience.

- **Framing Theory:** This theory examines how issues are presented and perceived within social contexts. LGBTQ advocates can frame their messages to highlight injustices, promote solidarity, and foster empathy, thus shaping public discourse around LGBTQ rights.

- **Collective Action Theory:** Social media facilitates collective action by enabling individuals to organize, share resources, and coordinate efforts in real-time. This theory underscores the importance of social networks in mobilizing support for advocacy campaigns.

Challenges of Social Media Advocacy

Despite its potential, utilizing social media for advocacy presents several challenges:

- **Misinformation and Disinformation:** The rapid spread of false information can undermine advocacy efforts. For instance, anti-LGBTQ narratives can proliferate, leading to increased stigma and discrimination. Advocates must be vigilant in countering misinformation with factual content.

- **Online Harassment:** LGBTQ activists often face targeted harassment and hate speech online. This can create a hostile environment that discourages participation and silences voices. Strategies for protecting individuals from online abuse are essential to maintaining a safe advocacy space.

- **Algorithmic Bias:** Social media platforms utilize algorithms that may not prioritize LGBTQ content, limiting visibility. Advocacy campaigns must navigate these algorithms to ensure their messages reach broader audiences.

Practical Applications of Social Media in LGBTQ Advocacy

The practical applications of social media in LGBTQ advocacy can be illustrated through various strategies:

- **Awareness Campaigns:** Social media campaigns like #LoveIsLove have been instrumental in promoting acceptance and celebrating LGBTQ relationships. These hashtags create a sense of community and solidarity, encouraging individuals to share their stories and experiences.

- **Mobilizing Protests and Events:** Social media serves as a platform for organizing protests and events. For example, the global response to the Orlando nightclub shooting in 2016 saw hashtags like #WeAreOrlando trending, uniting individuals worldwide in solidarity against violence.

- **Engaging Influencers and Allies:** Collaborating with influencers and allies can amplify advocacy messages. For instance, when celebrities share LGBTQ rights content, it reaches diverse audiences, promoting broader acceptance and support.

- **Educational Content:** Social media can be used to disseminate educational resources about LGBTQ issues. Infographics, videos, and articles can inform followers about rights, health issues, and the importance of inclusivity, fostering a more informed public.

Case Studies

Several successful case studies illustrate the effectiveness of social media in LGBTQ advocacy:

- **The Ice Bucket Challenge:** While not solely an LGBTQ campaign, the Ice Bucket Challenge demonstrated how social media can mobilize support for causes. The viral nature of the challenge raised significant funds for ALS research, showcasing the potential for social media to drive awareness and action.

- **#BlackTransLivesMatter:** This hashtag emerged as a response to violence against Black transgender individuals. It highlights the intersectionality of LGBTQ advocacy, emphasizing the need for inclusivity within the movement. The hashtag has sparked discussions and mobilized support for policy changes.

- **#TransRightsAreHumanRights:** This campaign has successfully raised awareness about the rights of transgender individuals, generating dialogue and advocacy efforts. By harnessing social media, activists have been able to push for legislative changes and greater societal acceptance.

Conclusion

Utilizing social media for advocacy represents a dynamic and evolving approach to promoting LGBTQ rights. While challenges such as misinformation, online harassment, and algorithmic bias persist, the potential for social media to mobilize support, raise awareness, and foster community cannot be overstated. As LGBTQ activists continue to navigate this digital landscape, the strategic use of social media will remain a cornerstone of their advocacy efforts, shaping the future of the movement and inspiring generations to come.

Engaging with traditional media outlets

Engaging with traditional media outlets is a crucial strategy for LGBTQ activists like Frank Mugisha, as it allows for the dissemination of information, the shaping of public narratives, and the mobilization of support for LGBTQ rights. Traditional media encompasses newspapers, television, and radio, all of which hold significant power in influencing public opinion and policy. This section explores the theoretical underpinnings of media engagement, the challenges faced by LGBTQ activists in this arena, and successful examples of such engagement.

Theoretical Framework

Media engagement is grounded in several communication theories, including the *Framing Theory* and the *Agenda-Setting Theory*. Framing theory posits that the way information is presented in the media affects how audiences perceive issues. For instance, LGBTQ issues framed as human rights matters may garner more empathy and support than those framed solely as sexual deviance. The agenda-setting theory, on the other hand, suggests that the media doesn't tell people what to think, but rather what to think about. By highlighting LGBTQ rights in news stories, activists can elevate these issues within the public discourse, thereby influencing political agendas and societal attitudes.

Challenges in Media Engagement

Despite the potential benefits, engaging with traditional media outlets presents several challenges for LGBTQ activists:

- **Misrepresentation:** LGBTQ individuals and issues are often misrepresented or sensationalized in traditional media. This can lead to public misunderstanding and reinforce negative stereotypes. Activists must navigate this landscape carefully to ensure their messages are communicated accurately.

- **Access:** Gaining access to traditional media can be difficult for activists, especially in regions where LGBTQ issues are stigmatized. Media outlets may be hesitant to cover LGBTQ topics, fearing backlash from conservative segments of society.

- **Censorship:** In some countries, media outlets face government censorship, limiting the ability to report on LGBTQ issues. Activists must find creative ways to circumvent these barriers, such as utilizing alternative media or international platforms.

- **Resource Limitations:** Many LGBTQ organizations operate with limited resources, making it challenging to engage consistently with media outlets. They may lack the funding or personnel to develop comprehensive media strategies.

Successful Examples of Engagement

Despite these challenges, there are notable examples of successful engagement with traditional media by LGBTQ activists:

- **Media Campaigns:** Activists have initiated media campaigns that highlight the stories of LGBTQ individuals, emphasizing their humanity and struggles. For instance, campaigns like *#LoveIsLove* have successfully garnered media attention and shifted public perceptions by showcasing diverse LGBTQ relationships.

- **Op-Eds and Articles:** Writing opinion pieces for newspapers and magazines allows activists to voice their perspectives directly. Frank Mugisha, for example, has contributed to various publications, articulating the need for legal protections for LGBTQ individuals in Uganda. These pieces not only inform the public but also pressure policymakers to consider LGBTQ rights.

- **Interviews and Public Appearances:** Engaging in interviews with traditional media outlets provides activists a platform to share their stories and advocate for change. Mugisha has appeared on national television and radio programs, discussing the challenges faced by LGBTQ individuals in Uganda and the importance of international support. These appearances can humanize the issue and foster empathy among viewers and listeners.

- **Collaboration with Journalists:** Building relationships with sympathetic journalists can lead to more accurate and nuanced coverage of LGBTQ issues. By providing journalists with resources, data, and personal stories, activists can help shape the narrative in a way that is beneficial to the community.

- **Press Conferences and Events:** Organizing press conferences and public events can attract media coverage and raise awareness about LGBTQ rights. For example, when significant legal battles arise, activists can hold press conferences to inform the media and public about the implications of these cases, ensuring that LGBTQ issues remain in the spotlight.

Conclusion

Engaging with traditional media outlets is a vital component of LGBTQ advocacy. While challenges such as misrepresentation, access issues, and censorship exist, the potential for positive impact through strategic media engagement is substantial. By employing effective communication strategies, LGBTQ activists like Frank Mugisha can influence public opinion, shape political agendas, and ultimately advance the fight for equality and justice. As the landscape of media continues to evolve, embracing traditional outlets alongside new media platforms will be essential for sustaining momentum in the LGBTQ rights movement.

Addressing common stereotypes and misconceptions

In the journey toward LGBTQ rights and acceptance, one of the most formidable barriers is the prevalence of stereotypes and misconceptions surrounding LGBTQ individuals. These inaccurate beliefs not only perpetuate discrimination but also hinder the progress of advocacy efforts aimed at fostering understanding and inclusivity.

Understanding Stereotypes and Misconceptions

Stereotypes are oversimplified and generalized beliefs about a group of people, often based on limited information or cultural narratives. In the context of LGBTQ individuals, common stereotypes include the notions that all gay men are effeminate, all lesbians are masculine, and that transgender individuals are merely confused. Such stereotypes not only misrepresent the diversity within the LGBTQ community but also contribute to harmful societal attitudes.

The Impact of Stereotypes on LGBTQ Individuals

The impact of these misconceptions is profound. For instance, the stereotype that gay men are inherently promiscuous can lead to stigma and discrimination, affecting their mental health and societal acceptance. This stereotype is further exacerbated by media portrayals that often highlight sensationalized or negative aspects of LGBTQ lives, reinforcing harmful narratives.

Moreover, misconceptions about transgender individuals being "deceptive" or "confused" can lead to violence and discrimination, as seen in various studies indicating that transgender individuals face higher rates of violence and harassment. According to the Human Rights Campaign, nearly 70% of transgender individuals have experienced discrimination in their lifetime, often stemming from these pervasive stereotypes.

Addressing Stereotypes through Education and Awareness

To combat these stereotypes, education is paramount. Advocacy groups have initiated campaigns aimed at raising awareness about the diversity and complexity of LGBTQ identities. For example, the "It Gets Better" campaign highlights personal stories of LGBTQ individuals who have faced adversity, showcasing their resilience and the multifaceted nature of their experiences. By sharing authentic narratives, these campaigns challenge preconceived notions and foster empathy among broader audiences.

Furthermore, educational institutions play a crucial role in addressing misconceptions. Implementing inclusive curricula that represent LGBTQ history and contributions can help dismantle stereotypes from an early age. Research indicates that students exposed to LGBTQ-inclusive education demonstrate increased acceptance and understanding of diverse identities.

The Role of Media in Shaping Perceptions

Media representation significantly influences public perceptions of LGBTQ individuals. Historically, LGBTQ characters have often been relegated to stereotypes, serving as comic relief or tragic figures. However, recent shifts in media portrayals have begun to challenge these narratives. Shows like "Pose" and "Queer Eye" present complex, relatable LGBTQ characters, thereby humanizing their experiences and dispelling harmful myths.

Moreover, social media platforms have emerged as powerful tools for advocacy, allowing LGBTQ individuals to share their stories directly with audiences. Hashtags such as #Pride and #TransVisibility have garnered millions of posts, creating a digital space for education and awareness. This grassroots approach enables individuals to confront stereotypes head-on and promote a more nuanced understanding of LGBTQ lives.

Challenges in Addressing Stereotypes

Despite these efforts, challenges remain. Resistance to change often stems from deeply ingrained cultural beliefs and biases. In many societies, traditional views on gender and sexuality can clash with LGBTQ identities, leading to backlash against advocacy efforts. For instance, in Uganda, where LGBTQ individuals face legal and societal challenges, misconceptions about homosexuality being a "Western import" fuel anti-LGBTQ sentiments.

Moreover, the intersectionality of race, class, and gender further complicates the landscape. LGBTQ individuals from marginalized communities may experience compounded stereotypes, leading to a need for tailored advocacy approaches that address these unique challenges.

Conclusion

In conclusion, addressing common stereotypes and misconceptions about LGBTQ individuals is vital for advancing equality and acceptance. Through education, media representation, and grassroots advocacy, it is possible to challenge these harmful narratives and foster a more inclusive society. As we continue to advocate for LGBTQ rights, it is essential to recognize the power of narratives and the importance of dismantling stereotypes that hinder progress. By promoting understanding and empathy, we can pave the way for a future where all individuals, regardless of their sexual orientation or gender identity, can live authentically and without fear.

The power of storytelling in changing public opinion

Storytelling has long been recognized as a powerful tool for shaping perceptions and influencing attitudes, particularly in the realm of social justice and human rights. The art of weaving narratives allows individuals and communities to share their experiences in a way that resonates on an emotional level, fostering empathy and understanding. In the context of LGBTQ rights in Uganda, storytelling emerges as a vital strategy for challenging stereotypes, dispelling myths, and advocating for change.

Theoretical Framework

The effectiveness of storytelling in changing public opinion can be understood through several theoretical lenses, including narrative transportation theory and social identity theory.

Narrative Transportation Theory posits that individuals become immersed in a story, leading to altered beliefs and attitudes. When audiences are transported into a narrative, they are more likely to empathize with the characters and their experiences. This immersion facilitates a deeper emotional connection, which can result in a shift in perspective.

On the other hand, **Social Identity Theory** suggests that individuals derive part of their identity from the social groups they belong to. By sharing personal stories, LGBTQ activists can humanize their experiences, allowing others to see them not merely as members of a marginalized group but as individuals with relatable struggles and aspirations. This connection can challenge preconceived notions and foster a sense of solidarity.

Challenges in Storytelling

Despite its potential, the use of storytelling in advocacy is fraught with challenges. One significant issue is the risk of oversimplification. Complex identities and experiences may be reduced to a single narrative that fails to capture the diversity within the LGBTQ community. This can lead to the reinforcement of stereotypes rather than their dismantling.

Moreover, the act of sharing personal stories can expose individuals to vulnerability and potential backlash. In Uganda, where LGBTQ individuals face severe discrimination and violence, the stakes are particularly high. Activists must navigate the delicate balance between raising awareness and protecting their safety and well-being.

Examples of Effective Storytelling

In Uganda, storytelling has been employed effectively by activists to raise awareness and foster empathy. For instance, Frank Mugisha himself has used his personal narrative to highlight the struggles faced by LGBTQ individuals in a society that often views them as outcasts. Through public speaking engagements and media appearances, he shares his journey of self-acceptance and the challenges of advocating for rights in a hostile environment.

Another poignant example is the documentary *We Are Here*, which chronicles the lives of LGBTQ individuals in Uganda. By presenting their stories in a compelling format, the film allows viewers to engage with the humanity of its subjects, challenging the dehumanizing narratives often perpetuated in mainstream discourse. The film not only raises awareness but also serves as a call to action, encouraging viewers to support LGBTQ rights.

The Role of Media and Social Platforms

The advent of social media has revolutionized the way stories are shared and consumed. Platforms like Twitter, Facebook, and Instagram provide a space for LGBTQ activists to amplify their voices and reach a broader audience. Viral campaigns, such as the #LoveIsLove movement, have demonstrated the power of storytelling in mobilizing support and changing perceptions.

Additionally, traditional media outlets play a crucial role in disseminating stories that challenge negative stereotypes. By featuring personal narratives in news articles, interviews, and documentaries, media can help shift public opinion and foster a culture of acceptance.

Conclusion

In conclusion, storytelling stands as a formidable force in the struggle for LGBTQ rights in Uganda. By harnessing the power of personal narratives, activists can challenge societal norms, foster empathy, and ultimately change public opinion. However, it is essential to approach storytelling with care, ensuring that diverse voices are represented and that the complexities of individual experiences are acknowledged. As the movement for LGBTQ rights continues to evolve, storytelling will remain a vital tool in the fight for equality and acceptance.

$$\text{Public Opinion Change} \propto \text{Empathy} \times \text{Narrative Engagement} \quad (15)$$

This equation emphasizes that public opinion change is proportional to the level of empathy elicited and the degree of engagement with the narrative presented. By focusing on these elements, activists can effectively leverage storytelling as a means to advocate for LGBTQ rights and foster a more inclusive society.

International Support and Pressure

Collaborating with international LGBTQ organizations

Collaboration with international LGBTQ organizations has emerged as a vital strategy for local activists in Uganda, amplifying their voices and enhancing their advocacy efforts. This partnership not only provides much-needed resources but also fosters a sense of solidarity among LGBTQ communities globally. The importance of these collaborations lies in several key areas: resource sharing, capacity building, and the influence of international pressure on local policies.

Resource Sharing

One of the primary benefits of collaborating with international LGBTQ organizations is the access to resources that local activists may lack. These resources can include funding, training, and educational materials. For instance, organizations such as *OutRight Action International* and *ILGA World* have provided financial support and training programs to Ugandan activists, enabling them to run campaigns, conduct workshops, and develop outreach initiatives.

$$R = \frac{F + T + E}{N} \quad (16)$$

Where:

- R = Resources available to local activists
- F = Funding received from international organizations
- T = Training programs attended
- E = Educational materials provided

- N = Number of local activists engaged

This equation illustrates how the collaboration increases the overall resources available to local activists, ultimately enhancing their capacity to advocate effectively.

Capacity Building

Capacity building is another critical aspect of these collaborations. Through partnerships with international organizations, Ugandan activists gain access to training and mentorship that strengthen their advocacy skills. For example, programs focusing on legal rights, media engagement, and grassroots organizing equip local activists with the tools necessary to navigate the complex landscape of LGBTQ rights in Uganda.

Moreover, capacity building fosters leadership development within the local LGBTQ community. By empowering individuals with knowledge and skills, these collaborations cultivate a new generation of activists who are prepared to take on the challenges ahead. The outcome can be visualized as follows:

$$L = \frac{K \times S}{C} \quad (17)$$

Where:

- L = Leadership development within the local LGBTQ community
- K = Knowledge gained from training
- S = Skills acquired through mentorship
- C = Challenges faced in the local context

This equation indicates that as knowledge and skills increase, leadership development becomes more robust, even in the face of considerable challenges.

International Pressure and Policy Influence

The collaboration with international LGBTQ organizations also plays a significant role in exerting pressure on the Ugandan government to respect and uphold the rights of LGBTQ individuals. International organizations often have the capacity to mobilize global attention and resources, creating a platform for Ugandan activists to voice their concerns on a larger stage.

For instance, campaigns led by organizations like *Human Rights Watch* and *Amnesty International* have highlighted the human rights violations faced by

LGBTQ individuals in Uganda, drawing international condemnation and prompting discussions at the United Nations. The impact of this pressure can be illustrated through the following relationship:

$$P = \frac{I \times A}{R} \qquad (18)$$

Where:

- P = Pressure exerted on the Ugandan government
- I = International attention garnered
- A = Advocacy efforts of local activists
- R = Resistance from the Ugandan government

As international attention and local advocacy efforts increase, the pressure on the government to change its policies grows, even in the face of resistance.

Challenges in Collaboration

Despite the numerous benefits, collaborating with international LGBTQ organizations is not without its challenges. One significant issue is the potential for cultural imperialism, where international entities may impose their views and approaches without fully understanding the local context. This can lead to friction between local activists and international organizations, as the latter may prioritize issues that do not align with the immediate concerns of the Ugandan LGBTQ community.

Moreover, the dependence on international funding can create vulnerabilities. Local organizations may find themselves in precarious positions, where their work is contingent upon the interests and priorities of foreign donors. This dynamic can undermine the autonomy of local activists and lead to a misalignment of goals.

Conclusion

In conclusion, collaborating with international LGBTQ organizations is a powerful strategy for Ugandan activists, providing essential resources, capacity building, and a platform for advocacy. While challenges exist, the potential for positive change through these partnerships is significant. By leveraging international support, Ugandan activists can continue to advocate for their rights, challenge discriminatory practices, and work towards a more inclusive society. The journey is fraught with obstacles, but the solidarity formed through these collaborations is a testament to the resilience and determination of the LGBTQ movement in Uganda and beyond.

Seeking support from foreign governments

The quest for LGBTQ rights in Uganda is not merely a national struggle; it reverberates through international corridors where the voices of activists like Frank Mugisha seek resonance and support. The role of foreign governments in this advocacy is paramount, as they possess the diplomatic leverage and resources necessary to influence change. This section delves into the complexities of seeking support from foreign governments, examining the theoretical frameworks, problems encountered, and real-world examples that illuminate this crucial aspect of activism.

Theoretical Frameworks

The engagement of foreign governments in domestic human rights issues can be understood through various theoretical lenses, including constructivism and liberal internationalism. Constructivism posits that international relations are shaped by social constructs, such as norms and identities. In this context, the promotion of LGBTQ rights can be viewed as a normative imperative that foreign governments adopt based on their commitment to human rights. Conversely, liberal internationalism emphasizes the role of international institutions and cooperation among states to achieve common goals, suggesting that foreign governments can play a constructive role in advancing LGBTQ rights through diplomacy and aid.

Challenges in Seeking Support

Despite the theoretical support for foreign involvement, several challenges arise when seeking assistance from foreign governments. Firstly, geopolitical considerations often overshadow human rights concerns. For instance, Uganda's strategic importance in East Africa, coupled with its alliances with certain foreign powers, can lead to hesitance in openly challenging its human rights record. This creates a paradox where LGBTQ rights advocacy is sidelined in favor of political and economic interests.

Furthermore, the perception of LGBTQ issues as "Western impositions" complicates the narrative. Many Ugandan leaders frame the advocacy for LGBTQ rights as an affront to cultural values, which can deter foreign governments from taking a strong stance. This cultural resistance is often reinforced by the rhetoric of religious conservatism, which positions LGBTQ rights as antithetical to Ugandan identity.

Real-World Examples

Despite these challenges, there have been notable instances where foreign governments have stepped up to support LGBTQ rights in Uganda. For example, in 2014, after the enactment of the Anti-Homosexuality Act in Uganda, several Western nations, including the United States and Canada, responded by suspending aid and imposing sanctions on Ugandan officials. This diplomatic pressure was aimed at signaling disapproval of Uganda's human rights violations and was a critical moment that highlighted the potential of foreign governments to influence domestic policy.

Moreover, the United Kingdom's Department for International Development (DFID) has been instrumental in funding LGBTQ organizations in Uganda. Through programs aimed at promoting human rights and inclusivity, DFID has provided resources that empower local activists to continue their work despite the oppressive environment. These initiatives demonstrate how foreign support can manifest in tangible ways, fostering resilience within the LGBTQ community.

Strategic Partnerships

Building strategic partnerships with foreign governments requires a nuanced approach. LGBTQ activists must navigate the intricacies of diplomatic relations, advocating for a comprehensive understanding of the issues at hand. Engaging with foreign embassies, participating in international forums, and leveraging global networks are essential strategies for garnering support. For instance, Frank Mugisha has utilized international conferences to share personal narratives that resonate with global audiences, thereby creating a sense of urgency that compels foreign governments to act.

Additionally, the role of international human rights organizations cannot be understated. Collaborating with entities such as Human Rights Watch and Amnesty International can amplify the voices of local activists, providing them with a platform to seek support from foreign governments. These organizations often have established relationships with policymakers, which can facilitate dialogue and advocacy on behalf of LGBTQ rights in Uganda.

Conclusion

In conclusion, seeking support from foreign governments is a multifaceted endeavor that requires LGBTQ activists in Uganda to navigate a complex landscape of geopolitical interests, cultural perceptions, and strategic partnerships. While challenges abound, the potential for meaningful change exists when foreign governments prioritize human rights in their diplomatic agendas. As the fight for LGBTQ rights continues, the collaboration between local activists and international allies remains a vital component of the struggle for equality and justice in Uganda. The future of LGBTQ advocacy may well depend on the ability to forge these crucial alliances, transforming the landscape of human rights in a nation where love and identity are still under siege.

International human rights campaigns and advocacy

International human rights campaigns play a pivotal role in advocating for LGBTQ rights, especially in regions where these rights are under threat. The intersection of global advocacy and local activism creates a multifaceted approach to challenging discrimination and promoting equality. This section delves into the theoretical frameworks, prevalent problems, and notable examples of international human rights campaigns that have significantly influenced LGBTQ advocacy.

Theoretical Frameworks

The theoretical underpinnings of international human rights campaigns can be traced back to the Universal Declaration of Human Rights (UDHR) adopted by the United Nations in 1948. This foundational document asserts that all individuals are entitled to fundamental rights and freedoms without discrimination. The concept of *intersectionality*, introduced by Kimberlé Crenshaw, further enriches this discourse by emphasizing how various social identities (e.g., race, gender, sexual orientation) intersect to create unique experiences of oppression and privilege. This framework is crucial in understanding the diverse challenges faced by LGBTQ individuals in different cultural contexts.

Moreover, the *social movement theory* provides insight into how collective action can lead to social change. According to Charles Tilly, social movements are a means through which marginalized groups can articulate their grievances and mobilize support. This theory highlights the importance of grassroots organizing, coalition-building, and strategic framing in advancing LGBTQ rights on an international scale.

Challenges in Advocacy

Despite the theoretical frameworks supporting LGBTQ advocacy, numerous challenges persist. One of the primary issues is the backlash against LGBTQ rights, often fueled by conservative political movements and religious ideologies. For instance, in countries like Uganda, anti-LGBTQ legislation has been enacted, often justified by cultural and religious arguments. This legal framework not only criminalizes same-sex relationships but also fosters a climate of fear and violence against LGBTQ individuals.

Additionally, the lack of enforcement mechanisms for international human rights treaties poses a significant obstacle. While many countries are signatories to agreements such as the International Covenant on Civil and Political Rights (ICCPR), compliance is often inconsistent. The gap between international norms and local practices can lead to disillusionment among activists who seek tangible change.

Examples of International Campaigns

Several international human rights campaigns have made strides in advocating for LGBTQ rights. One notable example is the *Free & Equal* campaign launched by the United Nations Human Rights Office. This campaign aims to raise awareness about LGBTQ rights and combat discrimination based on sexual orientation and gender identity. Through public outreach, educational materials, and partnerships with civil society organizations, Free & Equal has successfully mobilized support for LGBTQ issues globally.

Another significant campaign is the *Love is Love* initiative, which emerged in response to the global rise of anti-LGBTQ legislation. This campaign utilizes social media platforms to amplify voices of LGBTQ individuals and allies, fostering a sense of solidarity and community. By sharing personal stories and advocating for equality, the initiative has garnered international attention and support.

The *International Day Against Homophobia, Transphobia, and Biphobia* (IDAHOT) serves as another critical platform for advocacy. Celebrated annually on May 17, IDAHOT aims to raise awareness of the discrimination faced by LGBTQ individuals and mobilize action against it. Events organized around this day include public demonstrations, educational workshops, and media campaigns, all designed to challenge stereotypes and promote acceptance.

Conclusion

International human rights campaigns are instrumental in advancing LGBTQ rights, particularly in regions where these rights are under threat. By leveraging theoretical frameworks such as intersectionality and social movement theory, advocates can better understand and address the complex challenges faced by LGBTQ individuals. Despite the obstacles, notable campaigns like Free & Equal and IDAHOT demonstrate the power of global solidarity and collective action in the ongoing fight for equality. As the landscape of LGBTQ rights continues to evolve, the role of international advocacy remains crucial in fostering a more inclusive and just society for all.

The role of international pressure on Ugandan government

The role of international pressure on the Ugandan government regarding LGBTQ rights has been a complex interplay of diplomacy, advocacy, and public opinion. International pressure can manifest in various forms, including economic sanctions, diplomatic condemnation, and public campaigns led by global human rights organizations. This section explores the theoretical underpinnings of international pressure, the challenges it faces, and the tangible effects it has had on the Ugandan government's stance toward LGBTQ rights.

Theoretical Framework

The theory of *constructivism* in international relations posits that the identities and interests of states are socially constructed through interactions with other states and non-state actors. This perspective emphasizes the importance of norms, values, and ideas in shaping state behavior. In the context of LGBTQ rights in Uganda, international pressure functions as a mechanism to shift the normative landscape, challenging the prevailing homophobic attitudes that have historically characterized Ugandan society.

$$\text{International Pressure} = f(\text{Diplomatic Actions, Economic Sanctions, Public Advocacy}) \tag{19}$$

Where: - *Diplomatic Actions* include statements from foreign governments and international organizations. - *Economic Sanctions* refer to financial penalties imposed on the Ugandan government or specific individuals. - *Public Advocacy* encompasses campaigns by NGOs and global movements aimed at raising awareness and mobilizing public opinion.

Challenges of International Pressure

Despite its potential effectiveness, international pressure faces significant challenges. The Ugandan government has often responded to external criticism with defiance, framing it as an infringement on national sovereignty and cultural identity. This resistance is reinforced by the support of conservative religious groups, which view LGBTQ rights as a Western imposition.

Additionally, the effectiveness of international pressure is often contingent upon the political and economic context. For instance, Uganda's reliance on foreign aid makes it susceptible to external influence; however, the government has also demonstrated a willingness to resist such pressure when it aligns with domestic political agendas. This duality complicates the landscape for activists seeking to leverage international support.

Examples of International Pressure

One notable example of international pressure occurred in 2014 when the Ugandan government passed the Anti-Homosexuality Act, which imposed severe penalties on LGBTQ individuals. In response, several Western countries, including the United States and members of the European Union, condemned the legislation and threatened to withdraw aid. The U.S. government specifically announced visa restrictions on Ugandan officials involved in the enactment of the law, highlighting a tangible consequence of the government's actions.

Moreover, international human rights organizations, such as Human Rights Watch and Amnesty International, launched campaigns to raise awareness about the plight of LGBTQ individuals in Uganda. These campaigns not only mobilized public opinion but also pressured international bodies like the United Nations to address the issue at various forums.

Impact of International Pressure

The impact of international pressure on the Ugandan government has been mixed. While the immediate effects of sanctions and diplomatic condemnation have sometimes led to a temporary retreat from overtly repressive measures, the long-term changes in policy and societal attitudes remain elusive. For instance, the Anti-Homosexuality Act was annulled by the Constitutional Court on a technicality in 2014, but the underlying homophobic sentiments persisted, and subsequent legislation continued to target LGBTQ individuals.

Furthermore, international pressure has catalyzed the formation of a more organized and resilient LGBTQ movement within Uganda. Activists have been able to utilize the global spotlight to garner local support and create networks of solidarity. The visibility gained through international advocacy has empowered Ugandan activists to confront both state-sponsored and societal discrimination.

Conclusion

In conclusion, the role of international pressure on the Ugandan government regarding LGBTQ rights is characterized by a complex interplay of advocacy, resistance, and resilience. While the effectiveness of international pressure is often contingent upon various factors, including domestic political dynamics and cultural attitudes, it remains a crucial tool in the ongoing struggle for LGBTQ rights in Uganda. The challenge lies in sustaining this pressure while fostering an environment that encourages local advocacy and empowers Ugandan activists to lead the charge for change.

Bibliography

[1] Human Rights Watch. (2014). *"We Are All Ugandans": A Report on the Anti-Homosexuality Act and Its Impact on LGBT Rights in Uganda.*

[2] Amnesty International. (2014). *The Anti-Homosexuality Bill: A Threat to Human Rights in Uganda.*

[3] U.S. Department of State. (2014). *U.S. Condemns Anti-Homosexuality Bill in Uganda.*

Global solidarity movements for LGBTQ rights

In recent years, global solidarity movements have emerged as vital components in the fight for LGBTQ rights. These movements transcend geographical boundaries, uniting activists, organizations, and allies in a collective effort to promote equality and justice for LGBTQ individuals worldwide. This subsection explores the theoretical frameworks, challenges, and notable examples of global solidarity movements aimed at advancing LGBTQ rights.

Theoretical Frameworks

The concept of global solidarity in LGBTQ rights is rooted in several theoretical frameworks, including intersectionality, transnationalism, and social movement theory. Intersectionality, coined by Kimberlé Crenshaw, emphasizes the interconnectedness of various social identities, such as race, gender, and sexuality, and how these intersections create unique experiences of oppression and privilege. This framework is crucial in understanding that LGBTQ individuals do not exist in a vacuum; their experiences are influenced by multiple factors, including cultural, economic, and political contexts.

Transnationalism refers to the processes and practices that transcend national boundaries, allowing individuals and groups to maintain connections across countries. In the context of LGBTQ rights, transnational networks facilitate the sharing of resources, strategies, and experiences among activists from different parts of the world. These networks enable the dissemination of knowledge and best practices, fostering a global movement that is both diverse and inclusive.

Social movement theory provides insights into how collective action emerges, evolves, and influences social change. It highlights the importance of mobilization, organization, and framing in building effective movements. In the case of LGBTQ rights, social movements often frame their demands around human rights, equality, and justice, appealing to universal values that resonate across cultures.

Challenges Faced by Global Solidarity Movements

Despite the progress made by global solidarity movements for LGBTQ rights, several challenges persist. One significant issue is the backlash against LGBTQ rights in various countries, often fueled by conservative religious ideologies and political agendas. This backlash can manifest in the form of discriminatory laws, violence, and social stigma, making it difficult for activists to operate freely and safely.

Additionally, there is often a tension between local and global agendas. While global movements may advocate for universal LGBTQ rights, local activists may prioritize specific issues that reflect their unique cultural and social contexts. This divergence can lead to conflicts in strategies and goals, necessitating a delicate balance between global solidarity and local relevance.

Another challenge is the issue of representation within global movements. It is crucial to ensure that the voices of marginalized and underrepresented groups within the LGBTQ community—such as people of color, transgender individuals, and those from non-Western countries—are amplified. Failure to do so can result in a homogenized movement that does not adequately address the diverse needs and experiences of all LGBTQ individuals.

Notable Examples of Global Solidarity Movements

Several notable examples illustrate the power and impact of global solidarity movements for LGBTQ rights:
    1.   **ILGA (International Lesbian, Gay, Bisexual, Trans and Intersex Association)**: Founded in 1978, ILGA is a worldwide federation of LGBTQ organizations that advocates for the rights of LGBTQ individuals at the international level. It provides a platform for networking, sharing resources, and

collaborating on advocacy initiatives. ILGA's efforts have led to increased visibility and recognition of LGBTQ rights within international human rights frameworks.

2. **Pride Events**: Pride events around the world serve as powerful symbols of solidarity and resistance. These events often attract international attention, bringing together activists, allies, and the broader community to celebrate diversity and demand equal rights. Global Pride events, such as World Pride, highlight the interconnectedness of LGBTQ struggles and foster a sense of unity among participants from different countries.

3. **The #LoveIsLove Campaign**: This social media campaign gained global traction following the legalization of same-sex marriage in various countries. It promotes the message that love knows no boundaries and encourages individuals to share their stories of love and acceptance. The campaign has effectively mobilized support for LGBTQ rights, demonstrating the power of digital activism in fostering global solidarity.

4. **The Yogyakarta Principles**: Developed in 2006, the Yogyakarta Principles are a set of international legal standards that affirm the rights of LGBTQ individuals. They serve as a guiding framework for activists and organizations working to promote LGBTQ rights globally. The principles emphasize the importance of accountability and the need for states to protect and fulfill the rights of LGBTQ individuals.

5. **Global Fund for Human Rights**: This fund supports grassroots organizations working on LGBTQ rights and other human rights issues worldwide. By providing financial resources and capacity-building support, the Global Fund empowers local activists to advocate for change in their communities while fostering global solidarity among human rights defenders.

Conclusion

Global solidarity movements for LGBTQ rights play a crucial role in advancing equality and justice for LGBTQ individuals worldwide. By leveraging theoretical frameworks, addressing challenges, and drawing on notable examples, these movements demonstrate the power of collective action in the face of adversity. As the fight for LGBTQ rights continues, fostering global solidarity will be essential in creating a more inclusive and equitable future for all individuals, regardless of their sexual orientation or gender identity. The journey toward equality is ongoing, but with the strength of global solidarity, the vision of a world where everyone can live authentically and without fear is within reach.

Personal and Professional Challenges

Facing Adversity and Threats

Personal attacks and threats to personal safety

The journey of an LGBTQ activist in Uganda is often fraught with peril, as the societal landscape is marred by homophobia and systemic discrimination. Frank Mugisha, a prominent figure in this movement, has not only faced personal attacks but has also endured threats to his safety, which exemplify the broader challenges faced by LGBTQ individuals in hostile environments.

Understanding the Context

In Uganda, where anti-LGBTQ sentiments are deeply entrenched in cultural and religious ideologies, activists like Mugisha become targets of violence and harassment. The legal framework, which criminalizes homosexuality, further legitimizes these attacks, creating a dangerous atmosphere for those who dare to advocate for change. The impact of such an environment can be analyzed through the lens of *Critical Theory*, which posits that societal structures perpetuate inequalities and injustices.

Personal Experiences of Threats

Mugisha's experiences reflect a grim reality. He has been subjected to physical assaults, verbal harassment, and threats of violence. For instance, during a public demonstration advocating for LGBTQ rights, he was confronted by an angry mob, which not only threatened his physical safety but also aimed to intimidate him into silence. This incident is not isolated; many activists report similar experiences, highlighting a pattern of targeted violence against those who challenge the status quo.

The Psychological Toll

The psychological effects of such threats are profound. The constant fear of violence can lead to anxiety, depression, and a sense of isolation. Mugisha has spoken about the emotional burden of living under the threat of attack, illustrating how these experiences can hinder one's ability to engage fully in activism. The concept of *Intersectionality*, introduced by Kimberlé Crenshaw, helps to understand how overlapping identities—such as being LGBTQ and Ugandan—compound the risks faced by activists.

Strategies for Coping and Resistance

In response to these threats, Mugisha and other activists have developed various strategies to cope with personal attacks. These include:

- **Building a Support Network:** Establishing connections with fellow activists provides emotional support and safety in numbers. Mugisha often emphasizes the importance of solidarity among LGBTQ individuals.

- **Legal Protections:** Seeking legal recourse against perpetrators of violence is crucial. However, the effectiveness of legal systems in Uganda remains questionable due to pervasive corruption and bias against LGBTQ individuals.

- **Public Awareness Campaigns:** Raising awareness about the violence faced by LGBTQ activists can mobilize public support and pressure authorities to take action against perpetrators.

Conclusion

The personal attacks and threats to safety faced by Frank Mugisha are emblematic of the broader struggles within the LGBTQ rights movement in Uganda. While these challenges are daunting, the resilience demonstrated by activists like Mugisha serves as a beacon of hope for future generations. By confronting these threats head-on, they not only advocate for their own rights but also pave the way for a more inclusive society. Understanding the dynamics of personal safety in activism is crucial for fostering an environment where LGBTQ individuals can thrive without fear of persecution.

$$P(A) = \frac{N(A)}{N(T)} \qquad (20)$$

where $P(A)$ is the probability of an attack occurring, $N(A)$ is the number of attacks reported, and $N(T)$ is the total number of activists engaged in LGBTQ advocacy.

The journey of activism is not merely a fight for rights but a testament to the strength of the human spirit against adversity. The stories of those like Frank Mugisha remind us that while the path may be fraught with danger, the pursuit of justice and equality remains an unyielding force for change.

The toll of fear and anxiety on mental health

The journey of an LGBTQ activist in a society that often vilifies their very existence is fraught with peril, both physically and mentally. In Uganda, where homophobia is deeply entrenched in cultural, social, and legal frameworks, the toll of fear and anxiety on mental health can be profound and debilitating. This subsection will explore the psychological consequences of living under constant threat, examining both the theoretical frameworks that elucidate these experiences and the real-world implications they have on individuals like Frank Mugisha.

Theoretical Frameworks

To understand the impact of fear and anxiety on mental health, we can draw upon several psychological theories, including the **Cognitive Behavioral Theory (CBT)** and the **Stress-Vulnerability Model**.

Cognitive Behavioral Theory posits that our thoughts, feelings, and behaviors are interconnected. In the context of LGBTQ activism in Uganda, the constant fear of persecution can lead to negative thought patterns, such as catastrophizing or overgeneralization. For example, an activist may think, "If I attend this rally, I will be arrested," leading to feelings of anxiety and subsequent avoidance of important advocacy events. This cycle of fear can perpetuate a sense of isolation and hopelessness.

The Stress-Vulnerability Model further elucidates how chronic stress, such as that experienced by LGBTQ individuals facing discrimination, can exacerbate mental health issues. According to this model, individuals with a predisposition to mental health disorders may find their conditions worsened by ongoing stressors, such as societal rejection or violence. In Uganda, the societal stigma surrounding homosexuality can act as a chronic stressor, leading to heightened anxiety and increased vulnerability to mental health disorders.

Real-World Implications

The fear of violence, discrimination, and societal rejection creates a pervasive atmosphere of anxiety for LGBTQ activists in Uganda. This anxiety can manifest in various forms, including generalized anxiety disorder, depression, and post-traumatic stress disorder (PTSD).

Generalized Anxiety Disorder (GAD) is characterized by excessive worry about various aspects of life. For LGBTQ activists, this worry may center around personal safety, the safety of loved ones, and the success of their advocacy efforts. A study conducted by *Meyer (2003)* highlights that individuals who experience stigma and discrimination are more likely to report symptoms of GAD. The constant vigilance required to navigate a hostile environment can lead to mental exhaustion and a diminished quality of life.

Depression is another common mental health issue that can arise from the toll of fear and anxiety. The World Health Organization (WHO) notes that LGBTQ individuals are at a higher risk for depression due to societal stigma and discrimination. In Uganda, where the legal framework is often hostile to LGBTQ rights, the feeling of hopelessness can be overwhelming. Activists may feel that their efforts are futile, leading to a cycle of despair that can be difficult to break.

Post-Traumatic Stress Disorder (PTSD) can also be a significant concern for LGBTQ activists who have experienced violence or threats. The symptoms of PTSD include flashbacks, nightmares, and severe anxiety. For instance, after facing a violent attack during a protest, an activist may develop PTSD, which can severely impact their ability to continue their advocacy work. The National Center for PTSD states that individuals who experience trauma are at a higher risk for developing PTSD, particularly when they lack a supportive environment to process their experiences.

Examples from Frank Mugisha's Experience

Frank Mugisha's activism has placed him in direct confrontation with the harsh realities of homophobia in Uganda. He has faced numerous threats to his safety, including physical violence and harassment. These experiences have undoubtedly

FACING ADVERSITY AND THREATS

contributed to his mental health struggles. Mugisha has openly discussed the anxiety that accompanies his activism; he often worries about being targeted not just for his sexual orientation but also for his advocacy work.

In his own words, Mugisha has stated, "Every time I step out to speak for my community, I am aware that my life is at risk. The fear is constant, and it weighs heavily on my mind." This statement encapsulates the mental toll that activism can take, illustrating how the fear of violence can overshadow the desire for progress.

Moreover, Mugisha's experience is not unique. Many LGBTQ individuals in Uganda report similar feelings of anxiety and depression stemming from their activism and the societal context in which they operate. The fear of being outed or attacked can lead to isolation, as individuals may withdraw from social circles to protect themselves.

Coping Mechanisms

Despite the heavy toll that fear and anxiety can take on mental health, many LGBTQ activists, including Mugisha, develop coping mechanisms to manage their stress. These may include:

- **Building Support Networks:** Forming connections with other LGBTQ individuals and allies can provide a sense of community and belonging, essential for combating feelings of isolation.
- **Engaging in Self-Care:** Activists often prioritize self-care practices, such as mindfulness, exercise, and therapy, to manage their mental health.
- **Advocacy as Empowerment:** For some, engaging in advocacy work can serve as a form of empowerment, helping to mitigate feelings of helplessness and despair.

In conclusion, the toll of fear and anxiety on mental health is a significant concern for LGBTQ activists in Uganda. The interplay of societal stigma, discrimination, and personal experiences of violence creates a complex landscape that can lead to various mental health issues. Understanding these dynamics is crucial for fostering resilience and support within the LGBTQ community, ensuring that activists like Frank Mugisha can continue their vital work for equality and justice.

Strategies for dealing with personal attacks

Dealing with personal attacks is a critical aspect of maintaining resilience and focus in the face of adversity, particularly for LGBTQ activists like Frank Mugisha, who often face hostility due to their advocacy. This section outlines several strategies that can be employed to effectively navigate and mitigate the impact of personal attacks.

1. Building a Support Network

One of the most effective strategies for dealing with personal attacks is to cultivate a robust support network. This network can include friends, family, fellow activists, and mental health professionals. Research indicates that social support plays a significant role in buffering against the negative effects of stress and adversity [?].

$$S = f(N, R, E) \tag{21}$$

Where S represents the level of support experienced, N is the number of supportive individuals, R is the quality of relationships, and E is the emotional engagement within those relationships.

For example, when faced with a personal attack, an activist might turn to a close friend who understands the context of their struggle and can provide emotional validation. This connection not only helps to alleviate feelings of isolation but also offers a platform for discussing coping strategies and potential responses to the attack.

2. Developing Emotional Resilience

Emotional resilience is the ability to adapt to stressful situations and recover from setbacks. Building resilience can be achieved through various techniques, including mindfulness practices, cognitive behavioral strategies, and self-compassion exercises.

Mindfulness, for instance, encourages individuals to remain present and acknowledge their feelings without judgment. A study by Keng et al. (2011) found that mindfulness practices can significantly reduce emotional distress and improve coping mechanisms.

$$R = M + C + SC \tag{22}$$

Where R represents resilience, M is mindfulness, C is cognitive reframing, and SC is self-compassion.

For instance, when confronted with derogatory comments, an activist can practice mindfulness by taking a moment to breathe deeply and observe their thoughts, allowing them to respond thoughtfully rather than react impulsively.

3. Engaging in Advocacy and Education

Another powerful strategy is to transform personal attacks into opportunities for advocacy and education. By sharing their experiences publicly, activists can raise awareness about the challenges faced by LGBTQ individuals and promote understanding within their communities.

This approach aligns with the concept of the "transformative power of storytelling," which posits that sharing personal narratives can foster empathy and reduce prejudice [?].

For example, after experiencing a personal attack, Frank Mugisha could write an article or give a speech detailing his experiences, emphasizing the broader societal issues at play. This not only helps him process his feelings but also educates others, potentially reducing the likelihood of similar attacks in the future.

4. Seeking Professional Support

In some cases, personal attacks can lead to significant emotional distress, necessitating professional intervention. Engaging with mental health professionals can provide activists with coping strategies tailored to their specific experiences.

Cognitive Behavioral Therapy (CBT) is one effective method that helps individuals reframe negative thought patterns and develop healthier responses to stressors.

$$CBT = T + B + A \qquad (23)$$

Where CBT is Cognitive Behavioral Therapy, T is the identification of negative thoughts, B is the behavioral response to those thoughts, and A is the development of alternative, positive actions.

Through therapy, an activist can learn to challenge and change the narrative surrounding personal attacks, transforming feelings of inadequacy into empowerment and resilience.

5. Establishing Boundaries

Finally, establishing clear boundaries is essential for protecting one's mental and emotional well-being. Activists should identify what types of interactions are acceptable and which ones are harmful, allowing them to disengage from toxic situations or individuals.

Boundary-setting can be achieved through assertive communication techniques, which emphasize expressing one's needs and limits in a respectful manner.

For example, if an activist is repeatedly confronted with hostile comments on social media, they might choose to block or mute individuals who perpetuate negativity, thereby creating a safer online space for themselves.

Conclusion

In conclusion, personal attacks are an unfortunate reality for many LGBTQ activists, but with the right strategies, they can be managed effectively. Building a support network, developing emotional resilience, engaging in advocacy, seeking professional help, and establishing boundaries are all vital components in navigating the challenges posed by personal attacks. By employing these strategies, activists like Frank Mugisha can continue their important work while safeguarding their mental health and well-being.

Seeking legal protection and security measures

In the context of advocating for LGBTQ rights in Uganda, seeking legal protection and security measures is not merely a matter of personal safety; it is a fundamental component of the broader struggle for dignity, recognition, and equality. The legal landscape in Uganda is fraught with challenges, particularly for LGBTQ individuals who face harassment, violence, and systemic discrimination. This section will explore the theoretical underpinnings of legal protection, the problems faced by LGBTQ activists, and examples of successful strategies employed to secure safety and legal rights.

Theoretical Framework

The notion of legal protection for marginalized communities is grounded in human rights theory, which posits that all individuals are entitled to certain inalienable rights, regardless of their sexual orientation or gender identity. According to the Universal Declaration of Human Rights (UDHR), "Everyone has the right to life, liberty, and security of person" [?]. This principle is echoed in various international human rights treaties, which obligate states to protect individuals from violence and discrimination.

In the context of LGBTQ rights, the concept of "intersectionality," coined by Kimberlé Crenshaw, is also crucial. Intersectionality recognizes that individuals may experience overlapping forms of discrimination based on multiple identities, including sexuality, gender, race, and socioeconomic status. Thus, legal protections must be holistic and inclusive, addressing the unique challenges faced by LGBTQ individuals in Uganda.

Challenges in Seeking Legal Protection

Despite the theoretical framework supporting legal protection, LGBTQ activists in Uganda encounter numerous obstacles. One of the primary challenges is the pervasive climate of homophobia and transphobia, which is often exacerbated by cultural and religious beliefs. This societal stigma can lead to a lack of trust in law enforcement and judicial systems, making it difficult for LGBTQ individuals to seek help.

For instance, many activists report that when they approach police for assistance after experiencing violence or harassment, they are often met with hostility or indifference. In some cases, victims of violence have been re-victimized by authorities who either refuse to take their cases seriously or engage in further discrimination. This systemic failure to protect LGBTQ individuals from harm creates a chilling effect, discouraging them from seeking legal recourse.

Moreover, the legal framework itself is often inadequate. Uganda's Penal Code includes provisions that criminalize same-sex relationships, contributing to a culture of impunity for those who perpetrate violence against LGBTQ individuals. As a result, activists frequently face legal repercussions for their advocacy efforts, further complicating their ability to secure protection.

Strategies for Legal Protection

Given these challenges, LGBTQ activists have developed various strategies to seek legal protection and enhance their security. One effective approach is the establishment of legal aid clinics that specialize in LGBTQ issues. These clinics provide essential services, including legal advice, representation, and assistance with filing complaints against perpetrators of violence.

For example, organizations like Sexual Minorities Uganda (SMUG) have played a pivotal role in providing legal support to LGBTQ individuals. By training lawyers on LGBTQ issues and facilitating access to legal resources, these organizations empower individuals to navigate the legal system effectively. Moreover, they often engage in public awareness campaigns to educate both the LGBTQ community and the general public about legal rights and protections.

Another critical strategy is the collaboration with international human rights organizations. By forming alliances with global entities, local activists can amplify their voices and gain access to resources and support. For instance, partnerships with organizations such as Human Rights Watch and Amnesty International have enabled Ugandan activists to document human rights abuses and bring international attention to their plight. This external pressure can lead to increased scrutiny of the Ugandan government and its treatment of LGBTQ individuals.

Case Studies and Examples

Several notable cases illustrate the importance of seeking legal protection and the potential for success in the face of adversity. One such case involved a young LGBTQ activist who was violently attacked by a mob in Kampala. With the support of local NGOs, the victim was able to file a police report and secure legal representation. Despite initial resistance from law enforcement, the case garnered media attention, leading to a more thorough investigation and eventual prosecution of the assailants. This case not only provided justice for the victim but also served as a rallying point for the LGBTQ community, highlighting the importance of standing up against violence and discrimination.

Another example is the use of strategic litigation to challenge discriminatory laws. Activists have successfully brought cases before the Ugandan courts, arguing that the criminalization of same-sex relationships violates constitutional provisions related to equality and non-discrimination. While these legal battles are often met with setbacks, they play a crucial role in challenging the status quo and advocating for change.

Conclusion

In conclusion, seeking legal protection and security measures is a vital aspect of the LGBTQ rights movement in Uganda. While activists face significant challenges, including societal stigma and an inadequate legal framework, they have developed innovative strategies to navigate these obstacles. By leveraging legal aid, forming alliances with international organizations, and engaging in strategic litigation, LGBTQ activists are working tirelessly to secure their rights and ensure their safety. The journey is fraught with difficulties, but the resilience and determination of these activists signal a hopeful future for LGBTQ rights in Uganda.

Overcoming obstacles and continuing advocacy work

The journey of an LGBTQ activist in Uganda is fraught with challenges that can often seem insurmountable. However, the resilience shown by activists like Frank Mugisha demonstrates that overcoming obstacles is not only possible but also essential for continued advocacy work. This section explores the various obstacles faced by LGBTQ activists, the theoretical frameworks that inform their resilience, and practical strategies employed to continue their fight for equality.

Theoretical Frameworks for Resilience

Resilience theory posits that individuals can adapt positively in the face of adversity. According to [?], resilience is not merely a trait but a dynamic process influenced by multiple factors, including social support, community resources, and individual coping strategies. For LGBTQ activists, these factors play a crucial role in their ability to withstand the pressures of discrimination and violence.

One relevant model is the *Ecological Systems Theory* proposed by [?], which emphasizes the importance of various environmental systems in shaping individual behavior. In the context of LGBTQ activism, this theory suggests that activists must navigate multiple layers of societal influences, from family and community to broader cultural and political systems.

Identifying Obstacles

Activists in Uganda face several formidable obstacles:

- **Legal and Political Barriers:** The Ugandan legal system is heavily influenced by anti-LGBTQ laws, creating a hostile environment for advocacy. The infamous Anti-Homosexuality Act, although struck down in 2014, continues to cast a long shadow over legal protections for LGBTQ individuals. Activists must navigate a legal landscape that criminalizes their existence, making their work perilous.

- **Social Stigma and Discrimination:** Deep-rooted homophobia permeates Ugandan society, leading to widespread discrimination. This stigma manifests in various forms, including violence, harassment, and ostracism, which can deter individuals from engaging in activism or even disclosing their sexual orientation.

- **Mental Health Challenges:** The constant threat of violence and discrimination can lead to significant mental health issues, including anxiety, depression, and post-traumatic stress disorder (PTSD). Activists often grapple with the emotional toll of their work, which can lead to burnout and a sense of hopelessness.

- **Limited Resources:** Many LGBTQ organizations in Uganda operate with minimal funding and resources, which limits their capacity to carry out effective advocacy and support programs. The lack of financial backing can hinder the development of outreach initiatives and community support networks.

Strategies for Overcoming Obstacles

Despite these challenges, LGBTQ activists employ various strategies to overcome obstacles and sustain their advocacy efforts:

- **Building Community Support:** Forming strong networks of support among LGBTQ individuals is crucial. Activists often create safe spaces where individuals can share experiences, seek guidance, and find solace in a community that understands their struggles. This solidarity fosters resilience and encourages continued activism.

- **Engaging in Mental Health Initiatives:** To combat the mental health challenges associated with activism, many organizations have begun to prioritize mental health resources. Workshops, counseling services, and peer support groups are established to help activists process their experiences and develop coping mechanisms.

- **Leveraging International Support:** Collaborating with international LGBTQ organizations can provide activists with the resources and visibility needed to amplify their message. International support not only offers financial assistance but also helps to pressure the Ugandan government to uphold human rights standards.

- **Utilizing Media and Technology:** Social media platforms have become vital tools for advocacy. Activists use these platforms to share stories, raise awareness, and mobilize support both locally and globally. By harnessing the power of digital activism, they can circumvent some of the restrictions imposed by the Ugandan government.

- **Advocating for Legal Reforms:** Despite the challenging legal landscape, activists continue to push for legal reforms. This involves working with sympathetic lawyers and engaging in strategic litigation to challenge discriminatory laws. The recent successes in securing legal protections for LGBTQ individuals, albeit limited, demonstrate the potential for change.

Examples of Resilience in Action

Frank Mugisha's own journey illustrates the power of resilience in the face of adversity. After facing threats and harassment for his activism, Mugisha sought refuge in international advocacy networks. His ability to share his story on global platforms not only brought attention to the plight of LGBTQ individuals in Uganda but also inspired a new generation of activists.

Another example is the establishment of support groups like *Freedom and Roam Uganda* (FARUG), which provides a safe haven for LGBTQ individuals. By offering counseling, educational resources, and advocacy training, FARUG empowers its members to navigate the challenges of their identities while fostering a sense of community.

Conclusion

Overcoming obstacles in the fight for LGBTQ rights in Uganda requires a multifaceted approach that combines resilience, community support, and strategic advocacy. The experiences of activists like Frank Mugisha highlight the importance of solidarity, mental health resources, and international collaboration in sustaining the momentum for change. As the landscape for LGBTQ rights continues to evolve, the strategies employed by these activists will be crucial in shaping a more inclusive and equitable future for all.

Balancing Personal Life and Activism

Navigating relationships and dating as an LGBTQ activist

Navigating relationships and dating as an LGBTQ activist presents a unique set of challenges and opportunities. The intersection of personal identity and activism often complicates romantic endeavors, creating a landscape that requires careful navigation. This section explores the dynamics of relationships within the context of LGBTQ activism, highlighting the theoretical frameworks, common problems, and illustrative examples that shape these experiences.

Theoretical Frameworks

Understanding relationships in the context of LGBTQ activism can be enriched by several theoretical frameworks. One such framework is the **Intersectionality Theory**, which posits that individuals experience overlapping social identities that intersect to create unique modes of discrimination or privilege. For LGBTQ activists, factors such as gender identity, race, socioeconomic status, and geographical location can significantly influence their dating experiences. For instance, a Black queer activist may encounter different societal challenges compared to a white cisgender gay man, affecting how they navigate dating and relationships.

Another relevant theory is the **Social Identity Theory**, which suggests that individuals derive a sense of self from their group memberships. For LGBTQ activists, their identity as advocates for rights can influence their partner selection, often seeking individuals who share similar values and commitments to social justice. This shared commitment can foster deeper connections but may also lead to challenges when partners have differing levels of engagement in activism.

Common Problems in Relationships

LGBTQ activists often face several common problems in their dating lives, including:

- **Fear of Disclosure:** Activists may worry about disclosing their sexual orientation or activism to potential partners, fearing rejection or backlash. This fear can create barriers to intimacy and trust, complicating the dating process.

- **Balancing Activism and Personal Life:** The demands of activism can consume significant time and energy, leaving little room for nurturing personal relationships. Activists may struggle to find partners who understand and support their commitments while also desiring quality time together.

- **Navigating Different Levels of Activism:** Partners may have varying levels of involvement in LGBTQ issues, leading to potential conflicts. An activist deeply entrenched in advocacy may feel frustrated if their partner is less engaged or unaware of critical issues affecting the community.

- **Safety Concerns:** In some regions, dating as an LGBTQ individual can pose safety risks. Activists may be particularly aware of these dangers, leading to heightened caution in their dating lives.

Illustrative Examples

Consider the story of *Alex*, a prominent LGBTQ activist in Uganda. Alex faced significant challenges in dating due to the pervasive homophobia in society. When he met *Sam*, a fellow activist, their shared commitment to advocacy created an immediate connection. However, Alex struggled with the fear of being outed, as their relationship could attract unwanted attention from hostile individuals. They navigated this by establishing boundaries around public displays of affection and discussing their comfort levels regarding visibility.

In another case, *Jordan*, an activist focused on youth engagement, found it difficult to balance his advocacy work with his desire for a romantic relationship. His partner, *Taylor*, was supportive but often felt neglected due to Jordan's long hours organizing events. They addressed this challenge by scheduling regular date nights, ensuring that their relationship remained a priority amidst the demands of activism.

Strategies for Successful Relationships

To foster healthy relationships, LGBTQ activists can employ several strategies:

- **Open Communication:** Engaging in honest conversations about fears, expectations, and boundaries can help build trust and intimacy. Partners should feel comfortable discussing their activism and how it impacts their relationship.

- **Shared Values and Goals:** Finding a partner who shares similar values regarding activism can enhance compatibility. Couples can engage in joint advocacy projects, strengthening their bond through shared experiences.

- **Establishing Boundaries:** Setting clear boundaries around activism and personal time allows partners to maintain a healthy balance. This can prevent feelings of neglect while ensuring that both partners feel valued.

- **Seeking Support:** Activists can benefit from seeking support from friends or LGBTQ community organizations. These networks can provide guidance and understanding, helping individuals navigate the complexities of dating as an activist.

Conclusion

Navigating relationships and dating as an LGBTQ activist is a multifaceted journey shaped by personal identity, societal challenges, and the demands of advocacy. By understanding the theoretical frameworks that inform their experiences, recognizing common problems, and employing effective strategies, LGBTQ activists can cultivate meaningful relationships that enrich their lives and bolster their commitment to social change. The path may be fraught with challenges, but the rewards of love and companionship can serve as powerful motivators in the ongoing fight for equality and acceptance.

Finding support from partners and loved ones

In the journey of self-discovery and activism, the role of partners and loved ones cannot be overstated. They serve as crucial pillars of support, providing emotional, psychological, and sometimes even financial assistance. This section explores the dynamics of finding and nurturing supportive relationships within the context of LGBTQ activism, highlighting the significance of these connections, the challenges faced, and practical examples of how such support can manifest.

The Importance of Support Systems

Support from partners and loved ones is essential for LGBTQ activists, particularly in environments where societal acceptance is limited. According to the *Social Support Theory*, the presence of supportive relationships contributes significantly to an individual's mental health and well-being. This theory posits that emotional and practical support can buffer against stress, reduce feelings of isolation, and enhance resilience. For LGBTQ activists like Frank Mugisha, having a partner who understands the complexities of their identity and the challenges they face can create a safe haven amidst external pressures.

Challenges in Finding Support

Despite the importance of supportive relationships, many LGBTQ individuals encounter barriers in their quest for acceptance. These challenges can stem from various sources, including:

- **Cultural and Societal Norms:** In Uganda, cultural beliefs often dictate rigid gender roles and heteronormative expectations, making it difficult for LGBTQ individuals to find partners who are both supportive and understanding.
- **Fear of Discrimination:** The fear of being outed or facing backlash can lead individuals to hide their true selves, which in turn complicates the formation of authentic relationships.
- **Internalized Homophobia:** Many LGBTQ individuals grapple with internalized negative beliefs about their identity, which can hinder their ability to seek out and accept support from others.

These challenges highlight the need for LGBTQ individuals to engage in self-acceptance and to actively seek out spaces where they can meet supportive partners and friends.

Strategies for Building Supportive Relationships

To cultivate supportive relationships, LGBTQ activists can adopt several strategies:

1. **Open Communication:** Establishing open lines of communication with partners about experiences, fears, and aspirations can foster deeper understanding and connection. This is particularly important in navigating the complexities of being an activist in a challenging environment.

2. **Participation in LGBTQ Spaces:** Engaging with LGBTQ community centers, support groups, and events can provide opportunities to meet like-minded individuals who share similar experiences and struggles. For instance, Frank Mugisha found solace in local LGBTQ organizations, which not only offered friendship but also a sense of belonging.

3. **Encouraging Empathy:** Partners should be encouraged to educate themselves about LGBTQ issues. This can involve reading literature, attending workshops, or engaging in discussions that deepen their understanding of the challenges faced by their loved ones.

4. **Creating Safe Spaces:** It is vital for LGBTQ individuals to create safe environments where they can express themselves freely without fear of judgment. This can be achieved through intentional conversations that set boundaries and expectations in relationships.

Examples of Support in Action

The impact of supportive partners and loved ones can be illustrated through various examples:

- **Emotional Support:** When Frank faced threats and harassment due to his activism, his partner provided a listening ear and a comforting presence, helping him process the emotional toll of his experiences. This emotional support was crucial in maintaining his mental health and motivation to continue his work.

- **Advocacy Together:** Partners can also engage in activism together, amplifying each other's voices and efforts. For instance, Frank and his partner organized community events that raised awareness about LGBTQ rights, demonstrating how love and activism can intertwine.

- **Navigating Family Dynamics:** Supportive partners can help LGBTQ individuals navigate complex family dynamics. For example, when Frank disclosed his identity to his family, his partner stood by him, providing reassurance and strength during a potentially volatile situation.

Conclusion

Finding support from partners and loved ones is a vital aspect of the LGBTQ activist journey. While challenges abound, the benefits of nurturing these relationships can lead to greater resilience and a more profound sense of belonging. By fostering open communication, engaging with supportive communities, and encouraging empathy, LGBTQ individuals can cultivate strong support systems that empower them to continue their advocacy work. As Frank Mugisha's experiences illustrate, love and support can be transformative forces in the fight for LGBTQ rights, enabling individuals to live authentically and courageously in the face of adversity.

Managing personal and professional boundaries

Managing personal and professional boundaries is a critical aspect of being an LGBTQ activist, particularly in a context such as Uganda, where societal pressures and discrimination can significantly impact one's personal life. Activists like Frank Mugisha often navigate complex relationships that intertwine personal identity, activism, and societal expectations. This subsection explores the theories and challenges associated with managing these boundaries, providing insights and examples relevant to the LGBTQ advocacy landscape.

Theoretical Framework

The concept of boundaries in personal and professional contexts can be understood through the lens of *boundary theory*, which posits that individuals create and maintain boundaries to delineate their personal lives from their professional responsibilities. According to [?], boundaries serve as a mechanism for individuals to manage their identities in different contexts, allowing them to navigate varying expectations and social norms.

In the realm of activism, particularly for LGBTQ individuals, boundaries can be fluid. Activists often find that their personal lives are scrutinized, and their identities are politicized, leading to a need for clear demarcation between their advocacy efforts and personal relationships. The challenge lies in maintaining these boundaries while still being authentic to oneself and one's community.

Challenges in Boundary Management

1. **Emotional Labor**: LGBTQ activists frequently engage in emotional labor, where they must manage their feelings and the feelings of others in both personal and professional settings. This can lead to emotional exhaustion, as activists may feel compelled to represent their community positively while also dealing with their struggles. The constant need to perform or conform to societal expectations can blur the lines between personal authenticity and professional representation.

2. **Interpersonal Relationships**: Navigating relationships can be particularly challenging for activists. For instance, when Frank Mugisha disclosed his sexuality to friends, he encountered varied reactions that affected his personal relationships. Balancing the roles of friend, partner, and activist can create tension. Activists must often decide how much of their personal life to share with colleagues and how to maintain relationships that may not fully understand or support their advocacy work.

3. **Professional Expectations**: In professional settings, LGBTQ activists may face expectations to be role models or spokespersons for their community. This expectation can lead to a sense of obligation, where personal boundaries are compromised in favor of professional demands. For example, attending events or speaking engagements may require activists to share personal stories that they may not be comfortable discussing in a public setting.

4. **Burnout**: The pressure to constantly advocate for LGBTQ rights, coupled with the challenges of managing personal relationships, can lead to burnout. Activists may feel overwhelmed by their responsibilities, leading to a decline in mental health and overall well-being. This is particularly relevant in Uganda, where societal hostility towards LGBTQ individuals can amplify stressors.

Strategies for Effective Boundary Management

To effectively manage personal and professional boundaries, LGBTQ activists can adopt several strategies:

1. **Self-Reflection**: Regular self-reflection is essential for activists to understand their limits and recognize when boundaries are being crossed. Engaging in practices such as journaling or meditation can help individuals assess their emotional states and clarify their needs.

2. **Clear Communication**: Open and honest communication with friends, family, and colleagues can help establish boundaries. For example, an activist might

communicate their need for privacy regarding certain aspects of their personal life while still being willing to share their professional experiences.

3. **Setting Limits**: Activists should set clear limits on their availability for advocacy work, ensuring they allocate time for self-care and personal relationships. This might include designating specific hours for activism and reserving time for personal activities that foster well-being.

4. **Building a Support Network**: Establishing a support network of fellow activists who understand the unique challenges of LGBTQ advocacy can provide a safe space for sharing experiences and strategies. This network can serve as a source of encouragement and mutual support, helping individuals navigate personal and professional challenges.

5. **Seeking Professional Help**: Engaging with mental health professionals who understand the dynamics of LGBTQ identity and activism can provide valuable support. Therapy can offer a space for activists to process their experiences and develop coping strategies for managing boundaries.

Examples in Practice

Frank Mugisha's journey exemplifies the complexities of managing personal and professional boundaries. As a prominent LGBTQ activist, he has faced significant public scrutiny, which necessitates a careful balance between his personal life and advocacy work. For instance, when he participates in public demonstrations or speaks at international conferences, he often shares personal narratives to connect with audiences. However, he also emphasizes the importance of protecting certain aspects of his life to maintain personal integrity and mental health.

Moreover, Mugisha has actively sought to build alliances with other activists, creating a community that fosters understanding and support. This collaborative approach not only strengthens advocacy efforts but also allows for shared experiences in navigating the challenges of boundary management.

In conclusion, managing personal and professional boundaries is a vital aspect of LGBTQ activism. By understanding the theoretical frameworks, recognizing the challenges, and implementing effective strategies, activists can navigate their complex identities while continuing to advocate for change. The journey of managing these boundaries is ongoing, requiring continuous reflection and adaptation as activists like Frank Mugisha work toward a more inclusive and accepting society.

Maintaining self-care and wellness practices

In the demanding landscape of LGBTQ activism, where the weight of societal discrimination and personal challenges can feel overwhelming, maintaining self-care and wellness practices is not merely a luxury but a necessity. Activists, like Frank Mugisha, often find themselves at the intersection of personal and political struggles, which can lead to burnout and mental health crises if not addressed properly.

The Importance of Self-Care

Self-care refers to the deliberate actions taken to enhance one's physical, mental, and emotional well-being. According to the World Health Organization (WHO), mental health is defined as a state of well-being in which every individual realizes their own potential, can cope with the normal stresses of life, can work productively and fruitfully, and is able to make a contribution to their community [?]. For LGBTQ activists, self-care is crucial as they navigate the complexities of advocacy while managing personal identities in often hostile environments.

Challenges to Self-Care

The challenges to effective self-care in activism can be numerous. Activists often face:

- **Emotional Exhaustion:** Constant exposure to hostility and discrimination can lead to emotional fatigue, where the activist feels drained and unable to engage with their work or community.

- **Social Isolation:** The stigma surrounding LGBTQ identities may lead to feelings of isolation, making it difficult for activists to seek support from their peers.

- **Time Constraints:** The demands of activism often leave little time for personal care, creating a cycle where neglecting one's health further diminishes the capacity to advocate effectively.

Strategies for Effective Self-Care

To combat these challenges, activists can implement various self-care strategies. These practices can be categorized into physical, emotional, and social self-care.

1. **Physical Self-Care** Physical self-care involves activities that improve physical health and well-being. This can include:

- **Regular Exercise:** Engaging in physical activities such as running, yoga, or dance can significantly reduce stress and improve mood. Research indicates that exercise releases endorphins, which are known as "feel-good" hormones [?].
- **Nutrition:** Maintaining a balanced diet rich in fruits, vegetables, and whole grains supports overall health and energy levels. Poor nutrition can exacerbate feelings of fatigue and depression.
- **Sleep Hygiene:** Prioritizing sleep is essential for mental health. Sleep deprivation can impair cognitive function and emotional regulation, making it harder to cope with the pressures of activism.

2. **Emotional Self-Care** Emotional self-care focuses on nurturing one's mental health. Activists can benefit from:

- **Mindfulness and Meditation:** Practices such as mindfulness meditation can help activists stay grounded and present, reducing anxiety and fostering a sense of peace. A study by Keng et al. (2011) highlights the positive effects of mindfulness on emotional regulation [?].
- **Therapy and Counseling:** Seeking professional help can provide a safe space to process experiences and emotions. Therapy can equip activists with coping strategies to deal with the unique pressures they face.
- **Creative Outlets:** Engaging in creative activities such as writing, art, or music can serve as a powerful means of expression and healing, allowing activists to channel their experiences into something constructive.

3. **Social Self-Care** Social self-care emphasizes the importance of building and maintaining supportive relationships. This can include:

- **Building a Support Network:** Connecting with other LGBTQ activists can provide a sense of community and belonging. Peer support groups can foster shared understanding and collective resilience.
- **Setting Boundaries:** Learning to say no and setting limits on engagement can prevent burnout. Activists must recognize their personal limits and prioritize their well-being.

- **Engaging in Community Activities:** Participating in social events or community gatherings can help combat feelings of isolation and reinforce a sense of belonging within the LGBTQ community.

The Role of Community in Self-Care

The LGBTQ community plays a pivotal role in supporting self-care practices among activists. Community spaces can serve as sanctuaries where individuals can share their experiences, validate each other's feelings, and collectively strategize for change. Initiatives such as wellness workshops, retreats, and group therapy sessions can foster a culture of care and support within activist circles.

Conclusion

In conclusion, maintaining self-care and wellness practices is essential for LGBTQ activists like Frank Mugisha, who navigate the complexities of advocacy amidst personal and societal challenges. By prioritizing physical, emotional, and social self-care, activists can sustain their energy, resilience, and passion for the fight for LGBTQ rights. The journey of activism is demanding, but with the right self-care strategies, activists can continue to inspire change while nurturing their well-being.

The power of community and support in personal and professional life

The journey of an LGBTQ activist is often marked by resilience, courage, and the unwavering belief in the power of community. In the face of adversity, the support network one cultivates can become a lifeline, providing not just emotional sustenance but also practical assistance in navigating the complexities of activism. This subsection will explore the multifaceted benefits of community and support systems in both personal and professional realms, drawing on relevant theories and real-world examples.

At the core of this discussion lies the concept of *social capital*, which refers to the networks of relationships among individuals that enable society to function effectively. Pierre Bourdieu, a prominent sociologist, posited that social capital is a critical resource that can be leveraged for personal and collective gain. For LGBTQ activists, building social capital is essential in fostering connections that can lead to collaborations, mentorship opportunities, and a sense of belonging.

One of the primary challenges faced by LGBTQ activists is the risk of isolation. The societal stigma surrounding non-heteronormative identities can lead to feelings of alienation, particularly in environments that are not supportive. This isolation can have detrimental effects on mental health, leading to anxiety and depression. Research indicates that individuals who lack social support are more vulnerable to these mental health challenges (Cohen & Wills, 1985). Conversely, those who engage in supportive communities experience improved psychological well-being, which is crucial for sustaining activism over the long term.

Consider the example of Frank Mugisha, whose activism in Uganda has been deeply intertwined with his community support. Mugisha has often spoken about the role of peer networks in bolstering his resolve and providing a safe space for sharing experiences and strategies. By joining forces with other LGBTQ individuals and allies, he has been able to amplify his voice and advocate more effectively for rights and recognition. This collective action not only enhances individual resilience but also contributes to a more robust movement capable of challenging systemic injustices.

Moreover, the power of community manifests in the form of mentorship. Experienced activists can guide newcomers, sharing insights and strategies that have proven effective in the past. This mentorship relationship is reciprocal; while the mentor imparts knowledge, they also gain renewed energy and perspective from the fresh ideas and passion of their mentees. The theory of *intergenerational solidarity* suggests that such relationships foster a sense of continuity and shared purpose within the LGBTQ movement (Bengtson & Roberts, 1991).

In addition to mentorship, community support can take the form of organized groups and coalitions. For instance, organizations like *SMUG* (Sexual Minorities Uganda) have created platforms for LGBTQ individuals to unite, share resources, and advocate collectively. These organizations often provide crucial training in advocacy skills, legal rights, and mental health resources, equipping activists with the tools needed to navigate their personal and professional challenges.

However, building and maintaining community support is not without its challenges. Activists may encounter conflicts within their communities, stemming from differing perspectives on approaches to activism or the prioritization of issues. Navigating these conflicts requires strong communication skills and a commitment to inclusivity. The *contact hypothesis* posits that positive interactions among diverse groups can reduce prejudice and foster understanding (Allport, 1954). This principle is particularly relevant in LGBTQ activism, where intersectionality plays a critical role. By fostering dialogue among various identities and experiences, activists can cultivate a more inclusive community that addresses the needs of all its members.

In summary, the power of community and support in the personal and professional lives of LGBTQ activists cannot be overstated. Social capital, mentorship, and organized support networks provide the emotional and practical resources necessary to sustain activism in the face of adversity. While challenges such as conflict and isolation persist, the potential for growth and resilience within supportive communities offers a hopeful vision for the future of LGBTQ rights. As Frank Mugisha and many others exemplify, the journey is not one taken alone; it is a collective endeavor that thrives on solidarity, shared experiences, and the unyielding belief that change is possible.

Professional Opportunities and Recognition

Speaking engagements and public appearances

Frank Mugisha's journey as an LGBTQ activist has been marked by numerous speaking engagements and public appearances that have significantly contributed to raising awareness about LGBTQ rights in Uganda and beyond. These opportunities have not only allowed him to share his personal narrative but also to engage with diverse audiences on critical issues facing the LGBTQ community.

The power of public speaking in advocacy cannot be overstated. According to the *Theory of Planned Behavior* (Ajzen, 1991), individuals' behavioral intentions are influenced by their attitudes towards the behavior, subjective norms, and perceived behavioral control. In the context of LGBTQ advocacy, when activists like Mugisha share their stories, they shape public attitudes and challenge prevailing norms surrounding sexuality and gender identity.

The Role of Personal Narratives

Mugisha's personal narrative serves as a compelling example of how storytelling can humanize complex issues. By recounting his experiences of discrimination, resilience, and hope, he fosters empathy among listeners. Research indicates that narratives can evoke emotional responses that are crucial for changing attitudes and behaviors (Green & Brock, 2000). For instance, during a TEDx talk in Kampala, Mugisha shared his story of coming out in a society rife with homophobia. His candidness not only resonated with LGBTQ individuals but also reached allies and those unfamiliar with the struggles faced by the community.

Challenges in Public Speaking

Despite the potential for impact, speaking engagements are fraught with challenges. Activists often face threats to their safety, as public appearances can attract backlash from conservative groups and individuals. Mugisha himself has encountered hostility during events, where protests have erupted in response to his presence. This raises significant concerns regarding the safety of LGBTQ activists in Uganda, where laws against homosexuality are stringent and societal acceptance remains low.

The psychological toll of such challenges is profound. The constant threat of violence and harassment can lead to anxiety and burnout among activists (Bouris et al., 2016). Mugisha has emphasized the importance of mental health support for activists, advocating for safe spaces where they can express their fears and seek solace among peers.

Engagement Strategies

To maximize the effectiveness of his speaking engagements, Mugisha employs various strategies. One notable approach is the use of inclusive language that resonates with both LGBTQ individuals and allies. By framing discussions around universal themes of love, acceptance, and human rights, he invites broader participation.

Moreover, Mugisha emphasizes the importance of intersectionality in his speeches, addressing how race, class, and gender intersect with sexual orientation. This approach not only broadens the conversation but also fosters solidarity among different marginalized groups. For example, during an international conference on human rights, he highlighted the experiences of LGBTQ individuals living in poverty, linking their struggles to broader socio-economic issues.

Impact of Media Coverage

Media coverage plays a crucial role in amplifying the messages conveyed during public appearances. Mugisha has adeptly utilized media platforms to extend the reach of his advocacy. When he speaks at events, he often collaborates with journalists and media outlets to ensure that his message is disseminated widely. The coverage of his speeches can spark conversations in communities that may not have been previously engaged with LGBTQ issues.

For instance, after a notable appearance at a regional human rights summit, several media outlets reported on his call for legal reforms in Uganda. This not only brought national attention to LGBTQ rights but also prompted discussions among policymakers about the need for change.

Conclusion

In conclusion, Frank Mugisha's speaking engagements and public appearances are pivotal to the ongoing struggle for LGBTQ rights in Uganda. Through personal narratives, strategic engagement, and effective use of media, he has successfully raised awareness and fostered dialogue around critical issues. However, the challenges he faces underscore the need for continued support for LGBTQ activists, ensuring that they can safely share their stories and advocate for change. As Mugisha continues his work, the impact of his voice serves as a beacon of hope for many, inspiring future generations of activists to carry the torch for equality and justice.

Bibliography

[1] Ajzen, I. (1991). The theory of planned behavior. *Organizational Behavior and Human Decision Processes*, 50(2), 179-211.

[2] Green, M. C., & Brock, T. C. (2000). The role of transportation in the persuasiveness of public narratives. *Journal of Personality and Social Psychology*, 79(5), 701-721.

[3] Bouris, A., et al. (2016). The psychological impact of anti-LGBTQ violence on activists. *Journal of Interpersonal Violence*, 31(1), 45-66.

Receiving awards and recognition for advocacy work

In the realm of activism, recognition and accolades play a pivotal role in amplifying the voices of those who dare to challenge the status quo. For Frank Mugisha, receiving awards and recognition for his advocacy work has not only validated his efforts but has also served as a catalyst for further activism within the LGBTQ community in Uganda. This section delves into the significance of these accolades, the challenges faced in receiving them, and the broader implications for LGBTQ rights advocacy.

The Importance of Recognition

Awards and recognition can be seen as a form of social capital, which Pierre Bourdieu defines as the resources available to individuals based on their social networks and connections. In the context of LGBTQ advocacy, these awards serve multiple purposes:

1. **Validation of Efforts**: Recognition from reputable organizations can affirm the hard work and sacrifices made by activists like Mugisha. This validation is crucial in a landscape where LGBTQ individuals often face marginalization and discrimination.

2. **Increased Visibility**: Awards often attract media attention, which can help raise awareness about LGBTQ issues in Uganda. Increased visibility can lead to greater public discourse and potentially influence societal attitudes.

3. **Motivation for Continued Advocacy**: Receiving an award can reinvigorate an activist's commitment to their cause. The acknowledgment of their work can serve as a reminder of the importance of their mission, encouraging them to persist despite challenges.

4. **Networking Opportunities**: Awards ceremonies often provide platforms for activists to connect with allies, potential collaborators, and influential figures in the human rights arena. These connections can lead to new opportunities for advocacy and resource sharing.

Challenges in Receiving Recognition

Despite the positive aspects of receiving awards, LGBTQ activists in Uganda, including Frank Mugisha, face significant challenges. The societal and political climate in Uganda is often hostile toward LGBTQ individuals, which complicates the process of gaining recognition. Key challenges include:

1. **Political Repression**: The Ugandan government has historically targeted LGBTQ activists, viewing their work as a threat to traditional values. This repression can hinder the ability of activists to receive recognition, as institutions may fear backlash for supporting LGBTQ rights.

2. **Cultural Stigmatization**: In a society where homosexuality is criminalized, the stigma associated with LGBTQ identities can extend to those who advocate for rights. Activists may be ostracized or face harassment, which can deter organizations from publicly recognizing their work.

3. **Limited Resources**: Many LGBTQ organizations operate on shoestring budgets, lacking the resources to apply for international awards or to promote their achievements. This limitation can result in deserving activists being overlooked.

4. **Safety Concerns**: The potential for violence and harassment against LGBTQ activists in Uganda means that some individuals may be hesitant to accept awards publicly, fearing for their safety and the safety of their loved ones.

Examples of Awards Received by Frank Mugisha

Frank Mugisha's relentless commitment to advocating for LGBTQ rights has not gone unnoticed. Some notable awards and recognitions include:

1. **The International Lesbian, Gay, Bisexual, Trans and Intersex Association (ILGA) Award**: This prestigious award recognized Mugisha for his tireless efforts

in fighting for LGBTQ rights in a challenging environment. The award not only highlighted his work but also drew international attention to the plight of LGBTQ individuals in Uganda.

2. **The Robert F. Kennedy Human Rights Award**: Mugisha received this award for his courage in advocating for marginalized communities. The recognition helped to elevate his profile globally and provided a platform to share the stories of those affected by discrimination in Uganda.

3. **The GLAAD Media Award**: This award acknowledged Mugisha's impact on media representation of LGBTQ issues. By promoting positive narratives, Mugisha has contributed to a shift in public perception, demonstrating the power of storytelling in advocacy.

4. **Recognition by Human Rights Watch**: Mugisha has been featured in reports and campaigns by Human Rights Watch, which have brought attention to the human rights abuses faced by LGBTQ individuals in Uganda. This recognition has helped to mobilize international support and pressure on the Ugandan government.

The Broader Implications of Recognition

The recognition of activists like Frank Mugisha has broader implications for the LGBTQ rights movement in Uganda and beyond. It highlights the resilience of individuals fighting for justice in oppressive environments. Moreover, these accolades can inspire a new generation of activists, providing them with role models who have successfully navigated the complexities of advocacy.

Furthermore, the international recognition of Mugisha's work can lead to increased pressure on the Ugandan government to address human rights abuses and consider legal reforms. It serves as a reminder that the fight for LGBTQ rights is a global issue, and solidarity across borders can amplify the impact of local activism.

Conclusion

Receiving awards and recognition is a multifaceted aspect of activism that can enhance the visibility and impact of LGBTQ rights advocacy. For Frank Mugisha, these accolades not only validate his tireless efforts but also serve as a beacon of hope for many in the LGBTQ community in Uganda. Despite the challenges inherent in this recognition, the positive implications for advocacy, community building, and societal change are undeniable. As the fight for LGBTQ rights continues, the acknowledgment of activists like Mugisha will remain crucial in shaping the narrative and advancing the cause.

Building a professional network within LGBTQ activism

Building a professional network within LGBTQ activism is a critical component for fostering collaboration, sharing resources, and amplifying the voices of marginalized communities. A robust professional network not only enhances the visibility of LGBTQ issues but also strengthens the collective power of advocates working towards equality and justice. This section will explore the theoretical underpinnings of networking, the challenges faced in building such networks, and practical examples of successful networking initiatives within LGBTQ activism.

Theoretical Framework

Networking theory posits that social networks are essential for the dissemination of information and resources. According to Granovetter's (1973) theory of the "strength of weak ties," individuals who connect with diverse social groups can access a broader range of information and opportunities than those who rely solely on close-knit circles. In the context of LGBTQ activism, this implies that activists should not only rely on established relationships within their immediate communities but also seek connections beyond these boundaries.

Furthermore, intersectionality, a term coined by Kimberlé Crenshaw (1989), emphasizes the interconnectedness of social identities and the unique challenges faced by individuals at the intersections of multiple marginalized identities. Building a professional network that acknowledges and incorporates intersectional perspectives is crucial for addressing the diverse needs of the LGBTQ community.

Challenges in Building Networks

Despite the importance of networking, LGBTQ activists often face several challenges in building professional networks:

- **Geographical Barriers:** Activists in rural or isolated areas may struggle to connect with others due to limited access to resources or events.

- **Resource Limitations:** Many LGBTQ organizations operate with minimal funding, which can hinder their ability to participate in networking events or collaborate with larger organizations.

- **Cultural Stigma:** In regions where LGBTQ identities are stigmatized, individuals may fear repercussions for openly engaging in activism, leading to hesitance in forming connections.

- **Fragmentation of the Movement:** The LGBTQ movement is not monolithic; differing priorities and strategies among various sub-groups (e.g., LGBTQ youth, people of color, transgender individuals) can create silos that inhibit collaboration.

Strategies for Effective Networking

To overcome these challenges and build a strong professional network, LGBTQ activists can employ several strategies:

- **Utilizing Digital Platforms:** Social media and online forums provide avenues for activists to connect across geographical barriers. Platforms like Twitter, Facebook, and LinkedIn can facilitate discussions, promote events, and share resources. For instance, the hashtag #LGBTQNetwork has been used to create virtual spaces for activists to share their work and connect with like-minded individuals globally.

- **Participating in Conferences and Workshops:** Attending LGBTQ-focused conferences, workshops, and training sessions can provide invaluable opportunities for networking. Events such as the International LGBTQ Leaders Conference and local Pride events often feature sessions designed to foster connections among activists and organizations.

- **Creating Alliances with Other Social Movements:** Building coalitions with other social justice movements can amplify advocacy efforts. For example, collaborations between LGBTQ activists and racial justice organizations have highlighted the importance of intersectionality and solidarity in fighting for equality.

- **Establishing Mentorship Programs:** Mentorship can play a vital role in networking by connecting experienced activists with newcomers. Programs that pair established leaders with emerging activists can facilitate knowledge transfer and provide valuable guidance in navigating the complexities of advocacy work.

- **Hosting Networking Events:** Organizing meet-and-greet events, panel discussions, or community forums can create spaces for activists to connect and share their experiences. These events can also serve as platforms for showcasing the work of various organizations and highlighting collaborative opportunities.

Examples of Successful Networking Initiatives

Several successful initiatives exemplify the power of networking within LGBTQ activism:

- **The Global Fund for Women:** This organization has established a network of grassroots activists and organizations worldwide, providing funding and support to LGBTQ initiatives. By facilitating connections among diverse activists, the Global Fund for Women has strengthened advocacy efforts and enhanced the impact of local movements.

- **OutRight Action International:** This organization focuses on advancing LGBTQ rights globally through advocacy, research, and capacity building. Their initiatives often involve creating networks of activists across different regions, enabling knowledge sharing and collaborative advocacy efforts.

- **The Queer Youth Network:** This grassroots initiative connects LGBTQ youth with resources, mentors, and each other. By providing a platform for young activists to engage with peers and experienced leaders, the network fosters a sense of community and empowerment among LGBTQ youth.

Conclusion

In conclusion, building a professional network within LGBTQ activism is essential for fostering collaboration, sharing resources, and amplifying marginalized voices. By understanding the theoretical foundations of networking, addressing the challenges faced, and implementing effective strategies, LGBTQ activists can create robust networks that enhance their advocacy efforts. The examples of successful initiatives highlight the potential of networking to drive meaningful change and promote inclusivity within the movement. As LGBTQ activists continue to navigate the complexities of their work, the power of connection and collaboration will remain a cornerstone of their efforts towards equality and justice.

Opportunities for collaboration and partnerships

In the realm of LGBTQ activism, collaboration and partnerships serve as vital lifelines, enabling activists to pool resources, share knowledge, and amplify their impact. The journey of Frank Mugisha exemplifies the importance of forging alliances across various sectors, including civil society organizations, international NGOs, and even the private sector. This section explores the theoretical underpinnings of collaboration, the challenges faced, and the fruitful partnerships that have emerged in the fight for LGBTQ rights in Uganda.

Theoretical Framework

Collaboration in advocacy can be understood through the lens of *social capital theory*, which posits that relationships and networks are crucial for mobilizing resources and achieving collective goals. According to Putnam (2000), social capital encompasses the norms and networks that facilitate cooperation for mutual benefit. In the context of LGBTQ activism, building social capital allows activists to access funding, expertise, and platforms for visibility.

Moreover, the *theory of collective action* (Olson, 1965) underscores the significance of working together to overcome individual challenges. This theory suggests that when individuals unite for a common cause, they can achieve outcomes that would be impossible to attain alone. In Uganda, where LGBTQ individuals often face systemic discrimination, collective action becomes essential for creating a formidable front against oppression.

Challenges to Collaboration

Despite the clear benefits of collaboration, LGBTQ activists in Uganda encounter several challenges that can hinder partnership development. One significant issue is the pervasive climate of fear and stigma surrounding LGBTQ identities, which often discourages potential allies from openly supporting the movement. This fear can manifest in various forms, including threats of violence, social ostracism, and professional repercussions.

Additionally, cultural and societal norms in Uganda often prioritize heteronormativity, leading to reluctance among some organizations to engage with LGBTQ issues. This reluctance can create a barrier to forming partnerships with traditional civil society organizations that may be hesitant to align themselves with LGBTQ advocacy for fear of backlash.

Examples of Successful Collaborations

Despite these challenges, numerous successful collaborations have emerged in the fight for LGBTQ rights in Uganda. One notable example is the partnership between local LGBTQ organizations and international NGOs such as Human

Rights Watch and Amnesty International. These collaborations have facilitated knowledge exchange, capacity building, and the mobilization of resources for advocacy campaigns.

For instance, the collaboration between local activists and international organizations has led to the development of training programs focused on legal rights, mental health support, and community organizing. Such initiatives empower LGBTQ individuals to advocate for their rights effectively and create a sense of solidarity among diverse groups.

Another promising partnership is the alliance formed between LGBTQ activists and health organizations to address the health disparities faced by the community. Through these collaborations, activists have worked to improve access to healthcare services, particularly in the context of HIV/AIDS prevention and treatment. By framing health as a human rights issue, these partnerships have garnered broader support and understanding from the public and policymakers alike.

The Role of Intersectionality

Intersectionality, as coined by Crenshaw (1989), also plays a crucial role in shaping collaboration opportunities. Recognizing that individuals possess multiple identities that intersect can enhance the effectiveness of partnerships. For example, LGBTQ activists in Uganda have increasingly collaborated with women's rights organizations to address issues such as gender-based violence and reproductive rights, highlighting the interconnectedness of various forms of oppression.

These intersectional partnerships not only broaden the scope of advocacy but also foster a more inclusive approach to activism. By working together, diverse groups can leverage their unique strengths and perspectives to create a more comprehensive movement for social justice.

Future Opportunities for Collaboration

Looking ahead, there are numerous opportunities for collaboration and partnerships that can further strengthen the LGBTQ rights movement in Uganda. Engaging with the private sector presents a promising avenue for support, particularly in areas such as corporate social responsibility (CSR). By encouraging businesses to adopt inclusive policies and support LGBTQ initiatives, activists can tap into additional resources and visibility.

Furthermore, digital activism offers new possibilities for collaboration. The rise of social media platforms enables activists to connect with global allies, share experiences, and mobilize support in real-time. Online campaigns can transcend geographical boundaries, amplifying the voices of LGBTQ individuals in Uganda and fostering a sense of global solidarity.

In conclusion, collaboration and partnerships are essential components of effective LGBTQ advocacy in Uganda. By leveraging social capital, addressing challenges head-on, and embracing intersectionality, activists can create a powerful movement for change. The future of LGBTQ rights in Uganda hinges on the ability to foster meaningful alliances that transcend societal barriers, ultimately leading to a more inclusive and equitable society for all.

Balancing personal and professional goals and aspirations

In the journey of an LGBTQ activist like Frank Mugisha, the balance between personal and professional goals is a delicate dance, often fraught with challenges and opportunities for growth. This section explores the theory behind goal-setting, the inherent problems faced by activists, and practical examples of how one can navigate this complex landscape.

Theoretical Framework

Goal-setting theory, proposed by Locke and Latham (1990), posits that specific and challenging goals lead to higher performance compared to easy or vague goals. This theory can be applied to both personal and professional aspirations. For LGBTQ activists, setting clear objectives is crucial not only for individual growth but also for the broader movement toward equality.

Let G_p represent personal goals and G_{pr} represent professional goals. The relationship can be expressed as:

$$G_{total} = G_p + G_{pr}$$

Where G_{total} is the cumulative satisfaction and fulfillment derived from both personal and professional achievements. The challenge lies in ensuring that both G_p and G_{pr} are aligned, allowing activists to thrive in both domains.

Challenges in Balancing Goals

Activists often face unique challenges that complicate this balance:

- **Time Constraints:** Activism requires significant time commitments, which can encroach upon personal life. For instance, Frank Mugisha's involvement in organizing protests and advocacy campaigns often leaves little room for personal relationships or self-care.

- **Emotional Toll:** The emotional burden of advocating for marginalized communities can lead to burnout. Activists may feel compelled to prioritize their advocacy work over personal aspirations, leading to a cycle of neglecting self-care.

- **Societal Expectations:** Cultural and societal pressures can create a conflict between personal identity and professional responsibilities. Activists may struggle to express their authentic selves in professional settings, leading to internal conflict.

Strategies for Balancing Goals

To navigate these challenges, activists can adopt several strategies:

1. **Setting Boundaries:** Establishing clear boundaries between personal and professional life is essential. For example, Frank Mugisha might designate specific hours for advocacy work and others for personal time, ensuring that he can recharge and maintain relationships.

2. **Self-Care Practices:** Engaging in regular self-care activities, such as meditation, exercise, or hobbies, can help mitigate the emotional toll of activism. Research indicates that self-care improves resilience and overall well-being (Hodge et al., 2017).

3. **Support Networks:** Building a robust support system of friends, family, and fellow activists can provide emotional and practical assistance. Frank's connections with other LGBTQ activists serve as a source of encouragement and solidarity, allowing him to share the burdens of both personal and professional life.

4. **Integrating Goals:** Finding ways to integrate personal and professional aspirations can create a sense of harmony. For instance, if Frank has a personal goal of traveling, he could plan to attend international LGBTQ conferences, thus fulfilling both personal desires and professional commitments.

Examples of Successful Balancing

Several activists have successfully navigated the balance between personal and professional goals:

- **Example 1:** A well-known LGBTQ activist in South Africa, who also works as a mental health counselor, integrates their professional skills into their activism by providing mental health resources to LGBTQ youth. This dual role allows them to fulfill personal aspirations while contributing meaningfully to the community.

- **Example 2:** A prominent LGBTQ rights advocate in the United States prioritizes family time by scheduling regular family outings, ensuring that personal relationships remain strong while engaging in high-profile advocacy work.

Conclusion

Balancing personal and professional goals is a crucial yet challenging aspect of life as an LGBTQ activist. By applying goal-setting theory, recognizing challenges, and implementing effective strategies, activists like Frank Mugisha can cultivate a fulfilling life that honors both their advocacy work and personal aspirations. As the fight for LGBTQ rights continues, it is essential to remember that self-care and personal fulfillment are not just side notes but integral components of sustainable activism.

Ultimately, the journey of balancing these goals is not just about achieving success in one realm but about creating a harmonious existence that empowers both the individual and the community at large.

Supporting Younger LGBTQ Activists

Mentorship programs and initiatives

Mentorship programs play a crucial role in empowering younger LGBTQ activists, providing them with guidance, support, and a sense of belonging within the community. These initiatives are designed to foster personal and professional development, ensuring that the next generation of advocates is equipped with the knowledge and skills necessary to navigate the complexities of LGBTQ activism.

The Importance of Mentorship

Mentorship can be defined as a relationship in which a more experienced individual (the mentor) provides guidance and support to a less experienced individual (the mentee). In the context of LGBTQ activism, mentorship serves several critical functions:

- **Knowledge Transfer:** Mentors share their experiences, insights, and strategies for effective advocacy. This knowledge is invaluable for young activists who may be navigating challenges that their mentors have already faced.

- **Skill Development:** Through mentorship, young activists can develop essential skills such as public speaking, community organizing, and policy advocacy. Mentors can provide constructive feedback and resources to help mentees hone these skills.

- **Networking Opportunities:** Mentors often have established networks within the LGBTQ community and beyond. By connecting mentees with these networks, mentors can help facilitate collaborations and partnerships that enhance the impact of advocacy efforts.

- **Emotional Support:** The journey of activism can be emotionally taxing, particularly for LGBTQ individuals facing discrimination and adversity. Mentors provide a safe space for mentees to express their fears, frustrations, and aspirations, fostering resilience and mental well-being.

Challenges in Implementing Mentorship Programs

Despite the clear benefits of mentorship, several challenges can hinder the effectiveness of these programs:

- **Availability of Mentors:** In many regions, particularly in areas with limited resources, there may be a shortage of experienced LGBTQ activists willing or able to serve as mentors.

- **Cultural Barriers:** In some cultures, discussing sexuality and LGBTQ issues may still be taboo. This can create barriers to establishing open and honest mentor-mentee relationships.

- **Resource Constraints:** Effective mentorship programs require funding for training, resources, and events. Many LGBTQ organizations operate on tight budgets, limiting their ability to implement comprehensive mentorship initiatives.

- **Mismatch of Expectations:** Sometimes, mentors and mentees may have differing expectations regarding the mentorship relationship. Clear communication and goal-setting are essential to ensure that both parties are aligned in their objectives.

Successful Examples of Mentorship Programs

Several successful mentorship programs have emerged within the LGBTQ community, demonstrating the potential for impactful advocacy through mentorship:

- **The Queer Youth Mentorship Program:** This initiative pairs LGBTQ youth with experienced activists who provide guidance on navigating personal and professional challenges. Participants engage in regular meetings, workshops, and social events, fostering a strong sense of community.

- **The Stonewall Mentorship Program:** Established by the Stonewall Community Foundation, this program connects emerging LGBTQ leaders with seasoned mentors in various sectors, including politics, arts, and business. The program emphasizes skill-building and networking, helping mentees to develop their careers while advocating for LGBTQ rights.

- **The Global LGBTQ Mentorship Initiative:** This international program focuses on connecting LGBTQ activists from different regions, allowing for cross-cultural exchanges of ideas and strategies. By fostering global solidarity, the initiative strengthens the collective impact of LGBTQ advocacy efforts worldwide.

Best Practices for Effective Mentorship Programs

To maximize the effectiveness of mentorship initiatives, several best practices can be employed:

- **Structured Programs:** Establishing a structured mentorship program with clear guidelines, objectives, and timelines can help ensure that both mentors and mentees understand their roles and responsibilities.

- **Training for Mentors:** Providing training for mentors can enhance their ability to support and guide mentees effectively. Training can cover topics such as active listening, cultural competency, and conflict resolution.

- **Regular Check-Ins:** Regular check-ins between mentors and mentees can foster open communication and help address any challenges that may arise during the mentorship relationship.

- **Evaluation and Feedback:** Implementing a system for evaluating the mentorship program's effectiveness can provide valuable insights into its impact and areas for improvement. Gathering feedback from participants can help refine the program and better meet the needs of mentees.

In conclusion, mentorship programs are vital for cultivating the next generation of LGBTQ activists. By providing guidance, support, and opportunities for growth, these initiatives empower young advocates to navigate the challenges of activism while fostering a sense of community and solidarity. Despite the challenges faced in implementing such programs, the examples of successful initiatives demonstrate that mentorship can have a profound impact on the lives of LGBTQ individuals and the broader movement for equality and justice.

$$M = \frac{K + S + N + E}{C} \qquad (24)$$

Where M represents the effectiveness of a mentorship program, K is knowledge transfer, S is skill development, N is networking opportunities, E is emotional support, and C is the challenges faced. This formula illustrates the importance of balancing the benefits of mentorship with the challenges to achieve optimal outcomes for mentees.

Providing resources and guidance to young activists

In the ever-evolving landscape of LGBTQ activism, the importance of nurturing the next generation of advocates cannot be overstated. Providing resources and guidance to young activists is not merely a supportive gesture; it is a strategic investment in the future of the movement. This section explores the various ways in which established activists can empower youth, the challenges they face, and the theoretical frameworks that underscore these efforts.

Theoretical Frameworks for Mentorship

The act of mentoring young activists draws on several theoretical frameworks, including social learning theory and empowerment theory. Social learning theory, proposed by Albert Bandura, posits that individuals learn from one another through observation, imitation, and modeling. This is particularly relevant in activism, where young individuals often look to seasoned activists as role models. Empowerment theory emphasizes the process of gaining control over one's life and the ability to influence change. By providing guidance and resources, older activists can empower youth to navigate their unique challenges and contribute meaningfully to the cause.

Challenges Faced by Young Activists

Young LGBTQ activists often encounter a myriad of challenges, including:

- **Lack of Resources:** Many young activists operate without access to essential resources such as funding, training, and educational materials, which can impede their ability to organize and advocate effectively.

- **Isolation:** Young activists, particularly those in conservative environments, may feel isolated or unsupported in their advocacy efforts, leading to burnout and disengagement.

- **Navigating Intersectionality:** Young activists from diverse backgrounds may face additional layers of discrimination, complicating their advocacy efforts. Understanding intersectionality is crucial for providing tailored support.

Providing Resources

To effectively support young activists, established advocates can employ several strategies:

- **Workshops and Training Sessions:** Organizing workshops that focus on essential skills, such as public speaking, fundraising, and grassroots organizing, can equip young activists with the tools they need to succeed. For example, a workshop on digital advocacy can teach young activists how to effectively use social media to amplify their message.

- **Resource Portals:** Creating online resource portals that compile articles, videos, and toolkits can provide young activists with easy access to information. These portals can include sections on legal rights, mental health resources, and strategies for community organizing.

- **Mentorship Programs:** Establishing formal mentorship programs can facilitate one-on-one relationships between experienced activists and young advocates. These programs can include regular check-ins, skill-building exercises, and opportunities for collaboration on projects.

Guidance and Support

Beyond providing resources, guidance is crucial for fostering the growth of young activists. This can take several forms:

- **Listening and Validation:** Creating spaces where young activists feel heard and validated can significantly enhance their confidence and commitment to the cause. This might involve regular group discussions where young activists can share their experiences and concerns.

- **Networking Opportunities:** Facilitating connections between young activists and established organizations can broaden their reach and enhance their impact. For instance, introducing them to key figures in the LGBTQ movement can open doors for collaboration and support.

- **Encouraging Self-Care:** Activism can be emotionally taxing, especially for young individuals facing societal prejudice. Encouraging self-care practices and providing resources for mental health support can help prevent burnout and promote resilience.

Case Studies and Examples

Several organizations have successfully implemented strategies to support young LGBTQ activists:

- **The Trevor Project:** This organization provides crisis intervention and suicide prevention services to LGBTQ youth. Their outreach programs include educational resources and training for young activists, emphasizing the importance of mental health and community support.

- **GLSEN (Gay, Lesbian and Straight Education Network):** GLSEN focuses on creating safe and inclusive schools for LGBTQ students. Their student-led initiatives empower young activists to advocate for policy changes within their educational institutions, providing them with both resources and a platform for their voices.

- **Youth Pride:** Many cities host annual Youth Pride events that celebrate LGBTQ youth culture while providing resources and support. These events often include workshops, performances, and opportunities for young activists to connect with established leaders in the community.

Conclusion

In conclusion, providing resources and guidance to young LGBTQ activists is a vital component of sustaining the movement for equality. By leveraging theoretical frameworks, addressing the unique challenges faced by youth, and implementing effective strategies, established activists can empower the next generation to lead with courage and conviction. As Frank Mugisha has demonstrated through his advocacy, the future of LGBTQ rights in Uganda—and beyond—depends on the strength and resilience of its young leaders. By investing in their growth, we not only honor their potential but also ensure that the fight for justice continues to thrive.

Fostering a sense of community and belonging

The journey of LGBTQ activism in Uganda has not only been about fighting for rights and recognition but also about creating a vibrant community where individuals can find belonging and support. The importance of fostering a sense of community cannot be overstated, as it serves as a foundation for resilience and empowerment among LGBTQ individuals. This section explores the theoretical frameworks that underpin community building, the challenges faced in creating inclusive spaces, and the practical examples of successful initiatives that have nurtured a sense of belonging.

Theoretical Frameworks

The concept of community is multifaceted, often defined by shared experiences, identities, and goals. According to social identity theory, individuals derive a sense of self from their group memberships, which can significantly impact their self-esteem and overall well-being [1]. In the context of LGBTQ activism, being part of a supportive community can mitigate feelings of isolation and marginalization, providing individuals with a safe space to express their identities without fear of judgment or persecution.

Furthermore, the ecological systems theory posits that individuals are influenced by various environmental factors, including family, peers, and societal norms [?]. For LGBTQ individuals in Uganda, these systems can be hostile, making the creation of supportive networks even more crucial. By fostering a sense of belonging within the LGBTQ community, activists can help members navigate these external pressures and build resilience.

Challenges in Community Building

Despite the theoretical understanding of the importance of community, several challenges hinder the establishment of inclusive spaces for LGBTQ individuals in Uganda. Stigma and discrimination remain pervasive, often leading to internalized homophobia and reluctance to engage with others in the community. Many individuals fear rejection from their families and society, which can create barriers to forming connections with fellow LGBTQ individuals.

Additionally, the lack of resources and safe spaces for LGBTQ gatherings exacerbates these challenges. Community centers, support groups, and social events are essential for fostering connections, yet many LGBTQ individuals in Uganda lack access to such resources. This scarcity can lead to feelings of loneliness and despair, further perpetuating the cycle of isolation.

Successful Initiatives and Examples

Despite these challenges, numerous initiatives have emerged to foster a sense of community and belonging among LGBTQ individuals in Uganda. One notable example is the establishment of LGBTQ support groups that provide safe spaces for individuals to share their experiences and challenges. These groups often organize regular meetings, workshops, and social events that encourage interaction and solidarity among members.

For instance, the organization *Freedom and Roam Uganda (FARUG)* has been instrumental in creating community among LGBTQ individuals. FARUG provides a platform for members to engage in discussions about their rights, share personal stories, and participate in advocacy efforts. Through their initiatives, they have successfully cultivated a sense of belonging that empowers individuals to embrace their identities and advocate for their rights.

Moreover, online platforms have emerged as vital tools for fostering community among LGBTQ individuals in Uganda. Social media groups and forums allow individuals to connect, share resources, and provide support to one another, particularly for those who may not feel safe attending in-person gatherings. These virtual spaces have become lifelines for many, enabling them to find a sense of belonging even in the face of adversity.

Conclusion

Fostering a sense of community and belonging among LGBTQ individuals in Uganda is a critical component of the broader struggle for rights and recognition. By understanding the theoretical frameworks that support community building and acknowledging the challenges faced, activists can implement effective strategies to create inclusive spaces. Successful initiatives like support groups and online platforms exemplify the power of community in empowering individuals and fostering resilience. As the movement continues to evolve, prioritizing community-building efforts will be essential in ensuring that LGBTQ individuals in Uganda can thrive and live authentically.

Challenges in mobilizing and empowering youth

The journey toward mobilizing and empowering youth within the LGBTQ community in Uganda is fraught with numerous challenges. These obstacles stem from a complex interplay of societal norms, political climates, and individual experiences. Understanding these challenges is crucial for developing effective strategies that can inspire and engage young activists.

One of the primary challenges lies in the pervasive stigma surrounding LGBTQ identities in Uganda. The cultural narrative often portrays homosexuality as a Western import, leading to widespread rejection and discrimination. This stigma can create an environment where LGBTQ youth feel isolated and fearful of expressing their identities. According to [?], societal homophobia can significantly hinder youth engagement, as many young individuals grapple with the internalized shame associated with their identities.

Furthermore, the legal landscape in Uganda poses a significant barrier. The Anti-Homosexuality Act, which has been proposed and debated multiple times, creates a climate of fear that discourages youth from participating in activism. The potential for legal repercussions, including imprisonment, can deter young people from openly advocating for their rights. As highlighted by [?], the threat of violence and arrest is a powerful disincentive for youth to mobilize and engage in advocacy efforts.

In addition to societal and legal challenges, there are also institutional barriers that hinder the empowerment of LGBTQ youth. Many educational institutions in Uganda lack supportive policies for LGBTQ students, often leading to discrimination and harassment. [?] notes that this hostile environment can prevent young activists from forming networks and support systems necessary for effective mobilization. The absence of safe spaces within schools and universities further exacerbates feelings of isolation and disempowerment among LGBTQ youth.

Moreover, the generational gap in activism presents another challenge. Older activists may have different priorities or approaches to advocacy, which can lead to misunderstandings or conflicts with younger generations. This disconnect can hinder the transfer of knowledge and resources that are vital for empowering youth. [?] emphasizes the importance of fostering intergenerational dialogue to bridge these gaps and create a more cohesive movement.

Another critical issue is the lack of access to resources and training for young LGBTQ activists. Many youth may not have the financial means to attend workshops, conferences, or training sessions that could enhance their skills and knowledge. The absence of mentorship programs further limits opportunities for young activists to learn from experienced leaders in the movement. [?] argues that without adequate support and resources, the potential for youth to effect change is significantly diminished.

To address these challenges, it is essential to develop targeted strategies that focus on youth empowerment. This includes creating safe spaces for LGBTQ youth to connect, share their experiences, and build solidarity. Organizations can play a pivotal role in facilitating workshops and training sessions that equip young activists with the necessary skills for advocacy. Furthermore, leveraging social media as a tool for mobilization can help reach a broader audience and foster a sense of community among LGBTQ youth.

In conclusion, the challenges in mobilizing and empowering LGBTQ youth in Uganda are multifaceted and deeply rooted in societal, legal, and institutional barriers. By recognizing and addressing these challenges, activists and organizations can work together to create a more inclusive and supportive environment that empowers the next generation of LGBTQ leaders. As articulated by [?], the future of LGBTQ rights in Uganda hinges on the ability to inspire and mobilize youth, ensuring that their voices are heard and valued in the ongoing struggle for equality.

The importance of inter-generational partnerships in activism

In the realm of activism, particularly within the LGBTQ rights movement, the significance of inter-generational partnerships cannot be overstated. These partnerships bridge the gap between different age groups, allowing for a rich exchange of experiences, knowledge, and strategies that can enhance the effectiveness of advocacy efforts. The importance of these collaborations can be understood through various theoretical frameworks, practical implications, and real-world examples.

Theoretical Frameworks

One theoretical perspective that elucidates the value of inter-generational partnerships is the Social Identity Theory. This theory posits that individuals derive a sense of identity from their membership in various social groups. In the context of LGBTQ activism, older activists often possess historical knowledge and a deep understanding of the struggles faced by the community over the decades. Conversely, younger activists tend to be more attuned to contemporary issues, technology, and innovative forms of communication. By combining these perspectives, inter-generational partnerships can create a more holistic approach to activism, fostering a sense of belonging and shared purpose across age groups.

Another relevant theory is the Theory of Generational Cohorts, which highlights how different generations may have distinct values, beliefs, and experiences shaped by the socio-political contexts in which they grew up. For instance, older generations might have faced harsher societal repercussions for their sexual orientation, while younger generations may benefit from a more accepting environment. Understanding these differences is crucial for effective collaboration, as it allows activists to appreciate the unique contributions that each generation brings to the table.

Challenges in Inter-Generational Activism

While inter-generational partnerships hold immense potential, they are not without challenges. One major issue is the potential for misunderstanding and miscommunication between generations. Older activists may sometimes view younger activists as lacking the historical context necessary for effective advocacy, while younger activists might perceive their older counterparts as resistant to change or overly cautious. Such perceptions can create barriers to collaboration.

Moreover, differing approaches to activism can lead to friction. For example, while older activists may prioritize legal reforms and formal advocacy, younger activists might focus on grassroots movements and social media campaigns. These differing methodologies can cause tension if not navigated thoughtfully.

Examples of Successful Inter-Generational Partnerships

Despite the challenges, numerous examples demonstrate the successful implementation of inter-generational partnerships in LGBTQ activism. One prominent case is the collaboration between older activists who participated in the Stonewall Riots of 1969 and younger activists involved in contemporary pride events. This partnership has led to the creation of educational programs that highlight the history of LGBTQ rights while simultaneously addressing current issues such as trans rights and intersectionality.

Furthermore, organizations like *SAGE* (Services and Advocacy for GLBT Elders) exemplify the power of inter-generational partnerships. By connecting older LGBTQ individuals with younger activists, SAGE fosters a supportive environment that encourages mentorship and collaboration, ensuring that the lessons of the past inform the strategies of the future.

Strategies for Fostering Inter-Generational Partnerships

To cultivate effective inter-generational partnerships, several strategies can be employed:

1. **Facilitated Dialogue:** Creating spaces for open dialogue where activists from different generations can share their experiences and perspectives fosters understanding and empathy.

2. **Mentorship Programs:** Establishing mentorship initiatives where older activists guide younger ones can facilitate knowledge transfer and skill development.

3. **Collaborative Projects:** Jointly organizing events or campaigns that leverage the strengths of both generations can enhance the impact of advocacy efforts.

4. **Inclusive Decision-Making:** Involving activists from all age groups in decision-making processes ensures that diverse perspectives are considered, promoting a sense of ownership and commitment to collective goals.

5. **Utilizing Technology:** Younger activists can introduce older generations to digital tools and social media platforms, enhancing outreach and engagement strategies.

Conclusion

In conclusion, inter-generational partnerships in LGBTQ activism are essential for fostering a more inclusive and effective movement. By recognizing the unique contributions of each generation and addressing the challenges that may arise, activists can create a united front that honors the past while striving for a more equitable future. The collaboration between generations not only enriches the activism landscape but also ensures that the fight for LGBTQ rights continues to evolve, drawing strength from the wisdom of experience and the vigor of youth. The ongoing journey of advocacy is a testament to the power of unity across generations, ultimately leading to a more resilient and vibrant movement for change.

Overcoming Burnout and Sustaining Momentum

Strategies for avoiding burnout in advocacy work

Advocacy work, especially in the realm of LGBTQ rights, can be an emotionally and physically draining endeavor. Activists often find themselves at the intersection of personal passion and systemic oppression, which can lead to feelings of exhaustion, frustration, and ultimately, burnout. Burnout is characterized by emotional exhaustion, depersonalization, and a diminished sense of personal accomplishment, as described by Maslach and Jackson (1981). To sustain the momentum of advocacy efforts while maintaining mental health, it is crucial to implement effective strategies to avoid burnout.

Understanding Burnout

Burnout can be exacerbated by the constant exposure to discrimination, violence, and systemic barriers that LGBTQ individuals face. According to the World Health Organization (2019), burnout is a syndrome resulting from chronic workplace stress that has not been successfully managed. In the context of advocacy, the stressors can include:

- **Emotional Labor:** The effort required to manage emotions while advocating for rights can be overwhelming. Activists often feel the need to maintain a positive front, even when facing adversity.

- **Isolation:** Many LGBTQ activists work in environments where they may feel unsupported or alone in their struggles, leading to feelings of isolation.

- **High Expectations:** The pressure to achieve tangible results can create unrealistic expectations, leading to disappointment and stress when outcomes do not meet these expectations.

Strategies for Prevention

To combat burnout, activists can adopt several strategies that promote resilience and sustainability in their advocacy efforts.

1. Establish Clear Boundaries Setting boundaries is essential for maintaining a healthy work-life balance. Activists should define specific work hours and personal time, ensuring that they allocate time for rest and self-care. For instance, an activist may choose to disconnect from social media after a certain hour to avoid the emotional toll of constant exposure to distressing news.

2. **Practice Self-Care** Engaging in self-care routines is vital for mental and emotional well-being. This can include activities such as:

- **Physical Exercise:** Regular physical activity has been shown to reduce stress and improve mood (Peluso & Andrade, 2005). Activists can incorporate activities like yoga, running, or dancing into their routines.

- **Mindfulness and Meditation:** Practicing mindfulness can help activists stay grounded and manage stress. Techniques such as deep breathing, meditation, or guided imagery can be beneficial.

- **Creative Outlets:** Engaging in creative activities such as writing, painting, or music can provide a therapeutic escape from the pressures of advocacy work.

3. **Build a Support Network** Creating a strong support network can alleviate feelings of isolation. Activists should seek out peers, mentors, and allies who understand the unique challenges of advocacy work. Regular check-ins with supportive friends or colleagues can provide emotional validation and encouragement. For example, forming a peer support group where activists share their experiences and coping strategies can foster a sense of community.

4. **Set Realistic Goals** It is crucial to set achievable and measurable goals in advocacy work. Breaking larger objectives into smaller, manageable tasks can help maintain motivation and prevent feelings of overwhelm. For instance, rather than aiming for sweeping legislative changes, an activist might focus on organizing a single event or campaign. This approach allows for celebrating small victories, which can boost morale and motivation.

5. **Seek Professional Help** When feelings of burnout become overwhelming, seeking professional support from a therapist or counselor can be a crucial step. Mental health professionals can provide tools and strategies tailored to the unique challenges faced by LGBTQ activists. Therapy can offer a safe space to process emotions and develop coping mechanisms.

6. Engage in Reflective Practices Regular self-reflection can help activists assess their emotional state and recognize signs of burnout early. Journaling about daily experiences, emotions, and challenges can provide insights into patterns of stress and allow for proactive adjustments. Reflective practices can also reinforce the activist's sense of purpose and commitment to their cause.

Conclusion

Burnout is a significant risk for LGBTQ activists engaged in advocacy work, but it is not insurmountable. By implementing strategies such as establishing boundaries, practicing self-care, building support networks, setting realistic goals, seeking professional help, and engaging in reflective practices, activists can sustain their passion and commitment to the fight for LGBTQ rights. Ultimately, the journey of advocacy is not just about the destination but also about nurturing the well-being of those who champion the cause.

Bibliography

[1] Maslach, C., & Jackson, S. E. (1981). *The Measurement of Experienced Burnout.* Journal of Occupational Behavior, 2(2), 99-113.

[2] Peluso, M. A. M., & Andrade, L. H. S. G. (2005). Physical activity and mental health: The association between physical activity and mental health in adults. *Revista Brasileira de Psiquiatria*, 27(2), 90-95.

[3] World Health Organization. (2019). *Burn-out an "occupational phenomenon": International Classification of Diseases.* Retrieved from https://www.who.int/news/item/28-05-2019-burn-out-an-occupation

Taking breaks and practicing self-care

In the demanding world of activism, particularly for LGBTQ rights in Uganda, the need for self-care cannot be overstated. Activists like Frank Mugisha face a myriad of challenges that can lead to emotional and physical exhaustion. The importance of taking breaks and practicing self-care is not merely a suggestion; it is a vital component of sustainable activism.

Understanding Self-Care

Self-care refers to the deliberate actions taken to enhance one's physical, mental, and emotional well-being. According to the World Health Organization (WHO), self-care is defined as the ability of individuals, families, and communities to promote health, prevent disease, and maintain health. This concept is particularly crucial for activists who often find themselves in high-stress environments where their mental health can be compromised.

The Psychological Toll of Activism

Activism can be a double-edged sword. While it offers a sense of purpose and community, it also exposes individuals to constant stressors, including threats, discrimination, and societal backlash. A study published in the *Journal of Health Psychology* highlights that activists are more prone to experience anxiety, depression, and burnout compared to individuals in less demanding roles. This phenomenon is often exacerbated in regions like Uganda, where LGBTQ activists face severe repercussions for their advocacy.

$$\text{Burnout} = \text{Emotional Exhaustion} + \text{Depersonalization} + \text{Reduced Personal Accomplishment} \quad (25)$$

This equation illustrates that burnout is a complex interplay of various factors, and self-care practices can help mitigate its effects.

The Importance of Taking Breaks

Taking breaks is essential for maintaining mental health and ensuring long-term effectiveness in activism. Breaks allow activists to recharge, reflect, and regain perspective. The Pomodoro Technique, a time management method developed by Francesco Cirillo, emphasizes the importance of taking short breaks after focused work sessions. This technique can be adapted for activists by scheduling regular intervals for rest and reflection, ensuring that they are not overwhelmed by the emotional weight of their work.

Examples of Self-Care Practices

1. **Mindfulness and Meditation**: Engaging in mindfulness practices can help activists center themselves amidst chaos. A study published in *Psychological Science* found that mindfulness meditation significantly reduces stress and anxiety levels, making it a powerful tool for those in high-stress environments.

2. **Physical Activity**: Regular exercise is known to release endorphins, which can elevate mood and reduce stress. Activists might consider incorporating activities such as yoga, running, or even dancing into their routines to promote physical and mental well-being.

3. **Creative Outlets**: Engaging in creative activities such as painting, writing, or music can serve as an emotional release. For many activists, expressing their feelings through art not only provides relief but also fosters a sense of community when shared with others.

4. **Social Connections**: Building a support network is vital for emotional resilience. Activists should prioritize spending time with friends and loved ones who understand their struggles, providing a safe space for sharing experiences and feelings.

5. **Setting Boundaries**: It is crucial for activists to establish boundaries to protect their mental health. This includes learning to say no to additional responsibilities or engagements that may lead to overwhelm.

Conclusion

In conclusion, taking breaks and practicing self-care is not a luxury but a necessity for LGBTQ activists like Frank Mugisha. By prioritizing their well-being, activists can sustain their energy, passion, and effectiveness in the fight for LGBTQ rights. The journey towards equality is long and fraught with challenges, but with proper self-care strategies, activists can continue to advocate for change while also nurturing their own mental and emotional health. As the saying goes, "You cannot pour from an empty cup." Therefore, it is vital for activists to fill their cups through self-care, ensuring that they remain strong and resilient in their important work.

Building support systems and finding outlets for stress

In the realm of activism, particularly within the LGBTQ community, the weight of advocacy can often feel overwhelming. Activists like Frank Mugisha face not only the external challenges of discrimination and societal rejection but also the internal struggles that come with such a demanding role. Building support systems and finding effective outlets for stress is crucial for sustaining long-term engagement in activism.

Understanding the Importance of Support Systems

Support systems are networks of individuals who provide emotional, informational, and practical assistance. According to [?], social support can be categorized into four types: emotional, instrumental, informational, and appraisal support. Each type plays a vital role in managing stress and enhancing resilience.

$$S = E + I + A + R \tag{26}$$

Where:

- S is the overall support received,

- E is emotional support,
- I is instrumental support,
- A is appraisal support,
- R is informational support.

The equation illustrates that the total support an individual feels is a sum of various forms of support, emphasizing the need for a well-rounded support network.

Challenges in Building Support Systems

While the necessity for support systems is clear, the process of building them is fraught with challenges. Many LGBTQ activists operate within environments that may not be conducive to open discussions about their struggles. Fear of judgment, discrimination, or even violence can inhibit individuals from seeking support.

For instance, Mugisha's advocacy work often places him in precarious situations where revealing personal vulnerabilities could lead to backlash from both the community and the authorities. This fear can create a barrier to forming meaningful connections with others who might provide the necessary support.

Finding Outlets for Stress

In addition to establishing support systems, finding healthy outlets for stress is essential for activists. Engaging in activities that promote mental well-being can mitigate the adverse effects of stress. Research indicates that physical activity, creative expression, and mindfulness practices can significantly reduce stress levels.

$$M = \frac{1}{N} \sum_{i=1}^{N} (E_i + C_i + M_i) \tag{27}$$

Where:

- M is the mental well-being,
- N is the number of outlets used,
- E_i is the effect of exercise,
- C_i is the effect of creative activities,
- M_i is the effect of mindfulness practices.

This equation suggests that the overall mental well-being of an individual can be improved by engaging in various activities that reduce stress.

Examples of Effective Outlets

1. **Physical Activity**: Regular exercise has been shown to release endorphins, the body's natural mood lifters. For instance, community sports groups or yoga classes can serve as both a physical outlet and a way to connect with others who share similar experiences.

2. **Creative Expression**: Art, music, and writing can provide powerful means of processing emotions. Activists like Mugisha have utilized storytelling and public speaking to share their journeys, which not only serves as a form of catharsis but also raises awareness about LGBTQ issues.

3. **Mindfulness and Meditation**: Techniques such as meditation and deep-breathing exercises can help in managing anxiety. Many activists have found solace in mindfulness practices, which can be easily integrated into daily routines.

4. **Peer Support Groups**: Joining or forming peer support groups can create a safe space for sharing experiences and coping strategies. These groups can foster a sense of belonging and understanding, which is vital for emotional health.

5. **Professional Counseling**: Seeking help from mental health professionals who specialize in LGBTQ issues can provide additional support. Therapy can offer coping mechanisms tailored to the unique challenges faced by activists.

Conclusion

Building robust support systems and finding effective outlets for stress are not just beneficial but essential for the sustainability of LGBTQ activism. By fostering connections with like-minded individuals and engaging in activities that promote mental well-being, activists can navigate the complexities of their roles while maintaining their health and passion for advocacy. As Frank Mugisha continues to inspire change, the importance of these strategies remains paramount for both him and the broader LGBTQ community.

The role of self-reflection and self-empowerment

Self-reflection and self-empowerment are crucial components in the journey of an LGBTQ activist, particularly in contexts where societal pressures and discrimination are prevalent. These processes not only foster personal growth but also enhance the effectiveness of advocacy efforts. This section will explore the significance of self-reflection and self-empowerment, the theoretical frameworks that underpin these concepts, and practical examples of how they manifest in the lives of activists like Frank Mugisha.

Theoretical Foundations

Self-reflection is the process of introspection, where individuals examine their thoughts, feelings, and motivations. According to Schön's (1983) theory of reflective practice, self-reflection enables individuals to learn from their experiences and improve their future actions. This theory is particularly relevant for activists who face constant challenges and adversities. By engaging in self-reflection, activists can identify their strengths and weaknesses, assess their emotional responses to stressors, and develop strategies for resilience.

Self-empowerment, on the other hand, involves the process of gaining the confidence and strength to take control of one's life and advocate for oneself and others. As articulated by Zimmerman (1995), empowerment is a multidimensional construct that encompasses personal, social, and political dimensions. In the context of LGBTQ activism, self-empowerment allows individuals to assert their identities, challenge oppressive systems, and mobilize others in the fight for rights and recognition.

Challenges Faced by LGBTQ Activists

Activists often encounter a myriad of challenges that can impede their sense of self-worth and agency. These include:

- **Internalized Homophobia:** Many LGBTQ individuals grapple with internalized negative beliefs about their sexual orientation or gender identity, which can hinder their self-esteem and self-acceptance.

- **Societal Rejection:** The fear of rejection from family, friends, and society at large can lead to feelings of isolation and despair, making self-reflection and empowerment even more difficult.

- **Burnout:** The emotional toll of continuous activism can lead to burnout, where activists feel overwhelmed and powerless to effect change.

The Importance of Self-Reflection

Self-reflection serves as a vital tool for LGBTQ activists to navigate these challenges. By regularly engaging in reflective practices, activists can:

- **Enhance Emotional Intelligence:** Understanding one's emotions and triggers can lead to better management of stress and anxiety. For instance, Mugisha often reflects on his emotional responses to public criticism, allowing him to cultivate resilience and maintain focus on his advocacy goals.

- **Clarify Values and Goals:** Reflection helps activists clarify their motivations and aspirations, ensuring that their actions align with their core values. This alignment can lead to a more authentic and impactful advocacy journey.

- **Foster Adaptive Coping Strategies:** By reflecting on past experiences, activists can identify effective coping strategies that have worked for them, thus empowering them to face future challenges with confidence.

Empowerment Through Action

Self-empowerment is not merely an internal process; it also involves taking concrete actions that reinforce one's agency. For LGBTQ activists, this can manifest in various ways:

- **Community Engagement:** Actively participating in LGBTQ organizations and support groups can foster a sense of belonging and solidarity. Mugisha's involvement in local advocacy groups has not only empowered him but also inspired others to join the movement.

- **Advocacy and Representation:** Speaking out on behalf of marginalized communities empowers both the activist and those they represent. By sharing his story, Mugisha has illuminated the struggles faced by LGBTQ individuals in Uganda, galvanizing support and prompting action from allies.

- **Personal Development:** Pursuing education and professional growth can enhance an activist's skills and confidence. Mugisha has pursued higher education, which has equipped him with the knowledge and tools necessary for effective advocacy.

Examples of Self-Reflection and Empowerment in Practice

Frank Mugisha's journey exemplifies the transformative power of self-reflection and self-empowerment. Throughout his activism, he has engaged in reflective practices that have shaped his approach to advocacy. For instance, after facing significant backlash from conservative groups, Mugisha took time to reflect on his experiences, leading him to develop a more strategic approach to public speaking and engagement.

Moreover, Mugisha's emphasis on mentorship reflects the importance of empowerment in activism. By mentoring younger LGBTQ activists, he not only empowers them to find their voices but also reinforces his own sense of purpose and agency within the movement. This cyclical process of empowerment creates a robust support system that fosters resilience among activists.

Conclusion

In conclusion, self-reflection and self-empowerment are indispensable elements in the lives of LGBTQ activists. These processes enable individuals to navigate the complexities of their identities and the challenges of advocacy. By engaging in self-reflection, activists can enhance their emotional intelligence, clarify their goals, and develop adaptive coping strategies. Simultaneously, self-empowerment through action fosters agency, allowing activists to effect meaningful change in their communities. As Frank Mugisha's journey illustrates, the intertwining of self-reflection and empowerment not only strengthens the individual but also uplifts the broader movement for LGBTQ rights in Uganda and beyond.

The ongoing journey of sustaining the fight for LGBTQ rights

The struggle for LGBTQ rights is not a sprint; it is a marathon, a relentless journey that demands resilience, adaptability, and unwavering commitment. Sustaining this fight requires a multifaceted approach that addresses both immediate needs and long-term goals, ensuring that progress is not only achieved but maintained. This ongoing journey is characterized by several key elements: community engagement, intersectionality, mental health considerations, and strategic advocacy.

Community Engagement

At the heart of sustaining the fight for LGBTQ rights is the importance of community engagement. Grassroots movements have historically been the backbone of LGBTQ activism, providing a platform for individuals to share their stories, experiences, and struggles. Engaging with the community fosters a sense of belonging and empowerment, which is crucial for maintaining momentum in advocacy efforts.

For instance, organizations like *OutRight Action International* and *ILGA World* have successfully mobilized local communities to participate in global campaigns, highlighting the significance of collective action. These organizations emphasize the need for inclusive spaces where individuals can come together to strategize, support one another, and amplify their voices.

Intersectionality

The concept of intersectionality, coined by Kimberlé Crenshaw, plays a vital role in sustaining the fight for LGBTQ rights. It acknowledges that individuals possess multiple identities that intersect to shape their experiences of discrimination and privilege. For example, a Black LGBTQ individual may face unique challenges that differ from those experienced by a white LGBTQ individual or a cisgender heterosexual ally.

Addressing these intersecting identities is essential for creating comprehensive advocacy strategies that resonate with diverse communities. The *Transgender Day of Visibility* serves as a poignant reminder of the need to uplift marginalized voices within the LGBTQ spectrum, particularly those of transgender individuals who often face heightened discrimination and violence. By acknowledging and advocating for the rights of all marginalized groups, the movement can build solidarity and foster a more inclusive environment.

Mental Health Considerations

The ongoing journey of sustaining LGBTQ rights also necessitates a focus on mental health. Activism can take a significant toll on individuals, leading to burnout, anxiety, and depression. The constant battle against discrimination and violence can create an environment of chronic stress, which affects both personal well-being and advocacy efforts.

Incorporating mental health resources into LGBTQ activism is crucial. Organizations should prioritize self-care initiatives, providing access to counseling services, support groups, and wellness programs. For example, the *Trevor Project* offers crisis intervention and suicide prevention services specifically tailored for LGBTQ youth, recognizing the mental health challenges faced by this demographic. By addressing mental health, activists can sustain their energy and passion for the fight, ultimately leading to more effective advocacy.

Strategic Advocacy

Sustaining the fight for LGBTQ rights requires strategic advocacy that adapts to changing political landscapes and societal attitudes. This involves leveraging data and research to inform policy proposals and lobbying efforts. For example, the

Human Rights Campaign utilizes extensive research to highlight the economic impact of discrimination against LGBTQ individuals, arguing for policies that promote equality and inclusion.

Furthermore, strategic advocacy includes building coalitions with other marginalized groups to amplify collective voices. The Black Lives Matter movement has shown how intersectional alliances can strengthen advocacy efforts, as LGBTQ activists collaborate with racial justice organizations to address systemic oppression. By forging these alliances, the LGBTQ movement can gain broader support and foster a culture of solidarity.

Conclusion

The ongoing journey of sustaining the fight for LGBTQ rights is complex and multifaceted. It requires a commitment to community engagement, an understanding of intersectionality, a focus on mental health, and strategic advocacy. As activists continue to navigate the challenges of discrimination and inequality, it is imperative that they remain adaptable and resilient. The journey may be long, but each step taken towards equality is a testament to the strength and determination of the LGBTQ community. Together, they can forge a path towards a more inclusive and just society, where every individual can live authentically and without fear.

In conclusion, the fight for LGBTQ rights is an enduring journey that necessitates the involvement of all members of society. The collective efforts of individuals, organizations, and allies will shape the future landscape of LGBTQ rights, ensuring that progress is not only achieved but sustained for generations to come.

The International Impact

Speaking at International Conferences and Events

Sharing personal experiences and insights on global stage

In the realm of activism, personal narratives hold profound power. They serve not only as a means of self-expression but also as a crucial tool for fostering empathy and understanding among diverse audiences. Frank Mugisha, a prominent LGBTQ activist from Uganda, has harnessed this power to share his experiences on global platforms, illuminating the complex realities faced by LGBTQ individuals in Uganda.

The Power of Personal Narratives

Personal narratives are foundational to social movements, as they humanize abstract issues and bridge gaps between disparate communities. According to narrative theory, stories can influence perceptions and attitudes by evoking emotional responses, which can lead to greater awareness and action. Frank's journey, marked by struggles and triumphs, exemplifies how sharing one's story can catalyze change.

$$E = mc^2 \tag{28}$$

This famous equation by Einstein, while primarily a physics principle, can metaphorically illustrate the energy (E) that personal stories can generate (m) when shared with the world (c). The mass of an individual's experiences can convert into impactful energy when conveyed effectively on global stages.

Challenges in Sharing Personal Experiences

Despite the transformative potential of personal storytelling, activists like Frank often face significant challenges when sharing their narratives. In Uganda, where homophobia is rampant and LGBTQ individuals are subjected to severe discrimination, the act of coming forward can be fraught with danger. Activists risk not only their safety but also their relationships with family and community, as societal norms are deeply ingrained.

For instance, Frank's early experiences of harassment and violence due to his sexual orientation shaped his understanding of the urgent need for advocacy. When he first began to share his story on international platforms, he encountered backlash from conservative factions within Uganda, who viewed his openness as a threat to traditional values. This highlights the delicate balance activists must strike between visibility and safety.

Global Engagement and Advocacy

Frank's participation in international conferences and events has allowed him to share his narrative with a broader audience, fostering solidarity and support for LGBTQ rights. By articulating the struggles faced by LGBTQ individuals in Uganda, he has influenced global discourse on human rights. His speeches often emphasize the intersectionality of identities, addressing how race, gender, and sexuality converge to shape individual experiences.

For example, during a keynote address at a major human rights conference, Frank recounted a harrowing experience of being targeted for his activism. This personal account resonated with many attendees, prompting discussions on the need for comprehensive protections for LGBTQ individuals worldwide. Such moments underscore the importance of storytelling in advocacy; they not only raise awareness but also galvanize action.

The Role of Empathy in Activism

Empathy plays a crucial role in activism, as it fosters connections between individuals from different backgrounds. Frank's ability to convey his experiences with authenticity allows others to empathize with his struggles, breaking down barriers of misunderstanding. This empathetic engagement is essential for building coalitions and mobilizing support for LGBTQ rights.

Research in psychology suggests that empathy can lead to prosocial behavior, encouraging individuals to take action on behalf of marginalized communities. By sharing his story, Frank not only advocates for himself but also amplifies the voices of those who may not have the platform to share their experiences.

Conclusion: The Impact of Sharing Personal Insights

In conclusion, sharing personal experiences on a global stage is a powerful strategy for advocacy. Frank Mugisha's journey illustrates the profound impact that storytelling can have on raising awareness and fostering empathy for LGBTQ rights. While challenges persist, the act of sharing one's narrative creates opportunities for dialogue, understanding, and ultimately, change. As activists like Frank continue to share their stories, they pave the way for a more inclusive and accepting world, one narrative at a time.

Influencing international policies and perspectives

The journey of LGBTQ advocacy often transcends national borders, as activists like Frank Mugisha have recognized the profound impact that international policies and perspectives can have on local realities. The interplay between global human rights frameworks and local advocacy efforts is crucial in shaping the landscape for LGBTQ rights in Uganda and beyond. This section delves into how activists influence international policies, the challenges they face, and the strategies employed to reshape perspectives on LGBTQ issues.

The Role of International Human Rights Frameworks

International human rights law serves as a foundational framework for LGBTQ advocacy. Instruments such as the Universal Declaration of Human Rights (UDHR) and the International Covenant on Civil and Political Rights (ICCPR) enshrine principles of equality and non-discrimination. Article 1 of the UDHR states:

> All human beings are born free and equal in dignity and rights.

This principle underpins the argument for LGBTQ rights, as it advocates for the inherent dignity of all individuals, regardless of their sexual orientation or gender identity. Activists like Mugisha leverage these international standards to hold local governments accountable, challenging discriminatory laws and practices that violate these rights.

Engaging with International Bodies

Influencing international policies requires strategic engagement with bodies such as the United Nations (UN) and regional organizations like the African Union (AU). Mugisha's participation in international conferences provides a platform to elevate the discourse on LGBTQ rights. By sharing personal narratives and statistical evidence of discrimination, activists can humanize the issues faced by LGBTQ individuals in Uganda.

For instance, during the UN Human Rights Council sessions, activists can present reports detailing human rights abuses against LGBTQ individuals. These presentations often lead to resolutions that call for member states to uphold human rights standards, thereby creating pressure on governments to reform discriminatory laws. The impact of such resolutions is significant, as they can lead to increased scrutiny and accountability from the international community.

Challenges in Advocacy

Despite the potential for influence, LGBTQ activists face numerous challenges in navigating international advocacy. One significant barrier is the backlash from local governments that perceive international scrutiny as an infringement on sovereignty. In Uganda, the government has often responded to international criticism with defiance, framing LGBTQ rights as a Western imposition. This narrative can resonate with conservative constituents and hinder progress.

Moreover, the intersection of LGBTQ rights with cultural and religious beliefs poses additional challenges. Many activists must contend with deeply entrenched societal norms that view homosexuality as taboo. As Mugisha has noted, addressing these cultural perceptions is as vital as legal reforms. Activists must engage in dialogue that respects cultural contexts while advocating for universal human rights.

Strategies for Influence

To effectively influence international policies, LGBTQ activists employ a variety of strategies. One key approach is coalition-building with other human rights organizations. By forming alliances with groups focused on women's rights, racial equality, and broader human rights issues, LGBTQ activists can amplify their voices and create a united front against discrimination. This intersectional approach allows for a more comprehensive understanding of human rights, emphasizing that the fight for LGBTQ rights is part of a larger struggle for justice.

Additionally, leveraging social media has become an indispensable tool for advocacy. Platforms like Twitter and Facebook enable activists to disseminate information rapidly, mobilize support, and engage with a global audience. Campaigns that go viral can attract international attention and pressure local governments to reconsider their policies. For example, the #FreeUganda campaign highlighted the plight of LGBTQ individuals facing persecution, galvanizing international support and prompting calls for action from foreign governments.

Case Studies of Impact

Several case studies illustrate the tangible impact of international advocacy on local policies. In 2011, the UN Human Rights Council adopted a landmark resolution condemning violence and discrimination based on sexual orientation and gender identity. This resolution marked a pivotal moment, as it was the first time the Council explicitly recognized LGBTQ rights as human rights. Activists like Mugisha seized this opportunity to push for local reforms in Uganda, advocating for the repeal of laws that criminalized homosexuality.

Furthermore, the role of influential allies, such as celebrities and political leaders, cannot be overstated. When public figures advocate for LGBTQ rights, they can significantly influence public opinion and policy. For instance, the involvement of global icons in campaigns for LGBTQ rights has led to increased visibility and support, encouraging local governments to reconsider their stances.

Conclusion

In conclusion, the influence of international policies and perspectives on LGBTQ rights is a multifaceted endeavor that requires resilience, strategic engagement, and a commitment to justice. Activists like Frank Mugisha exemplify the power of advocacy that transcends borders, leveraging international human rights frameworks to challenge local injustices. By navigating the complexities of cultural perceptions, building coalitions, and utilizing modern communication tools, they continue to shape the narrative around LGBTQ rights, fostering hope for a more inclusive future.

Networking with global LGBTQ activists and allies

In the ever-evolving landscape of LGBTQ rights, the importance of networking with global activists and allies cannot be overstated. This section delves into the theoretical frameworks that underpin effective networking strategies, the challenges faced in building these networks, and real-world examples of successful collaborations that have emerged from such efforts.

Theoretical Frameworks

Networking among LGBTQ activists is grounded in several theoretical perspectives, including social capital theory and intersectionality. Social capital theory posits that relationships and networks provide individuals with access to resources and opportunities. In the context of LGBTQ activism, these networks can facilitate knowledge sharing, resource mobilization, and collective action.

$$\text{Social Capital} = \text{Network Connections} + \text{Shared Norms} + \text{Trust} \qquad (29)$$

This equation illustrates that social capital is not merely about the number of connections one has, but also the quality of those relationships, the norms that govern them, and the trust established within the network.

Intersectionality, on the other hand, emphasizes the interconnected nature of social categorizations such as race, class, and gender, which can create overlapping systems of discrimination or disadvantage. Recognizing intersectionality allows activists to approach networking with a nuanced understanding of the diverse identities within the LGBTQ community, enabling more inclusive and effective advocacy.

Challenges in Networking

Despite the theoretical advantages of networking, activists often encounter significant challenges. Geographic barriers, differing political climates, and cultural variations can hinder communication and collaboration. For instance, LGBTQ activists in regions with oppressive regimes may face severe repercussions for engaging with international allies, leading to a climate of fear that stifles open dialogue.

Moreover, language barriers can create misunderstandings and limit the effectiveness of communication. Activists may find it difficult to convey their messages or to fully understand the experiences of their counterparts from different cultural backgrounds. This can lead to a lack of solidarity and hinder the development of a unified global movement.

Real-World Examples

Despite these challenges, there are numerous examples of successful networking that have had a profound impact on the global LGBTQ movement. One notable instance is the collaboration between Ugandan activists and international organizations such as Human Rights Watch and Amnesty International. These partnerships have facilitated the sharing of resources, legal expertise, and advocacy strategies, empowering local activists to address human rights abuses effectively.

In 2014, Frank Mugisha attended the International Lesbian, Gay, Bisexual, Trans and Intersex Association (ILGA) conference in Mexico City, where he connected with activists from around the world. This networking opportunity allowed him to share his experiences and learn from others facing similar challenges. The relationships forged during this conference led to the establishment of a global coalition that advocated for the decriminalization of homosexuality in Uganda, demonstrating the power of international solidarity.

Another example is the use of social media platforms to create virtual networks. Activists can engage in real-time discussions, share resources, and mobilize support for campaigns. Hashtags such as #FreeUganda and #LGBTQRights have galvanized international attention and support, illustrating how digital platforms can transcend geographic barriers and foster global connections.

Conclusion

In conclusion, networking with global LGBTQ activists and allies is a vital component of successful advocacy. By leveraging social capital and embracing intersectionality, activists can build robust networks that enhance their capacity to effect change. While challenges such as geographic barriers and cultural differences persist, the examples of successful collaborations demonstrate the transformative potential of global networking. As the fight for LGBTQ rights continues, fostering these connections will be essential for creating a more inclusive and equitable world for all.

Bibliography

[1] Bourdieu, P. (1986). *The Forms of Capital*. In J. Richardson (Ed.), Handbook of Theory and Research for the Sociology of Education (241-258). Greenwood.

[2] Crenshaw, K. (1989). Demarginalizing the Intersection of Race and Sex: A Black Feminist Critique of Antidiscrimination Doctrine, Feminist Theory and Antiracist Politics. *University of Chicago Legal Forum*, 1989(1), 139-167.

[3] International Lesbian, Gay, Bisexual, Trans and Intersex Association. (2014). *ILGA World Conference 2014 - Report*. Retrieved from https://ilga.org/.

[4] Human Rights Watch. (2014). *"We Are All Ugandans": LGBT Rights in Uganda*. Retrieved from https://www.hrw.org/report/2014/02/12/we-are-all-ugandans/lgbt-rights-uganda.

The power of storytelling and personal narratives

Storytelling is an age-old practice, a method through which individuals convey their experiences, beliefs, and emotions. In the context of LGBTQ activism, personal narratives hold profound significance, serving as powerful tools for advocacy, awareness, and change. This section explores the multifaceted impact of storytelling in the realm of LGBTQ rights, highlighting its theoretical underpinnings, the challenges faced, and illustrative examples of its effectiveness.

Theoretical Framework

The theoretical foundation for the power of storytelling can be traced to narrative theory, which posits that stories are fundamental to human experience and understanding. According to Bruner (1991), narratives provide a framework through which individuals make sense of their lives and the world around them. In LGBTQ activism, personal narratives allow for the articulation of identity, the sharing of struggles, and the celebration of resilience. They serve as a means of bridging gaps between disparate communities, fostering empathy, and challenging stereotypes.

Moreover, the concept of *counter-narratives* emerges as a critical aspect of LGBTQ storytelling. As defined by Solórzano and Yosso (2002), counter-narratives are stories that challenge dominant cultural narratives. In Uganda, where homophobia is pervasive, LGBTQ individuals often face narratives that dehumanize and vilify them. By sharing their own experiences, activists like Frank Mugisha disrupt these harmful narratives, asserting their humanity and right to exist.

Challenges in Storytelling

Despite the power of storytelling, LGBTQ activists in Uganda encounter numerous challenges when sharing their narratives. One significant issue is the fear of backlash and violence. The societal climate in Uganda is fraught with hostility towards LGBTQ individuals, and sharing personal stories can lead to harassment, discrimination, or even physical harm. This fear often results in self-censorship, where individuals may choose to remain silent rather than risk their safety.

Additionally, there is the challenge of authenticity. Activists must navigate the complexities of their identities and experiences, determining what aspects of their stories to share publicly. The pressure to represent the LGBTQ community accurately can be overwhelming, as individuals may feel that their narratives must encapsulate the entirety of the community's struggles and triumphs.

Examples of Effective Storytelling

Despite these challenges, many activists have harnessed the power of storytelling to effect change. For instance, during international conferences, Frank Mugisha has shared his personal journey of coming to terms with his identity in a hostile environment. His narrative not only highlights the struggles faced by LGBTQ individuals in Uganda but also emphasizes the importance of love, acceptance, and resilience. By articulating his experiences, Mugisha humanizes the LGBTQ struggle, inviting empathy and understanding from a global audience.

Another poignant example is the use of social media platforms to amplify personal narratives. Activists have utilized hashtags like #LoveIsLove and #LGBTQUganda to share stories of love, loss, and perseverance. These online narratives create a sense of community and solidarity among LGBTQ individuals, while also educating allies and challenging misconceptions.

The Impact of Storytelling on Policy and Public Perception

The impact of storytelling extends beyond individual experiences; it plays a crucial role in shaping public perception and influencing policy. Research indicates that personal narratives can evoke emotional responses that drive social change (Green & Brock, 2000). When individuals hear personal stories of struggle and resilience, they are more likely to empathize with the storyteller and support their cause.

In Uganda, the visibility of LGBTQ stories has prompted discussions about human rights and legal protections. Activists have successfully leveraged personal narratives to engage with policymakers, illustrating the real-life consequences of discriminatory laws. By presenting their stories in legislative settings, activists like Mugisha have been able to advocate for change, emphasizing that LGBTQ rights are human rights.

Conclusion

In conclusion, the power of storytelling and personal narratives in LGBTQ activism cannot be overstated. Through the lens of narrative theory, we understand that stories are not merely recounts of experiences; they are transformative tools that challenge societal norms, foster empathy, and drive advocacy. Despite the challenges faced by LGBTQ activists in Uganda, the impact of their narratives resonates deeply, influencing public perception and policy. As Frank Mugisha and others continue to share their stories, they illuminate the path towards a more inclusive and accepting society, inspiring future generations of activists to embrace their voices and advocate for change.

Bibliography

[1] Bruner, J. (1991). *The Narrative Construction of Reality*. Critical Inquiry, 18(1), 1-21.

[2] Solórzano, D. G., & Yosso, T. J. (2002). *A Critical Race Theory Methodology: Counter-Storytelling as an Analytical Framework for Education Research*. Qualitative Inquiry, 8(1), 23-44.

[3] Green, M. C., & Brock, T. C. (2000). *The Role of Transportation in the Persuasiveness of Public Narratives*. Journal of Personality and Social Psychology, 79(5), 701-721.

The international impact of Frank Mugisha's advocacy

Frank Mugisha's advocacy for LGBTQ rights in Uganda has transcended national borders, resonating on an international scale and inspiring movements across the globe. His journey is a testament to the power of individual activism in the face of systemic oppression, illustrating how localized struggles can gain global attention and support. This section explores the multifaceted international impact of Mugisha's work, examining theoretical frameworks, challenges, and real-world examples that highlight his influence.

Theoretical Frameworks

To understand the international impact of Mugisha's advocacy, it is essential to consider the theories of transnational advocacy networks (TANs) and global civil society. According to Keck and Sikkink (1998), TANs consist of activists from various sectors who collaborate across borders to promote social change. Mugisha's efforts exemplify this theory, as he has successfully mobilized international support for LGBTQ rights in Uganda, creating a network of allies that transcends geographic boundaries.

$$\text{Impact} = \text{Advocacy} \times \text{Network Strength} \times \text{Global Awareness} \quad (30)$$

This equation illustrates that the impact of advocacy is not solely dependent on the efforts of the activist but is significantly amplified by the strength of the networks they build and the level of global awareness they generate.

Challenges in International Advocacy

Despite the positive outcomes of Mugisha's advocacy, numerous challenges persist. One significant problem is the backlash from conservative groups and governments that view LGBTQ rights as a Western imposition. This perspective is often rooted in cultural and religious beliefs that reject non-heteronormative identities. Mugisha has faced threats and hostility not only from local authorities but also from international actors who oppose the global LGBTQ rights movement.

Moreover, the intersectionality of Mugisha's advocacy presents additional challenges. As Crenshaw (1991) posits, individuals experience discrimination differently based on their multiple identities, including race, gender, and sexuality. Mugisha's work highlights the importance of addressing these intersecting issues to create a more inclusive movement.

Real-World Examples of Impact

Mugisha's advocacy has led to tangible outcomes on the international stage. For instance, his participation in the United Nations Human Rights Council sessions has brought attention to the plight of LGBTQ individuals in Uganda. In 2016, he delivered a powerful speech that galvanized support from various countries, leading to a resolution condemning human rights violations against LGBTQ individuals.

Another notable example is the collaboration between Mugisha and international organizations such as Human Rights Watch and Amnesty International. These partnerships have facilitated global campaigns that not only raise awareness but also apply pressure on the Ugandan government to change discriminatory laws. The "#FreeUganda" campaign, which gained traction on social media, is a prime example of how Mugisha's advocacy has mobilized global support and solidarity.

The Role of Media and Storytelling

The media plays a pivotal role in amplifying the international impact of Mugisha's advocacy. Through interviews, documentaries, and social media platforms, his story has reached a wide audience, fostering empathy and understanding. The power of storytelling, as posited by narrative theory, allows individuals to connect with experiences that may differ from their own, creating a sense of shared humanity.

For example, the documentary *Call Me Kuchu* chronicles Mugisha's life and activism, shedding light on the challenges faced by LGBTQ individuals in Uganda. This film not only educates viewers but also humanizes the struggle for rights, encouraging international audiences to engage with the cause.

Global Solidarity Movements

Mugisha's advocacy has also contributed to the emergence of global solidarity movements that unite activists from diverse backgrounds. The International Day Against Homophobia, Transphobia, and Biphobia (IDAHOT) serves as a platform for activists worldwide to raise awareness about LGBTQ rights. Mugisha's involvement in this event has further solidified his status as a leader in the global fight for equality.

In conclusion, the international impact of Frank Mugisha's advocacy is profound and multifaceted. By leveraging transnational networks, overcoming challenges, and utilizing the power of storytelling, he has inspired a global movement for LGBTQ rights. His work exemplifies the interconnectedness of local and global struggles, reminding us that the fight for equality knows no borders. As we look to the future, Mugisha's legacy will undoubtedly continue to influence and inspire generations of activists worldwide.

Collaborating with Global LGBTQ Organizations

Partnering with international NGOs and nonprofits

In the realm of LGBTQ advocacy, establishing partnerships with international non-governmental organizations (NGOs) and nonprofits is not merely beneficial; it is essential. These collaborations can amplify local efforts, provide critical resources, and foster a global network of support. This section delves into the significance of such partnerships, the challenges faced, and real-world examples that illustrate their impact.

The Importance of Partnerships

Collaborating with international NGOs and nonprofits allows local activists to leverage expertise, funding, and visibility that may not be available within their own countries. Theories of social capital suggest that networks of relationships among people who live and work in a particular society enable that society to function effectively. By partnering with global organizations, local activists can access a wealth of knowledge and resources, enhancing their capacity for advocacy and activism.

$$\text{Social Capital} = \text{Networks} + \text{Trust} + \text{Reciprocity} \qquad (31)$$

This equation illustrates that social capital is not just about the number of connections but also the quality of these relationships, which can be enriched through international partnerships.

Challenges in Collaboration

Despite the clear benefits, partnering with international NGOs and nonprofits is fraught with challenges. One significant issue is the potential for cultural imperialism, where foreign organizations impose their values and priorities on local communities. This can lead to resistance from local activists who feel that their unique contexts and needs are overlooked. Moreover, funding dependency can create a power imbalance, where local organizations become reliant on foreign support, potentially compromising their autonomy.

Additionally, navigating the bureaucratic landscape of international partnerships can be cumbersome. Differences in operational procedures, reporting requirements, and communication styles can hinder effective collaboration. It is crucial for local activists to advocate for equitable partnerships that prioritize mutual respect and shared goals.

Examples of Successful Partnerships

One notable example of effective partnership is the collaboration between the Ugandan LGBTQ organization, Sexual Minorities Uganda (SMUG), and international entities such as the International Gay and Lesbian Human Rights Commission (IGLHRC). This partnership has facilitated legal support, advocacy training, and international visibility for Ugandan LGBTQ issues. Through joint campaigns, they have successfully raised awareness about human rights violations against LGBTQ individuals in Uganda, garnering global attention and support.

Another example is the collaboration between Rainbow Railroad, a Canadian nonprofit, and local Ugandan activists. Rainbow Railroad assists LGBTQ individuals facing persecution by providing emergency relocation services. This partnership not only offers immediate safety to those in danger but also emphasizes the importance of international solidarity in the fight for LGBTQ rights.

Theoretical Frameworks Supporting Partnerships

Theories of transnational advocacy networks emphasize the role of global civil society in influencing local contexts. According to Keck and Sikkink (1998), these networks can mobilize resources and support for marginalized groups, creating a ripple effect that empowers local actors. By forming alliances with international NGOs, local activists can tap into these transnational networks, gaining access to funding, expertise, and advocacy platforms that can amplify their voices.

$$\text{Transnational Advocacy} = \text{Local Action} + \text{Global Support} \quad (32)$$

This equation highlights the symbiotic relationship between local and global efforts, underscoring the importance of collaboration in achieving meaningful change.

Conclusion

In conclusion, partnering with international NGOs and nonprofits presents both opportunities and challenges for LGBTQ activists in Uganda. While these collaborations can enhance advocacy efforts and provide critical resources, it is vital to approach them with a mindset of equity and mutual respect. By fostering genuine partnerships that prioritize local voices, the LGBTQ movement in Uganda can continue to grow stronger, more resilient, and more effective in its fight for equality and justice. The journey toward LGBTQ rights is undoubtedly complex, but through strategic alliances, activists can navigate these challenges and work towards a brighter future for all.

Sharing resources and best practices

In the realm of LGBTQ advocacy, sharing resources and best practices is essential for fostering a cohesive movement that can effectively address the myriad challenges faced by the community. This collaborative approach not only enhances the capacity of local organizations but also strengthens the global LGBTQ rights movement.

The Importance of Resource Sharing

The sharing of resources among LGBTQ organizations can take many forms, including the dissemination of educational materials, toolkits for advocacy, legal frameworks, and successful campaign strategies. By pooling knowledge and experiences, organizations can avoid duplicating efforts, thereby maximizing their impact. This concept aligns with the theory of collective efficacy, which posits that groups that work together towards a common goal are more likely to succeed than individuals working in isolation.

Challenges in Resource Sharing

Despite the clear benefits, several challenges hinder effective resource sharing. These include:

- **Geographical Barriers:** Many organizations operate in isolation due to geographical constraints, making it difficult to share information and resources effectively.

- **Language Differences:** The diversity of languages spoken within the LGBTQ community can create barriers to understanding and implementing shared resources.

- **Cultural Sensitivities:** Different cultural contexts may require tailored approaches to advocacy, which can complicate the sharing of best practices.

- **Funding Limitations:** Limited financial resources can restrict organizations' ability to create and disseminate materials or to participate in collaborative efforts.

Strategies for Effective Resource Sharing

To overcome these challenges, LGBTQ organizations can adopt several strategies:

1. **Creating Digital Platforms:** Utilizing online platforms to share resources can mitigate geographical barriers. Websites, social media groups, and dedicated online forums can serve as repositories for toolkits, research papers, and advocacy guides.

2. **Developing Multilingual Resources:** By creating materials in multiple languages, organizations can ensure that resources are accessible to a wider

audience. This approach not only promotes inclusivity but also respects cultural diversity.

3. **Encouraging Intercultural Exchanges:** Facilitating exchanges between organizations from different cultural backgrounds can enrich the advocacy landscape. These exchanges allow groups to learn from each other's successes and challenges, fostering a more nuanced understanding of LGBTQ issues.

4. **Collaborative Grant Writing:** By forming coalitions, organizations can pool their resources to apply for grants that support collaborative projects. This not only increases the chances of funding but also encourages joint initiatives that can lead to impactful change.

Examples of Successful Resource Sharing Initiatives

Several initiatives have successfully demonstrated the power of resource sharing within the LGBTQ community:

- **The Global Fund for Women:** This organization provides grants to women's rights groups, including LGBTQ organizations, and encourages the sharing of successful grant applications and project proposals to enhance funding opportunities.

- **ILGA World:** The International Lesbian, Gay, Bisexual, Trans and Intersex Association (ILGA) serves as a global network that facilitates the sharing of legal resources, advocacy toolkits, and best practices among its members, thereby strengthening the global LGBTQ movement.

- **The Human Rights Campaign (HRC):** HRC has developed a series of best practice guides for organizations to implement effective advocacy campaigns, which are made available to LGBTQ groups worldwide. These guides cover topics such as lobbying techniques, community engagement, and media strategies.

Conclusion

Sharing resources and best practices is not merely an act of generosity; it is a strategic necessity in the fight for LGBTQ rights. By overcoming barriers and fostering collaboration, organizations can amplify their voices and create a more unified front against discrimination and injustice. As the LGBTQ movement continues to evolve, the commitment to sharing knowledge and resources will be vital in shaping a future where all individuals can live authentically and without fear.

Collective Impact = Shared Vision+Mutually Reinforcing Activities+Continuous Comm
(33)

This equation encapsulates the essence of successful resource sharing in advocacy. When organizations unite under a shared vision, engage in mutually reinforcing activities, and maintain continuous communication, they can achieve a collective impact that transcends individual efforts.

The global network of LGBTQ activists and allies

The global network of LGBTQ activists and allies serves as a vital lifeline for individuals and organizations advocating for LGBTQ rights across diverse cultural and political landscapes. This interconnected web of support fosters collaboration, sharing of resources, and the amplification of voices that are often marginalized. Understanding the dynamics of this network reveals both its strengths and challenges, as well as its critical role in advancing the cause of LGBTQ rights worldwide.

At its core, the global network of LGBTQ activists operates on principles of solidarity and mutual aid. Activists from various regions come together to share strategies, experiences, and knowledge. This collaboration is often facilitated by international LGBTQ organizations, such as ILGA (International Lesbian, Gay, Bisexual, Trans and Intersex Association) and OutRight Action International, which provide platforms for dialogue and resource exchange. The significance of these organizations cannot be overstated; they serve as conduits for information, funding, and moral support, enabling local activists to amplify their impact.

One theoretical framework that can be applied to understand the functioning of this global network is the concept of **transnational activism**. According to Keck and Sikkink (1998), transnational advocacy networks (TANs) consist of various actors, including NGOs, social movements, and individuals, who collaborate across borders to promote social change. This framework highlights how LGBTQ activists utilize global connections to influence local contexts, advocating for policy changes, legal reforms, and social acceptance.

However, the global network is not without its challenges. Activists often face significant barriers, including cultural differences, language barriers, and varying levels of acceptance of LGBTQ identities within their respective societies. For instance, while Western nations may have made considerable strides in LGBTQ rights, activists in regions like Africa and the Middle East often contend with severe legal and societal repercussions. In Uganda, for example, the anti-LGBTQ legislation and societal stigma create an environment where activists must navigate a treacherous landscape of discrimination and violence.

Furthermore, the intersectionality of identities within the LGBTQ community complicates the dynamics of the global network. Activists representing diverse identities—such as race, gender, and socioeconomic status—may have differing priorities and experiences. For instance, the needs of LGBTQ individuals in rural areas may differ significantly from those in urban settings, necessitating a nuanced approach to advocacy that recognizes these differences. The challenge lies in ensuring that the voices of all marginalized groups within the LGBTQ community are heard and represented in the global discourse.

Despite these challenges, there are numerous examples of successful collaborations within the global network. The #BlackLivesMatter movement, for instance, has forged alliances with LGBTQ activists to address the unique challenges faced by Black LGBTQ individuals. This intersectional approach has not only raised awareness but has also fostered a sense of community among activists from different backgrounds, emphasizing the importance of solidarity in the fight for justice.

Moreover, the advent of digital technology has transformed the landscape of global LGBTQ activism. Social media platforms enable activists to connect, share their stories, and mobilize support on an unprecedented scale. Campaigns like #LoveIsLove and #TransRightsAreHumanRights have gained traction globally, demonstrating the power of collective action and the ability to transcend geographical boundaries. These online movements have created virtual spaces for dialogue, education, and advocacy, allowing activists to rally support and challenge oppressive systems.

In conclusion, the global network of LGBTQ activists and allies is a powerful force for change, uniting individuals and organizations in the pursuit of equality and justice. While challenges such as cultural differences and intersectionality persist, the strength of this network lies in its ability to adapt, learn, and grow. By fostering collaboration and amplifying diverse voices, the global LGBTQ movement continues to make strides toward a more inclusive and equitable world. As activists navigate the complexities of their respective contexts, the support of the global network remains crucial in sustaining their efforts and advancing the fight for LGBTQ rights.

> **Theorem**
>
> Let A be the set of LGBTQ activists and B be the set of allies. The global network G can be defined as the union of these two sets:
>
> $$G = A \cup B$$
>
> where A and B are interconnected through shared goals and mutual support.

> **Proof**
>
> The elements of set A represent activists working directly on LGBTQ rights, while the elements of set B represent allies who support these efforts. The intersection $A \cap B$ represents individuals who identify as both activists and allies. The union G signifies the collective strength of both groups in advocating for LGBTQ rights globally.

Strengthening the international LGBTQ rights movement

The international LGBTQ rights movement has evolved significantly over the past few decades, gaining momentum through the collaboration of activists, organizations, and allies across the globe. Strengthening this movement is essential for advancing the rights and recognition of LGBTQ individuals worldwide. This section explores the theoretical frameworks, challenges, and practical examples that contribute to the fortification of the international LGBTQ rights movement.

Theoretical Frameworks

To understand the dynamics of the international LGBTQ rights movement, it is vital to consider various theoretical frameworks that inform activism. One such framework is **Intersectionality**, coined by Kimberlé Crenshaw, which emphasizes the interconnectedness of social categorizations such as race, class, gender, and sexuality. This approach helps activists recognize that LGBTQ individuals do not exist in a vacuum; rather, their experiences are shaped by multiple, overlapping identities that influence their access to rights and resources.

Another important theory is **Globalization**. The movement's expansion can be attributed to the increased interconnectedness of societies, facilitated by technology and communication. Globalization allows for the rapid dissemination of ideas, strategies, and solidarity across borders, enabling local activists to learn from the successes and challenges faced by their counterparts in different regions.

Furthermore, the **Human Rights Framework** serves as a foundational pillar for LGBTQ advocacy. This framework positions LGBTQ rights as human rights, emphasizing that all individuals, regardless of their sexual orientation or gender identity, deserve equal protection under the law. By framing LGBTQ issues within the broader context of human rights, activists can garner support from a diverse range of stakeholders, including governments, NGOs, and the general public.

Challenges in Strengthening the Movement

Despite the progress made, the international LGBTQ rights movement faces several challenges that hinder its effectiveness. One significant issue is the **Backlash against LGBTQ Rights**. In many regions, particularly in conservative and authoritarian states, there has been a resurgence of anti-LGBTQ sentiments, often fueled by political leaders and religious organizations. This backlash manifests in the form of discriminatory laws, social stigmatization, and violence against LGBTQ individuals.

Additionally, the movement grapples with the challenge of **Resource Inequity**. While some organizations have access to substantial funding and resources, others, particularly grassroots groups in the Global South, struggle to secure necessary support. This disparity can lead to a lack of representation and voice for marginalized LGBTQ populations, hindering the movement's overall impact.

Another critical challenge is the **Fragmentation of the Movement**. The diversity of LGBTQ identities and experiences can sometimes lead to divisions within the movement, as different groups prioritize distinct issues. For instance, the concerns of transgender individuals may not always align with those of gay men or lesbian women. This fragmentation can weaken collective efforts and dilute the movement's message.

Examples of Strengthening Initiatives

To address these challenges and strengthen the international LGBTQ rights movement, several initiatives have emerged that exemplify effective strategies for collaboration and advocacy.

One notable example is the >Global Equality Fund, established by the U.S. State Department. This fund provides financial support to LGBTQ organizations around the world, enabling them to implement programs that promote legal protections, advocacy, and community-building. By channeling resources to grassroots organizations, the fund helps bridge the resource gap and fosters local leadership in the fight for LGBTQ rights.

Another example is the >International Lesbian, Gay, Bisexual, Trans and Intersex Association (ILGA), which serves as a global network for LGBTQ organizations. ILGA facilitates information sharing, capacity building, and advocacy efforts across borders, empowering local activists to amplify their voices on the international stage. The association's annual reports on the state of LGBTQ rights worldwide provide critical data that informs advocacy strategies and highlights areas in need of attention.

Furthermore, the >OutRight Action International organization plays a crucial role in strengthening the movement by conducting research, advocating for policy changes, and providing technical assistance to LGBTQ groups globally. Their work emphasizes the importance of evidence-based advocacy, equipping activists with the tools they need to effectively engage with policymakers and stakeholders.

Conclusion

Strengthening the international LGBTQ rights movement requires a multifaceted approach that embraces theoretical frameworks, addresses challenges, and draws on successful examples of collaboration and advocacy. By fostering intersectionality, leveraging globalization, and adhering to human rights principles, activists can build a more cohesive and effective movement. As the fight for LGBTQ rights continues, it is imperative to recognize the importance of unity, resource equity, and inclusivity in advancing the cause of justice and equality for all LGBTQ individuals worldwide.

The role of transnational advocacy in advancing LGBTQ rights

Transnational advocacy plays a pivotal role in the advancement of LGBTQ rights across the globe, particularly in regions where local movements face significant challenges. This form of advocacy transcends national boundaries, uniting activists, organizations, and allies from various countries to address human rights violations and promote equality for LGBTQ individuals. The dynamics of transnational advocacy are complex and multifaceted, involving various strategies, theories, and real-world applications.

Theoretical Framework

The theoretical foundation of transnational advocacy is rooted in several key concepts, including global governance, human rights frameworks, and social movements. According to Keck and Sikkink's (1998) theory of transnational advocacy networks (TANs), these networks consist of a diverse array of actors—including non-governmental organizations (NGOs), grassroots activists, and international institutions—who collaborate to influence policy and public opinion across borders. TANs leverage their collective power to challenge oppressive regimes and advocate for marginalized communities, including LGBTQ individuals.

One of the critical elements of transnational advocacy is the concept of *norm diffusion*, which refers to the process through which norms and values related to human rights and LGBTQ equality spread from one context to another. This diffusion occurs through various mechanisms, such as international treaties, advocacy campaigns, and the sharing of best practices among activists. The success of this process often hinges on the ability of activists to frame their struggles in ways that resonate with global audiences, emphasizing shared values of dignity, equality, and justice.

Challenges in Transnational Advocacy

Despite its potential, transnational advocacy faces several challenges. One significant issue is the *local backlash* that can arise when foreign entities intervene in domestic matters. In many countries, LGBTQ rights are framed as Western impositions, leading to a rise in nationalism and anti-LGBTQ sentiment. This backlash can manifest in legislative measures, such as Uganda's Anti-Homosexuality Act, which seeks to criminalize LGBTQ identities and behaviors. Activists must navigate these complex political landscapes, balancing the need for international support with the risk of alienating local communities.

Additionally, there are disparities in resources and access to platforms among different LGBTQ organizations globally. While some groups may have robust connections with international bodies and funding sources, others may struggle to gain visibility and support. This inequality can hinder the effectiveness of transnational advocacy efforts, as not all voices are equally represented in the global discourse on LGBTQ rights.

Examples of Transnational Advocacy in Action

Several notable examples illustrate the impact of transnational advocacy in advancing LGBTQ rights. One prominent case is the collaboration between local activists in Uganda and international organizations such as Human Rights Watch and Amnesty International. These organizations have conducted extensive research and documentation of human rights abuses against LGBTQ individuals in Uganda, bringing global attention to the issue. Their reports have not only raised awareness but also pressured the Ugandan government to reconsider its stance on LGBTQ rights.

Another example is the role of international LGBTQ organizations, such as ILGA (International Lesbian, Gay, Bisexual, Trans and Intersex Association), in providing support and resources to local movements. ILGA has facilitated networking opportunities, knowledge sharing, and capacity-building workshops for LGBTQ activists in Uganda and other countries facing similar challenges. This support has empowered local activists to strengthen their advocacy efforts and engage more effectively with policymakers.

Furthermore, transnational advocacy has also manifested in the form of global campaigns, such as the "Love is Love" movement, which seeks to promote marriage equality worldwide. This movement has mobilized activists from various countries to share their stories and experiences, creating a sense of solidarity and shared purpose. By amplifying these narratives, transnational advocacy helps to challenge stereotypes and misconceptions about LGBTQ individuals, fostering a more inclusive global dialogue.

Conclusion

In conclusion, transnational advocacy is a vital component of the struggle for LGBTQ rights, serving as a bridge that connects local movements with the global community. While challenges such as local backlash and resource disparities persist, the collaborative efforts of activists and organizations across borders have the potential to effect meaningful change. By leveraging the power of collective action and shared narratives, transnational advocacy can advance the cause of LGBTQ rights, fostering a more inclusive and equitable world for all.

Bibliography

[1] Keck, M. E., & Sikkink, K. (1998). *Activists Beyond Borders: Advocacy Networks in International Politics*. Cornell University Press.

Advocacy on the World Stage

Addressing the United Nations and international bodies

In the realm of global advocacy for LGBTQ rights, addressing the United Nations (UN) and other international bodies serves as a pivotal platform for change. Frank Mugisha's journey in this arena exemplifies the intersection of personal narrative and global policy, where the power of advocacy transcends borders and resonates with universal human rights principles.

The UN, as a leading international organization, plays a crucial role in setting norms and standards for human rights, including the rights of LGBTQ individuals. The Universal Declaration of Human Rights (UDHR), adopted in 1948, asserts that all human beings are entitled to rights and freedoms without distinction of any kind, including sexual orientation and gender identity. This foundational document serves as a cornerstone for LGBTQ advocacy, providing a legal and moral framework for activists like Mugisha to address violations and push for recognition.

However, the path to engaging with the UN is fraught with challenges. One significant issue is the varying degrees of acceptance of LGBTQ rights among member states. While some countries have made substantial progress in recognizing and protecting LGBTQ rights, others maintain oppressive laws and cultural attitudes that perpetuate discrimination and violence. For instance, in Uganda, the Anti-Homosexuality Act of 2014 exemplified the harsh legal landscape that activists must navigate. Mugisha's own experiences of facing legal repercussions for his advocacy work highlight the risks involved in addressing international bodies while advocating for change in a repressive environment.

To effectively address the UN, activists must employ strategic approaches that resonate with both the organization's mandate and the realities faced by LGBTQ individuals. This includes:

1. **Utilizing Human Rights Mechanisms**: Activists can leverage UN mechanisms such as the Universal Periodic Review (UPR), which assesses the human rights records of all UN member states. By submitting reports and testimonies about the human rights violations faced by LGBTQ individuals in Uganda, Mugisha and his peers can bring international attention to their plight, urging the Ugandan government to comply with its human rights obligations.

2. **Engaging with Special Rapporteurs**: The UN appoints Special Rapporteurs to investigate and report on specific human rights issues, including violence against LGBTQ individuals. Activists can collaborate with these experts to present evidence and advocate for recommendations that promote legal reforms and protections for LGBTQ rights.

3. **Building Alliances with Other NGOs**: Collaboration with international non-governmental organizations (NGOs) enhances the visibility and impact of advocacy efforts. By aligning with established organizations that have access to UN forums, Mugisha can amplify his message, drawing on collective resources and networks to strengthen the call for LGBTQ rights.

4. **Participating in UN Conferences and Events**: Engaging in high-profile events, such as the UN Human Rights Council sessions, provides a platform for activists to share their stories, advocate for policy changes, and hold governments accountable. Mugisha's participation in these events not only raises awareness but also fosters dialogue among member states regarding the importance of LGBTQ rights as a fundamental aspect of human rights.

5. **Utilizing Media to Raise Awareness**: In the digital age, media plays a crucial role in shaping public opinion and influencing policy. Activists can harness the power of social media and traditional media outlets to share their narratives, mobilize support, and put pressure on international bodies to take action. Mugisha's ability to articulate the struggles of LGBTQ individuals in Uganda through compelling storytelling can resonate with a global audience, fostering empathy and understanding.

Despite these strategies, challenges persist. The backlash against LGBTQ rights at the international level, often fueled by conservative political agendas and religious ideologies, can undermine advocacy efforts. For instance, some member states may resist discussions on LGBTQ rights at the UN, arguing that such matters infringe upon their sovereignty or cultural values. This resistance underscores the importance of persistence and resilience in advocacy work, as activists like Mugisha continue to confront these barriers with determination.

In conclusion, addressing the United Nations and international bodies is a critical component of the fight for LGBTQ rights. Through strategic engagement, collaboration, and the power of personal narratives, activists can challenge oppressive regimes and advocate for the recognition and protection of LGBTQ individuals globally. Frank Mugisha's journey exemplifies the potential for change when personal experiences intersect with international advocacy, highlighting the ongoing struggle for dignity, equality, and justice for LGBTQ communities in Uganda and beyond.

Lobbying for LGBTQ rights in global forums

Lobbying for LGBTQ rights in global forums represents a critical avenue for advocacy, where activists like Frank Mugisha can leverage international platforms to influence policies and promote awareness on a global scale. This subsection will explore the theoretical framework of lobbying, the challenges faced by LGBTQ advocates in these arenas, and successful examples that illustrate the impact of this advocacy.

Theoretical Framework of Lobbying

Lobbying can be understood through several theoretical lenses, including the *Pluralist Theory* and the *Elite Theory*. The Pluralist Theory posits that multiple interest groups compete in the political arena, and the outcomes are a result of negotiation and compromise among these groups. This aligns with the LGBTQ movement's approach, where various organizations and activists come together to advocate for rights, seeking to balance the interests of diverse communities within the LGBTQ spectrum.

In contrast, the Elite Theory suggests that a small group of powerful elites control political decisions, often sidelining marginalized voices. This theory underscores the importance of LGBTQ activists not only to participate in lobbying efforts but also to challenge the existing power structures that perpetuate discrimination and inequality.

Challenges in Lobbying for LGBTQ Rights

Despite the potential for influence, LGBTQ activists face numerous challenges in global lobbying efforts:

- **Cultural Resistance:** Many nations exhibit strong cultural and religious opposition to LGBTQ rights, making it difficult for activists to gain traction. For instance, in countries where homophobic laws are entrenched, lobbying efforts may be met with hostility or outright rejection.

- **Political Barriers:** In some regions, political leaders may actively oppose LGBTQ rights, viewing them as a threat to traditional values. This creates a hostile environment for lobbying, where activists must navigate complex political landscapes and often confront governmental pushback.
- **Limited Resources:** Many LGBTQ organizations operate with limited funding and resources, which can hinder their ability to engage effectively in lobbying efforts. This is particularly true for grassroots organizations in developing countries, where financial support is crucial for sustained advocacy.
- **Safety Concerns:** Activists often face threats to their safety and well-being, especially in regions where LGBTQ identities are criminalized. The fear of persecution can deter individuals from participating in lobbying efforts or sharing their stories in global forums.

Successful Examples of Lobbying for LGBTQ Rights

Despite these challenges, there have been notable successes in lobbying for LGBTQ rights at global forums:

- **United Nations Human Rights Council:** Activists have successfully lobbied for the inclusion of LGBTQ rights in international human rights discussions. For example, the establishment of the *Independent Expert on Sexual Orientation and Gender Identity* in 2016 marked a significant victory, providing a platform for addressing human rights violations against LGBTQ individuals globally.
- **Global Fund for Women:** This organization has effectively mobilized resources to support LGBTQ activists worldwide, advocating for gender equality and sexual rights. Their initiatives have empowered local organizations to engage in lobbying efforts, amplifying their voices in international forums.
- **International LGBTQI+ Youth and Student Organisation (IGLYO):** This organization has played a pivotal role in lobbying for the rights of LGBTQ youth at the European level. Their campaigns have influenced policies within the European Union, promoting inclusive educational environments and combating discrimination against LGBTQ youth.

- **The Yogyakarta Principles:** Formulated in 2006, these principles articulate the application of international human rights law in relation to sexual orientation and gender identity. The principles have served as a lobbying tool for activists, guiding discussions in international forums and influencing legal reforms in various countries.

Conclusion

Lobbying for LGBTQ rights in global forums is a multifaceted endeavor that requires strategic planning, collaboration, and resilience. By understanding the theoretical frameworks that underpin lobbying efforts and recognizing the challenges faced, activists can better navigate these complex environments. The successes achieved through lobbying demonstrate the power of collective action and the potential for meaningful change on a global scale. As Frank Mugisha and others continue to advocate for LGBTQ rights, their efforts in international forums will remain vital in the ongoing struggle for equality and justice.

Engaging with international political leaders

Engaging with international political leaders is a vital component of advocating for LGBTQ rights on a global scale. This engagement not only amplifies the voices of marginalized communities but also influences policy changes that can lead to greater protections and rights for LGBTQ individuals. The intersection of global politics and human rights advocacy is complex, yet it offers unique opportunities for activists like Frank Mugisha to create impactful change.

Theoretical Framework

The engagement with political leaders can be understood through the lens of *advocacy coalition framework* (ACF), which emphasizes the role of various actors in influencing policy through collective action. In this context, LGBTQ activists form coalitions with international allies, human rights organizations, and sympathetic political figures to create a unified front. The ACF posits that policy change occurs when these coalitions successfully align their beliefs and resources to influence decision-makers.

Additionally, *Framing Theory* plays a crucial role in how LGBTQ issues are presented to political leaders. By framing LGBTQ rights as fundamental human rights, activists can appeal to the moral and ethical responsibilities of political leaders. This approach seeks to reshape the narrative surrounding LGBTQ issues, portraying them as integral to broader human rights discussions.

Challenges in Engagement

Despite the potential for positive outcomes, engaging with international political leaders is fraught with challenges. One significant barrier is the *political climate* in various countries, where leaders may be resistant to LGBTQ rights due to cultural, religious, or political ideologies. For instance, in many African nations, including Uganda, political leaders often leverage anti-LGBTQ rhetoric to galvanize support among conservative constituents. This resistance can hinder meaningful dialogue and policy change.

Moreover, the *diversity of political systems* complicates advocacy efforts. Different countries have varying degrees of receptiveness to LGBTQ rights, influenced by their historical, cultural, and socio-political contexts. Engaging with leaders in nations with authoritarian regimes can be particularly challenging, as these leaders may prioritize maintaining power over addressing human rights concerns.

Strategies for Effective Engagement

To navigate these challenges, LGBTQ activists employ several strategies when engaging with international political leaders:

1. **Building Relationships:** Establishing rapport with political leaders is essential. Activists often seek to meet with leaders personally, attending international conferences and forums where they can present their case directly. For example, Frank Mugisha has participated in various international human rights conferences, where he has had the opportunity to speak with political leaders about the realities faced by LGBTQ individuals in Uganda.

2. **Utilizing Data and Research:** Presenting empirical evidence and case studies can bolster the argument for LGBTQ rights. Activists can cite research demonstrating the positive impact of legal protections for LGBTQ individuals on public health, economic growth, and social stability. For instance, studies have shown that countries with more inclusive policies experience lower rates of mental health issues among LGBTQ populations.

3. **Leveraging Global Networks:** Collaborating with international NGOs and human rights organizations amplifies the message. By aligning with established entities, activists can gain access to resources, expertise, and platforms that enhance their advocacy efforts. For example, partnerships

with organizations like Human Rights Watch or Amnesty International can provide critical support in lobbying efforts.

4. **Engaging in Public Diplomacy:** Activists often utilize media campaigns to raise awareness of LGBTQ issues, thereby putting pressure on political leaders to respond. Public diplomacy efforts can include social media campaigns, public protests, and awareness-raising events that capture the attention of both the public and political figures.

5. **Highlighting International Norms:** Advocates can emphasize international human rights frameworks, such as the Universal Declaration of Human Rights, to hold political leaders accountable. By framing LGBTQ rights as aligned with these global standards, activists can challenge leaders to uphold their commitments to human rights.

Examples of Successful Engagement

Several successful examples illustrate the effectiveness of engaging with international political leaders. One notable instance is the advocacy work surrounding the United Nations Human Rights Council's resolution on LGBTQ rights. Activists, including Frank Mugisha, have played pivotal roles in lobbying for the adoption of this resolution, which recognizes LGBTQ rights as human rights and calls for an end to discrimination and violence based on sexual orientation and gender identity.

Another example is the collaboration between LGBTQ activists and political leaders in countries like Canada and the Netherlands, where progressive policies have been developed to support LGBTQ rights globally. These nations have often taken a stand against anti-LGBTQ legislation in other countries, using their diplomatic influence to advocate for change.

Conclusion

Engaging with international political leaders is a critical avenue for advancing LGBTQ rights. While challenges abound, strategic approaches grounded in advocacy theory can lead to meaningful dialogue and policy changes. The work of activists like Frank Mugisha exemplifies the power of this engagement, as they navigate complex political landscapes to advocate for the rights of LGBTQ individuals in Uganda and beyond. By continuing to foster relationships, utilize research, and leverage global networks, the movement for LGBTQ rights can gain momentum and achieve lasting change on the international stage.

The impact of international pressure on national policies

International pressure plays a pivotal role in shaping national policies, particularly in the context of LGBTQ rights. The dynamics of globalization and interconnectedness have allowed for a more robust dialogue between nations, enabling advocacy groups and international organizations to exert influence over domestic policies. This subsection explores the mechanisms through which international pressure affects national policies, the challenges faced by LGBTQ activists, and notable examples of this impact in Uganda.

Theoretical Framework

The influence of international pressure on national policies can be understood through the lens of several theoretical frameworks, including constructivism, liberalism, and the theory of transnational advocacy networks.

1. **Constructivism** posits that international norms and values shape state behavior. In the case of LGBTQ rights, the global discourse surrounding human rights has evolved to include sexual orientation and gender identity as fundamental rights. This shift in norms has pressured countries to reconsider their policies.

2. **Liberalism** emphasizes the role of international institutions and cooperation. Organizations such as the United Nations (UN) and the African Union (AU) advocate for human rights, including LGBTQ rights, and provide platforms for dialogue and accountability.

3. **Transnational Advocacy Networks** (TANs) consist of various actors, including NGOs, activists, and international bodies that collaborate to promote social change across borders. These networks facilitate the sharing of resources, strategies, and information, amplifying the voices of marginalized communities.

Mechanisms of Influence

International pressure manifests through several mechanisms:
   - **Diplomatic Engagement**: Foreign governments often engage in diplomatic discussions, urging nations to adopt more inclusive policies. For instance, during bilateral talks, Western nations have raised concerns about human rights violations in Uganda, linking aid and trade agreements to improvements in LGBTQ rights.
   - **Economic Sanctions and Incentives**: Economic pressure can be a powerful tool. The threat of sanctions or the promise of financial assistance can compel governments to reconsider discriminatory laws. For example, the U.S. has used foreign aid as leverage, conditioning assistance on the respect for human rights, including LGBTQ rights.

- **Public Campaigns and Media Attention**: International media coverage of human rights abuses can mobilize public opinion and pressure governments to change policies. High-profile cases of violence against LGBTQ individuals in Uganda have drawn global outrage, leading to increased scrutiny of the Ugandan government.
- **International Treaties and Agreements**: Participation in international human rights treaties obligates countries to adhere to certain standards. The Universal Declaration of Human Rights and other international covenants provide a framework for advocating LGBTQ rights, compelling states to align their laws with these principles.

Challenges Faced by Activists

Despite the potential benefits of international pressure, LGBTQ activists in Uganda face significant challenges:
- **Backlash from Governments**: Increased international scrutiny can provoke a backlash from national governments, which may adopt more repressive measures to assert sovereignty. In Uganda, the Anti-Homosexuality Act of 2014 was partly a reaction to international condemnation, as the government sought to reinforce its stance against perceived external interference.
- **Cultural Resistance**: Deeply ingrained cultural and religious beliefs often fuel resistance to LGBTQ rights. Activists must navigate a complex landscape where international pressure is viewed as a form of neocolonialism, leading to further entrenchment of anti-LGBTQ sentiments.
- **Safety and Security Risks**: Activists advocating for LGBTQ rights in the face of international pressure often encounter threats to their safety. Increased visibility can lead to harassment, violence, and even death, as seen in the tragic case of David Kato, a prominent Ugandan LGBTQ activist.

Examples of Impact

Several instances illustrate the impact of international pressure on national policies regarding LGBTQ rights in Uganda:
1. **The U.S. Government's Stance**: Following the introduction of the Anti-Homosexuality Bill in 2009, the U.S. government expressed strong opposition, threatening to cut aid to Uganda. This pressure contributed to the eventual withdrawal of support for the bill, showcasing the potential for international influence.

2. **United Nations Involvement**: The UN has actively condemned human rights abuses against LGBTQ individuals in Uganda. In 2016, the UN Human Rights Council adopted a resolution urging member states to protect LGBTQ individuals from violence and discrimination, thereby reinforcing international norms that challenge Uganda's anti-LGBTQ policies.

3. **Global Campaigns and Solidarity**: International campaigns, such as the #FreeUganda campaign, have galvanized support for LGBTQ rights, leading to increased awareness and pressure on the Ugandan government. These campaigns highlight the power of collective action in advocating for change.

Conclusion

The impact of international pressure on national policies, particularly regarding LGBTQ rights, is a complex interplay of advocacy, diplomacy, and cultural dynamics. While international mechanisms can foster positive change, they also present challenges for activists who must navigate a landscape fraught with resistance and danger. As the global discourse on human rights continues to evolve, the role of international pressure remains crucial in the ongoing struggle for LGBTQ rights in Uganda and beyond.

$$\text{Impact of International Pressure} = \text{Diplomatic Engagement} + \text{Economic Incentives} + \text{Publi} \tag{34}$$

This equation illustrates the multifaceted nature of international pressure and its potential to influence national policies positively. By harnessing these mechanisms, advocates can continue to push for meaningful change in the fight for LGBTQ rights.

Raising awareness and promoting change globally

In the contemporary landscape of LGBTQ rights advocacy, raising awareness and promoting change on a global scale has become paramount. The interconnectedness of our world, facilitated by technology and social media, presents both challenges and opportunities for activists like Frank Mugisha. This subsection delves into the strategies employed to elevate LGBTQ issues to international prominence, the theoretical frameworks that underpin these strategies, and the tangible impacts observed in various contexts.

Theoretical Frameworks

Central to understanding the dynamics of global LGBTQ advocacy is the concept of **social movement theory**. This framework posits that social movements arise when individuals collectively mobilize to address grievances and pursue social change. In the context of LGBTQ rights, the theory emphasizes the importance of collective identity, resource mobilization, and political opportunity structures. Activists leverage these elements to galvanize support and advocate for change.

$$\text{Social Change} = f(\text{Collective Identity, Resource Mobilization, Political Opportunities}) \tag{35}$$

This equation highlights that social change is a function of three interrelated components. Each component plays a crucial role in shaping the efficacy of advocacy efforts. For instance, a strong collective identity among LGBTQ individuals fosters solidarity and resilience, while resource mobilization ensures that activists have the tools and funding necessary to enact change.

Challenges in Raising Awareness

Despite the theoretical underpinnings that support global advocacy efforts, significant challenges persist. One of the foremost obstacles is the pervasive stigma and discrimination against LGBTQ individuals, which often manifests in violence, legal repercussions, and social ostracism. In countries like Uganda, where homophobia is institutionalized, raising awareness can be particularly perilous.

Moreover, misinformation and negative stereotypes about LGBTQ individuals continue to hinder progress. Activists frequently encounter narratives that portray LGBTQ identities as deviant or unnatural, perpetuating a cycle of fear and misunderstanding. Addressing these misconceptions is essential for fostering a more inclusive dialogue.

Strategies for Advocacy

To combat these challenges, activists employ a variety of strategies aimed at raising awareness and promoting change. These include:

- **Storytelling and Personal Narratives:** Sharing personal experiences has proven to be a powerful tool in advocacy. By humanizing LGBTQ issues, activists can dismantle stereotypes and foster empathy among audiences. Frank Mugisha's own story serves as a testament to the transformative power of personal narratives.

- **Utilizing Social Media:** Platforms like Twitter, Instagram, and Facebook have revolutionized the way activists communicate and mobilize support. Social media campaigns, hashtags, and viral content can reach global audiences, creating awareness and solidarity across borders. For example, campaigns such as #LoveIsLove have gained traction worldwide, promoting acceptance and equality.

- **International Partnerships:** Collaborating with global LGBTQ organizations enhances the visibility of local issues on the world stage. By forming alliances with international NGOs, activists can leverage resources, knowledge, and networks to amplify their voices. The collaboration between Ugandan activists and international bodies like ILGA (International Lesbian, Gay, Bisexual, Trans and Intersex Association) exemplifies this approach.

- **Public Demonstrations:** Organizing protests and marches not only raises awareness but also serves as a form of resistance against oppressive regimes. Events such as Pride parades have become symbols of resilience and solidarity, drawing attention to the struggles faced by LGBTQ individuals globally.

- **Engaging with Traditional Media:** Activists must also engage with traditional media outlets to shape public discourse. By securing interviews, op-eds, and feature stories, they can reach audiences who may not be active on social media. Frank Mugisha's appearances on international news programs have helped shed light on the plight of LGBTQ individuals in Uganda.

Examples of Global Impact

The efforts to raise awareness and promote change have yielded tangible results in various contexts. For instance, the global response to Uganda's Anti-Homosexuality Act in 2014 sparked international outrage and condemnation. Activists mobilized a coalition of global voices, leading to sanctions and diplomatic pressure on the Ugandan government. This collective action demonstrated the power of global solidarity in advancing LGBTQ rights.

Furthermore, the #MeToo movement's intersection with LGBTQ advocacy has highlighted issues of sexual violence and harassment faced by LGBTQ individuals. This intersectionality has broadened the conversation, emphasizing that the fight for LGBTQ rights is part of a larger struggle for human rights and dignity.

Conclusion

Raising awareness and promoting change globally is a multifaceted endeavor that requires strategic planning, collaboration, and resilience. As activists like Frank Mugisha continue to navigate the complexities of advocacy, the theoretical frameworks and practical strategies outlined in this subsection provide a roadmap for future efforts. The ongoing journey toward LGBTQ equality is not without its challenges, but through collective action and international solidarity, a more inclusive and accepting world is within reach.

Collaboration with Celebrities and Influential Voices

Leveraging celebrity endorsements for LGBTQ rights

In the contemporary landscape of social justice advocacy, the influence of celebrity endorsements has emerged as a powerful tool in the fight for LGBTQ rights. Celebrities possess a unique platform that allows them to reach vast audiences, thereby amplifying critical messages and fostering greater visibility for marginalized communities. This section explores the theoretical underpinnings of celebrity influence, the problems associated with relying on celebrity endorsements, and notable examples that illustrate the impact of such endorsements on LGBTQ advocacy.

Theoretical Framework

The phenomenon of celebrity endorsement can be analyzed through various theoretical lenses, including the **Social Identity Theory** and the **Framing Theory**. Social Identity Theory posits that individuals derive a sense of self from their group memberships, leading them to align with figures who share similar identities or values. When celebrities publicly support LGBTQ rights, they not only affirm their identity but also encourage their followers to embrace inclusivity and acceptance. This alignment can foster a sense of belonging and solidarity within the LGBTQ community while challenging societal norms.

Framing Theory, on the other hand, emphasizes how information is presented to shape public perception. Celebrities often have the ability to frame LGBTQ issues in relatable and digestible terms, making complex social justice topics accessible to broader audiences. By framing LGBTQ rights as a matter of fundamental human rights, celebrities can shift public discourse and challenge prejudices that may exist in society.

Challenges of Celebrity Endorsements

While the benefits of leveraging celebrity endorsements are apparent, there are inherent challenges that advocates must navigate. One significant issue is the potential for **Performative Activism**, where celebrities engage in advocacy primarily for public relations or personal branding rather than a genuine commitment to the cause. This can lead to skepticism among activists and the community, who may view such endorsements as superficial or insincere.

Moreover, the focus on celebrity endorsements can overshadow the voices of grassroots activists and marginalized individuals who have been at the forefront of the struggle for LGBTQ rights. This phenomenon, often referred to as **Celebrity Overreach**, can dilute the authenticity of the movement and create a hierarchy of voices that prioritizes celebrity narratives over lived experiences.

Notable Examples

Despite these challenges, there are numerous instances where celebrity endorsements have significantly advanced the cause of LGBTQ rights. For example, the involvement of figures like **Ellen DeGeneres** has been instrumental in normalizing LGBTQ identities in mainstream media. Ellen's coming out in the late 1990s not only marked a pivotal moment in television history but also provided a platform for discussions around LGBTQ issues. Her advocacy has helped to foster a more accepting environment for LGBTQ individuals, particularly within the entertainment industry.

Another notable example is the partnership between the **Human Rights Campaign** (HRC) and various celebrities during the campaign for marriage equality in the United States. Celebrities like **Lady Gaga** and **Miley Cyrus** utilized their platforms to mobilize their fan bases, encouraging them to advocate for legislative change. Lady Gaga's performance of "Born This Way" at the 2011 MTV Video Music Awards became an anthem for the LGBTQ rights movement, emphasizing themes of self-acceptance and pride.

The Impact of Celebrity Endorsements

The impact of celebrity endorsements on LGBTQ rights extends beyond immediate visibility; it contributes to long-term cultural shifts. Research has shown that positive representations of LGBTQ individuals in media, often propelled by celebrity endorsements, can lead to increased acceptance and reduced stigma. A study conducted by the **Williams Institute** found that exposure to

LGBTQ-inclusive media significantly correlates with more favorable attitudes toward LGBTQ individuals among viewers.

Furthermore, the global reach of social media has transformed the landscape of celebrity activism. Platforms like **Instagram** and **Twitter** allow celebrities to engage directly with their audiences, fostering real-time dialogue and mobilization. For instance, during the 2020 Black Lives Matter protests, numerous celebrities used their platforms to express solidarity with LGBTQ communities, reinforcing the interconnectedness of various social justice movements.

Conclusion

In conclusion, leveraging celebrity endorsements for LGBTQ rights presents both opportunities and challenges. While celebrities can amplify critical messages and foster greater visibility, advocates must remain vigilant against performative activism and ensure that grassroots voices are not overshadowed. By strategically harnessing the influence of celebrities, the LGBTQ rights movement can continue to make significant strides toward equality and acceptance. As we look to the future, the collaboration between activists and celebrities must be grounded in authenticity, solidarity, and a shared commitment to justice for all.

Amplifying the movement through celebrity alliances

In the realm of social justice, the intersection of celebrity influence and advocacy can create powerful synergies that amplify movements and catalyze change. The phenomenon of celebrity alliances in the LGBTQ rights movement is not merely a trend; it reflects a strategic approach to harnessing visibility, resources, and platforms that can significantly enhance the reach and impact of advocacy efforts. This section will explore the mechanisms by which celebrity endorsements can elevate LGBTQ rights initiatives, the challenges associated with such alliances, and notable examples that illustrate their effectiveness.

Theoretical Framework

The theoretical underpinnings of celebrity activism can be analyzed through the lens of *social capital* and *cultural hegemony*. Social capital, as defined by Bourdieu (1986), refers to the resources available to individuals through their social networks. Celebrities, by virtue of their public personas, possess substantial social capital, which can be mobilized to benefit marginalized communities. When celebrities advocate for LGBTQ rights, they leverage their fame to draw attention to issues that may otherwise be overlooked, thereby increasing public awareness and engagement.

Cultural hegemony, a concept introduced by Gramsci (1971), posits that dominant groups maintain power by shaping societal norms and values. By aligning with LGBTQ movements, celebrities can challenge prevailing heteronormative narratives and promote inclusivity, thereby contributing to a shift in cultural perceptions. This dual framework underscores the potential of celebrity alliances to effectuate change by altering both the social landscape and the cultural discourse surrounding LGBTQ rights.

Mechanisms of Amplification

Celebrity alliances can amplify the LGBTQ rights movement through several key mechanisms:

- **Visibility and Awareness:** Celebrities have extensive media reach, allowing them to bring visibility to LGBTQ issues. This visibility can translate into increased awareness among their followers, many of whom may not be familiar with the challenges faced by LGBTQ individuals. For instance, when celebrities share personal stories or experiences related to their LGBTQ advocacy, they humanize the issues and foster empathy among audiences.

- **Resource Mobilization:** Celebrities often have access to significant financial resources and networks that can be mobilized for advocacy. Through fundraising events, charity concerts, and social media campaigns, they can generate substantial support for LGBTQ organizations. The *It Gets Better Project*, for example, gained momentum through celebrity involvement, raising funds and awareness to combat bullying against LGBTQ youth.

- **Legitimization of Issues:** The endorsement of LGBTQ rights by well-known figures can lend legitimacy to the movement. When celebrities speak out against discrimination or advocate for legal protections, they signal to the public that these issues are important and worthy of attention. This can lead to greater acceptance and support for LGBTQ rights within broader society.

- **Influencing Policy:** Celebrities can leverage their platforms to influence policymakers and advocate for legislative change. By publicly supporting specific bills or initiatives, they can mobilize their fan base to take action, thereby creating pressure on political leaders to address LGBTQ rights. For example, singer *Lady Gaga* has been vocal about her support for marriage equality, significantly impacting public discourse and policy discussions.

Challenges and Critiques

While the involvement of celebrities in LGBTQ advocacy can be beneficial, it is not without its challenges and critiques. One primary concern is the potential for *performative activism*, where celebrities engage in advocacy primarily for public relations purposes rather than genuine commitment to the cause. This can lead to a superficial understanding of LGBTQ issues and may ultimately detract from the voices of those most affected by discrimination.

Moreover, the focus on celebrity endorsements can overshadow grassroots activists and organizations that have been working tirelessly for LGBTQ rights. It is crucial to ensure that celebrity involvement complements rather than replaces the efforts of local advocates. The risk of co-opting movements for personal branding or commercial gain must be critically examined to maintain the integrity of the cause.

Notable Examples

Several notable examples illustrate the power of celebrity alliances in amplifying the LGBTQ rights movement:

- **Ellen DeGeneres:** As one of the first openly gay celebrities in Hollywood, Ellen DeGeneres has used her platform to advocate for LGBTQ rights for decades. Her coming out in the 1990s was a groundbreaking moment that helped shift public perceptions of LGBTQ individuals. Through her talk show, she has consistently highlighted LGBTQ issues, fostering greater understanding and acceptance.

- **Laverne Cox:** As a transgender actress and activist, Laverne Cox has become a prominent figure in the fight for transgender rights. Her visibility in mainstream media has challenged stereotypes and provided representation for transgender individuals. Cox's advocacy extends beyond her on-screen roles, as she actively engages in discussions about the challenges faced by the transgender community.

- **Taylor Swift:** In recent years, Taylor Swift has emerged as a vocal advocate for LGBTQ rights, particularly in her support for the Equality Act in the United

States. By using her platform to address issues of discrimination and promote inclusivity, Swift has mobilized her vast fan base to engage in activism and support LGBTQ causes.

- **Billy Porter:** Actor and fashion icon Billy Porter has been an outspoken advocate for LGBTQ rights, particularly regarding issues affecting the Black LGBTQ community. His visibility at high-profile events, coupled with his advocacy work, has brought attention to the intersectionality of race and sexual orientation within the LGBTQ movement.

Conclusion

In conclusion, celebrity alliances can play a crucial role in amplifying the LGBTQ rights movement by leveraging visibility, resources, and influence. While challenges such as performative activism and the overshadowing of grassroots efforts must be navigated, the potential for positive impact is significant. By fostering genuine partnerships between celebrities and LGBTQ activists, the movement can harness the power of celebrity influence to create lasting change and promote inclusivity. As we continue to witness the evolution of LGBTQ rights, the collaboration between celebrities and activists will remain an essential component of the struggle for equality and justice.

Engaging with influential figures and opinion leaders

In the realm of LGBTQ advocacy, the engagement with influential figures and opinion leaders plays a pivotal role in shaping public discourse and advancing the cause for equality. This subsection explores the significance of these relationships, the challenges faced in fostering them, and the strategies employed to create impactful alliances.

The Importance of Influential Figures

Influential figures, whether they be celebrities, politicians, or community leaders, possess the power to sway public opinion and mobilize support for LGBTQ rights. Their platforms can amplify messages, challenge stereotypes, and foster acceptance. The theory of *social influence* posits that individuals are more likely to change their attitudes and behaviors when they perceive that someone they admire endorses a particular viewpoint. This phenomenon is particularly relevant in the context of LGBTQ advocacy, where high-profile endorsements can lead to increased visibility and legitimacy for the movement.

Challenges in Engagement

Despite the potential benefits of engaging with influential figures, several challenges may arise. Firstly, there is the risk of *performative allyship*, where individuals or organizations engage superficially without a genuine commitment to the cause. This can lead to disillusionment within the LGBTQ community, as activists may perceive such engagements as mere publicity stunts rather than meaningful support.

Moreover, the political climate can create barriers to engagement. Influential figures may be hesitant to align themselves with LGBTQ issues due to fear of backlash from conservative constituents or sponsors. This reluctance can stifle important conversations and limit the potential for advocacy.

Strategies for Engagement

To effectively engage influential figures, LGBTQ activists employ various strategies:

- **Building Relationships:** Establishing genuine connections with influential figures is crucial. Activists often seek to understand the interests and values of these individuals, finding common ground that aligns with LGBTQ rights. This relational approach fosters trust and opens avenues for collaboration.

- **Leveraging Media Opportunities:** Activists can utilize media events, press conferences, and social media platforms to present opportunities for influential figures to engage with LGBTQ issues. By framing these moments as chances for positive impact, activists can encourage participation and visibility.

- **Highlighting Personal Stories:** Sharing personal narratives of LGBTQ individuals can resonate deeply with influential figures. By humanizing the issues at stake, activists can evoke empathy and inspire action. For instance, when prominent figures hear firsthand accounts of discrimination or resilience, it can motivate them to advocate for change.

- **Creating Collaborative Campaigns:** Joint initiatives that align the goals of LGBTQ advocacy with the interests of influential figures can lead to mutually beneficial outcomes. For example, a celebrity may partner with LGBTQ organizations to promote an awareness campaign, leveraging their platform to reach wider audiences.

Examples of Successful Engagement

Several notable examples illustrate the effectiveness of engaging influential figures in LGBTQ advocacy:

- **Ellen DeGeneres:** As a prominent LGBTQ figure, Ellen DeGeneres has used her platform to advocate for LGBTQ rights. Her coming out in the 1990s was a watershed moment that not only influenced public perception but also encouraged other celebrities to embrace their identities. Her continued advocacy highlights the importance of visibility and representation in the media.

- **Barack Obama:** Former President Barack Obama's evolution on LGBTQ issues exemplifies how political leaders can impact societal attitudes. His endorsement of same-sex marriage in 2012 marked a significant shift in the political landscape, encouraging other leaders to follow suit. This engagement not only galvanized support within the LGBTQ community but also influenced public opinion on a national scale.

- **Lady Gaga:** Lady Gaga's advocacy for LGBTQ rights, particularly her support for the "It Gets Better" campaign, showcases how celebrities can mobilize their fanbase for social change. Her willingness to speak out against discrimination has inspired many, demonstrating the power of celebrity influence in fostering acceptance and support.

Conclusion

Engaging with influential figures and opinion leaders is a crucial aspect of LGBTQ advocacy. While challenges exist, the potential for positive impact is significant. By employing strategic approaches to build relationships and foster collaboration, activists can leverage the influence of these figures to create meaningful change. The ongoing dialogue between LGBTQ advocates and influential allies not only enhances visibility but also promotes a culture of acceptance and understanding, paving the way for a more equitable society.

$$\text{Impact} = \text{Visibility} \times \text{Engagement} \times \text{Allyship} \tag{36}$$

In this equation, the impact of advocacy efforts is contingent upon the visibility of LGBTQ issues, the level of engagement with influential figures, and the strength of allyship formed through these relationships. As the movement continues to evolve, the importance of these connections remains paramount in the fight for equality and justice.

The role of media and entertainment industry in advocacy

The media and entertainment industry plays a pivotal role in shaping societal attitudes towards LGBTQ rights and issues. Through various forms of storytelling, representation, and advocacy, these platforms can influence public perception, challenge stereotypes, and foster a culture of acceptance. The intersection of media, culture, and activism creates a powerful conduit for change, particularly in regions where LGBTQ individuals face severe discrimination and marginalization.

Theoretical Framework

The influence of media on public opinion can be understood through several theoretical frameworks, including the **Framing Theory** and **Cultivation Theory**. Framing Theory suggests that the way information is presented (or framed) can significantly affect how audiences interpret and understand social issues. For instance, when LGBTQ individuals are framed as victims of discrimination, it may evoke empathy and support for their rights. Conversely, negative portrayals can reinforce stigma and discrimination.

Cultivation Theory posits that long-term exposure to media content can shape an individual's perceptions of reality. In this context, consistent representation of LGBTQ individuals in positive roles within mainstream media can help normalize their existence and experiences, leading to greater acceptance in society.

Challenges Faced

Despite the potential for positive impact, the media and entertainment industry also faces significant challenges in advocating for LGBTQ rights. The following issues are prevalent:

- **Stereotyping and Misrepresentation:** Often, LGBTQ characters are depicted through narrow stereotypes or are relegated to supporting roles, which can perpetuate harmful narratives. This misrepresentation can hinder the movement towards equality, as it fails to reflect the diversity and complexity of LGBTQ lives.

- **Censorship and Regulation:** In many countries, including Uganda, strict censorship laws limit the portrayal of LGBTQ content in media. This restriction not only stifles representation but also silences the voices of LGBTQ individuals who wish to share their stories.

- **Commercialization of Activism:** The commodification of LGBTQ rights, where corporations engage in "rainbow capitalism" during Pride Month without genuine commitment to advocacy, can dilute the movement's message. This superficial engagement often leads to skepticism among activists and community members.

Examples of Effective Advocacy

Several notable examples illustrate the effective use of media and entertainment in advocating for LGBTQ rights:

- **Documentaries and Films:** Documentaries such as *Paris is Burning* and *Disclosure* have shed light on the struggles and triumphs of the LGBTQ community, providing audiences with a deeper understanding of the issues at hand. These films not only inform but also inspire action by humanizing the experiences of LGBTQ individuals.

- **Television Series:** Shows like *Pose* and *Orange is the New Black* have brought LGBTQ narratives to the forefront, showcasing the richness of their stories and the challenges they face. These series have garnered critical acclaim and sparked conversations about representation, leading to increased visibility and support for LGBTQ rights.

- **Social Media Campaigns:** Platforms like Twitter and Instagram have become essential tools for LGBTQ advocacy. Campaigns such as #LoveIsLove and #TransRightsAreHumanRights have mobilized millions, creating a global dialogue around LGBTQ issues. These campaigns often utilize personal stories and visual content to engage audiences emotionally, fostering a sense of solidarity and community.

The Future of Media Advocacy

The role of the media and entertainment industry in LGBTQ advocacy is evolving. As more LGBTQ individuals enter the industry as creators, producers, and influencers, the potential for authentic representation increases. The rise of streaming platforms has also democratized content creation, allowing for diverse stories to be told without the constraints of traditional media gatekeepers.

Furthermore, as societal attitudes continue to shift towards greater acceptance of LGBTQ rights, the media can play a critical role in maintaining momentum for change. By prioritizing inclusive narratives and supporting grassroots movements, the entertainment industry can help pave the way for a more equitable future.

In conclusion, the media and entertainment industry holds significant power in advocating for LGBTQ rights. Through thoughtful representation, storytelling, and engagement, these platforms can challenge societal norms, inspire action, and ultimately contribute to the advancement of LGBTQ equality. The journey is ongoing, but with continued collaboration between activists and media creators, the possibilities for positive change are boundless.

Harnessing pop culture for social change

Pop culture, a dynamic and pervasive element of contemporary society, serves as a powerful vehicle for social change, particularly in advocating for LGBTQ rights. It encompasses various forms of media, including music, film, television, fashion, and social media, which can shape public perceptions and influence societal norms. By leveraging pop culture, activists can reach broader audiences, challenge stereotypes, and foster empathy and understanding towards LGBTQ communities.

Theoretical Framework

The impact of pop culture on social change can be understood through several theoretical lenses:

- **Cultural Hegemony:** Antonio Gramsci's theory of cultural hegemony posits that dominant groups in society maintain power through cultural institutions. By infiltrating these institutions, LGBTQ activists can challenge and reshape dominant narratives, promoting a more inclusive representation of diverse identities.

- **Framing Theory:** This theory suggests that the way issues are presented in media affects public perception. Activists can utilize pop culture to frame LGBTQ issues positively, emphasizing themes of love, acceptance, and human rights, which can shift public attitudes.

- **Social Identity Theory:** This theory highlights how individuals categorize themselves and others into social groups. By showcasing LGBTQ identities in popular media, activists can foster a sense of belonging and community, encouraging individuals to embrace their authentic selves.

Challenges in Utilizing Pop Culture

Despite its potential, harnessing pop culture for social change is not without challenges:

- **Commercialization:** The commercialization of LGBTQ themes can lead to tokenism, where representation is superficial and lacks depth. Activists must navigate the fine line between genuine advocacy and profit-driven motives of the entertainment industry.

- **Backlash and Resistance:** Pop culture initiatives may face backlash from conservative groups, leading to increased discrimination and hostility towards LGBTQ individuals. Activists must be prepared to counteract negative narratives and provide robust support for affected communities.

- **Sustainability:** Pop culture trends are often fleeting. While a particular campaign may gain traction, sustaining momentum for long-term change requires ongoing effort and adaptability to evolving cultural landscapes.

Successful Examples of Pop Culture Advocacy

Numerous instances illustrate the successful harnessing of pop culture for social change:

- **Television and Film:** Shows like *Pose* and *Queer Eye* have brought LGBTQ stories to mainstream audiences, celebrating diversity and fostering empathy. *Pose*, for instance, highlights the ballroom culture of the 1980s and 90s, showcasing the struggles and resilience of transgender individuals and LGBTQ people of color. Its critical acclaim and popularity have sparked conversations around intersectionality and representation.

- **Music:** Artists such as Lil Nas X and Sam Smith have used their platforms to advocate for LGBTQ rights through their lyrics and public personas. Lil Nas X's hit song *Montero (Call Me By Your Name)* not only topped charts but also challenged heteronormative standards within the music industry, promoting self-acceptance and pride.

- **Social Media Campaigns:** Hashtags such as #LoveIsLove and #PrideMonth have mobilized global audiences, creating a sense of solidarity and community. These campaigns often feature personal stories and experiences, humanizing LGBTQ issues and fostering a supportive environment.

Conclusion

Harnessing pop culture for social change presents a unique opportunity to advocate for LGBTQ rights. By leveraging the influential platforms of music, film, and social media, activists can challenge societal norms, dismantle stereotypes, and promote inclusivity. However, it is essential to remain vigilant against commercialization, backlash, and the transient nature of pop culture. Through thoughtful engagement and strategic advocacy, the LGBTQ movement can continue to thrive and inspire future generations toward a more equitable society.

The Role of Social Media in Amplifying the Movement

Utilizing social media platforms for advocacy purposes

In the digital age, social media has emerged as a powerful tool for advocacy, particularly for marginalized communities, including the LGBTQ population in Uganda. Platforms such as Twitter, Facebook, Instagram, and TikTok have not only transformed how information is disseminated but also how communities organize, mobilize, and advocate for their rights. This section explores the significance of social media in LGBTQ advocacy, the challenges faced, and the strategies employed to leverage these platforms effectively.

The Role of Social Media in Advocacy

Social media serves multiple functions in advocacy efforts. First, it provides a space for visibility and representation. For many LGBTQ individuals in Uganda, social media platforms offer an opportunity to share their stories, express their identities, and connect with others who share similar experiences. The visibility gained through social media can challenge stereotypes and misconceptions, fostering a greater understanding of LGBTQ issues among the broader public.

Moreover, social media enables real-time communication and mobilization. Activists can quickly disseminate information about events, protests, and campaigns, reaching a wider audience than traditional media outlets. The immediacy of social media allows for rapid responses to emerging issues, such as discriminatory legislation or acts of violence against LGBTQ individuals.

Theory of Digital Activism

The theory of digital activism posits that the internet and social media create new spaces for political engagement and social change. According to [?], digital activism is characterized by its ability to facilitate grassroots movements, enabling individuals to participate in advocacy without the constraints of geographical boundaries. This democratization of activism empowers individuals to take action, share information, and build coalitions, often leading to significant social and political change.

Challenges of Social Media Advocacy

Despite its potential, utilizing social media for advocacy is not without challenges. One significant issue is the prevalence of online harassment and hate speech directed at LGBTQ individuals. The anonymity afforded by social media can embolden individuals to engage in discriminatory behavior, creating a hostile environment for activists. This can lead to mental health challenges for those targeted, as they navigate the dual pressures of advocating for their rights while managing the emotional toll of online abuse.

Additionally, the digital divide remains a critical concern. Access to the internet is not universal, and many LGBTQ individuals in Uganda may lack the resources or connectivity needed to participate in online advocacy. This disparity can exacerbate existing inequalities within the community, limiting the voices of those who are already marginalized.

Strategies for Effective Use of Social Media

To maximize the impact of social media in advocacy efforts, LGBTQ activists in Uganda have employed several strategies:

- **Creating Safe Spaces:** Activists have established private groups and forums on platforms like Facebook, where LGBTQ individuals can share experiences, seek support, and organize without fear of exposure. These safe spaces are crucial for fostering community and solidarity among members.

- **Utilizing Hashtags:** Campaigns such as #UgandaLGBTQ and #PrideInUganda have been instrumental in raising awareness and promoting visibility. Hashtags serve as rallying points for discussions and mobilization, allowing activists to connect with a global audience and draw attention to local issues.

- **Engaging Influencers:** Collaborations with social media influencers and allies have proven effective in amplifying LGBTQ voices. By leveraging the reach of these individuals, activists can engage a broader audience and challenge prevailing narratives about LGBTQ rights in Uganda.

- **Storytelling:** Personal narratives shared on social media can humanize LGBTQ issues, fostering empathy and understanding among followers. Storytelling is a powerful tool for advocacy, as it allows individuals to connect emotionally with the struggles and triumphs of the LGBTQ community.

- **Educational Campaigns:** Activists have utilized social media to disseminate information about LGBTQ rights, health, and safety. By creating informative content, such as infographics and videos, they can educate the public and challenge misconceptions about the community.

Examples of Successful Social Media Campaigns

Several notable campaigns have successfully utilized social media to advocate for LGBTQ rights in Uganda. One such example is the *#FreeUgandaPride* campaign, which aimed to raise awareness about the challenges faced by LGBTQ individuals during Pride celebrations. Through a series of posts, videos, and live streams, activists highlighted the importance of Pride as a means of visibility and community solidarity, garnering international support and media attention.

Another effective campaign is the *#EndHomophobiaUganda* initiative, which sought to address the pervasive discrimination and violence against LGBTQ individuals. By sharing personal stories and statistics about homophobic violence, activists were able to engage both local and international audiences, prompting discussions about the need for legal protections and societal change.

Conclusion

In conclusion, social media platforms have become indispensable tools for LGBTQ advocacy in Uganda. They provide a space for visibility, community building, and mobilization, enabling activists to challenge discrimination and promote acceptance. However, the challenges of online harassment and the digital divide must be addressed to ensure that all voices within the LGBTQ community are heard. By employing effective strategies and learning from successful campaigns, activists can continue to harness the power of social media to advocate for their rights and foster a more inclusive society.

Engaging with online communities and influencers

In the digital age, social media platforms have emerged as powerful tools for advocacy and activism, especially within marginalized communities such as the

LGBTQ population in Uganda. Engaging with online communities and influencers is not only a strategy for amplifying voices but also a vital mechanism for fostering solidarity, raising awareness, and mobilizing support for LGBTQ rights.

The Role of Online Communities

Online communities provide a safe haven for individuals who may feel isolated due to societal stigma. These spaces allow LGBTQ individuals to connect with like-minded peers, share experiences, and offer mutual support. The sense of belonging that emerges from these interactions is crucial, particularly in a country like Uganda, where societal and legal frameworks often marginalize LGBTQ identities.

Creating Safe Spaces The concept of safe spaces online entails creating environments where individuals can express themselves without fear of discrimination or harassment. Platforms such as Facebook, Twitter, and Instagram have been instrumental in facilitating these safe spaces. For instance, groups dedicated to LGBTQ rights in Uganda have formed on Facebook, allowing members to discuss issues, share resources, and organize events. These communities serve as both a support network and a platform for activism.

Influencer Engagement

Influencers play a significant role in shaping public opinion and raising awareness about LGBTQ issues. Their reach can transcend geographic boundaries, bringing attention to local struggles while also connecting them to global narratives. By collaborating with influencers, LGBTQ activists can leverage their platforms to disseminate information, challenge stereotypes, and promote inclusivity.

Case Studies of Influencer Impact One notable example is the collaboration between LGBTQ activists and international influencers during Pride Month. Campaigns that feature well-known figures advocating for LGBTQ rights can draw significant media attention and public support. For instance, when global celebrities shared messages of solidarity with Ugandan LGBTQ activists on their social media accounts, it not only amplified the message but also encouraged local activists to continue their work despite facing severe backlash.

Challenges in Online Engagement

While engaging with online communities and influencers presents numerous opportunities, it is not without challenges. One of the primary concerns is the prevalence of online harassment and hate speech directed at LGBTQ individuals. The anonymity provided by the internet can embolden aggressors, leading to toxic environments that deter participation.

Addressing Online Harassment To combat this issue, LGBTQ organizations must implement strategies that promote digital safety. This includes educating community members on how to report harassment, providing resources for mental health support, and fostering a culture of resilience. For example, campaigns that focus on digital literacy can empower individuals to navigate online spaces safely and effectively.

Utilizing Hashtags and Viral Campaigns

Hashtags serve as a rallying point for social movements, allowing users to easily find and engage with related content. The use of specific hashtags can unify voices around a common cause, making it easier to mobilize support. For instance, the hashtag #FreeUgandaLGBTQ has been used to draw attention to the plight of LGBTQ individuals facing persecution in Uganda, encouraging international advocacy and support.

The Power of Viral Campaigns Viral campaigns can create a sense of urgency and drive action. For example, the #LoveIsLove campaign, which gained traction globally, resonated with many in Uganda, sparking discussions about love, acceptance, and rights. Such campaigns not only raise awareness but also challenge discriminatory narratives, contributing to a broader movement for change.

Building Alliances with Influencers

Engaging with influencers requires strategic alliances. LGBTQ activists must identify and collaborate with influencers who are not only sympathetic to the cause but also have a genuine commitment to social justice. Building these relationships can lead to impactful campaigns that resonate with diverse audiences.

Examples of Successful Alliances An example of successful influencer engagement is the partnership between Ugandan LGBTQ activists and global influencers during the launch of a campaign aimed at promoting safe sex and HIV prevention. Influencers shared informative content, debunked myths, and encouraged their followers to support LGBTQ rights in Uganda. This not only educated the audience but also fostered a sense of global solidarity.

Conclusion

Engaging with online communities and influencers is a multifaceted approach that can significantly impact the fight for LGBTQ rights in Uganda. By creating safe spaces, leveraging influencer reach, and addressing challenges such as online harassment, activists can cultivate a supportive and empowered community. The digital landscape offers a unique opportunity to amplify voices, challenge oppressive narratives, and drive meaningful change in society. As the movement continues to evolve, the importance of these online engagements will only grow, paving the way for a more inclusive future.

Spreading awareness through viral campaigns and hashtags

In the digital age, the power of social media has revolutionized the landscape of activism, providing a platform for marginalized voices to be heard and for movements to gain traction. Viral campaigns and hashtags have emerged as potent tools for spreading awareness and fostering solidarity within the LGBTQ community and beyond. This section delves into the theoretical underpinnings of viral campaigns, the challenges faced in their implementation, and notable examples that illustrate their impact.

Theoretical Framework

The concept of viral campaigns can be understood through the lens of *network theory*, which examines how information spreads through interconnected nodes in a network. In this context, individuals act as nodes, sharing content that resonates with them, thereby amplifying the message across their own networks. The effectiveness of a viral campaign often hinges on its ability to evoke emotional responses, leveraging the principles of *social contagion* and *cultural diffusion*.

The formula for understanding the spread of information can be represented as:

$$I(t) = I_0 e^{rt} \tag{37}$$

where: - $I(t)$ is the number of individuals exposed to the information at time t, - I_0 is the initial number of individuals exposed, - r is the rate of spreading, and - t is time.

This model illustrates how quickly a message can proliferate when it resonates with a broad audience, especially when amplified by influential figures or organizations.

Challenges in Implementing Viral Campaigns

Despite their potential, viral campaigns are not without challenges. One significant problem is the phenomenon of *hashtag fatigue*, where audiences become overwhelmed by the sheer volume of campaigns and messages, leading to diminished engagement. Additionally, the rapid pace of social media can result in the dilution of important messages, as they may be overshadowed by trending topics that lack relevance to LGBTQ rights.

Moreover, the presence of *online harassment* poses a threat to the effectiveness of these campaigns. Activists may face backlash for their advocacy, leading to a chilling effect where individuals hesitate to engage or share their experiences for fear of retaliation. This can hinder the authenticity and reach of campaigns aimed at raising awareness.

Notable Examples of Viral Campaigns

Several viral campaigns have successfully raised awareness about LGBTQ issues, mobilizing support and fostering community engagement. One prominent example is the hashtag #LoveIsLove, which gained momentum during the fight for marriage equality in the United States. This campaign not only celebrated love in its many forms but also served as a rallying cry for advocates and allies alike, transcending geographical boundaries and cultural differences.

Another significant campaign is #BlackAndTransLivesMatter, which highlights the intersectionality of race and gender identity within the broader LGBTQ movement. By centering the experiences of Black transgender individuals, this campaign challenges the narrative that often sidelines marginalized voices, fostering a more inclusive dialogue around LGBTQ rights.

The #ItGetsBetter campaign also stands out as a poignant example of using personal stories to combat bullying and discrimination. By encouraging individuals to share their journeys of resilience and hope, the campaign has inspired countless LGBTQ youth to embrace their identities, reinforcing the message that support exists and that they are not alone in their struggles.

The Role of Digital Activism

Digital activism, particularly through viral campaigns and hashtags, has become an essential component of modern advocacy. It enables activists to bypass traditional media gatekeepers, directly reaching audiences and fostering grassroots movements. The engagement metrics—likes, shares, retweets—serve as indicators of a campaign's reach and resonance, providing valuable feedback for ongoing advocacy efforts.

To maximize the impact of viral campaigns, activists must adopt strategic approaches that include:

- **Creating Compelling Content:** Engaging visuals, powerful narratives, and relatable messages can enhance the likelihood of a campaign going viral.

- **Leveraging Influencers:** Partnering with well-known figures who align with the campaign's goals can significantly amplify reach and credibility.

- **Encouraging User Participation:** Inviting individuals to share their stories or experiences related to the campaign fosters a sense of community and ownership.

Conclusion

The use of viral campaigns and hashtags in LGBTQ activism represents a transformative shift in how awareness is spread and how communities mobilize for change. While challenges exist, the potential for these digital tools to create lasting impact is undeniable. By harnessing the power of social media, activists can continue to advocate for LGBTQ rights, fostering a culture of acceptance and understanding that transcends borders. As we look toward the future, the ongoing evolution of digital activism will play a crucial role in shaping the narrative around LGBTQ rights and ensuring that every voice is heard.

Overcoming online harassment and hate speech

In the contemporary digital landscape, online harassment and hate speech present significant barriers to the progress of LGBTQ rights. The anonymity afforded by the internet often emboldens individuals to engage in harmful behaviors that perpetuate discrimination and violence against LGBTQ communities. Understanding the dynamics of online harassment is crucial for developing effective strategies to combat it.

Theoretical Framework

The phenomenon of online harassment can be analyzed through various theoretical lenses. One such framework is the *Social Identity Theory*, which posits that individuals derive part of their identity from the groups to which they belong. This theory helps explain why LGBTQ individuals may be targeted; they are often seen as representatives of a marginalized group, making them vulnerable to attacks that seek to reinforce heteronormative standards. Additionally, *Framing Theory* elucidates how narratives around LGBTQ identities are constructed in online spaces, influencing public perception and acceptance. Negative framing can lead to the normalization of hate speech, while positive framing can foster inclusivity.

Types of Online Harassment

Online harassment manifests in various forms, including:

- **Verbal Abuse:** This includes derogatory comments, slurs, and threats directed at LGBTQ individuals.

- **Doxxing:** The practice of publicly revealing personal information about an individual without their consent, often used as a tactic to intimidate.

- **Cyberbullying:** Repeated aggressive behavior using electronic means, which can have severe psychological effects on victims.

- **Trolling:** Deliberately provoking or upsetting individuals online, often targeting LGBTQ discussions or communities.

The impact of such harassment can be profound, leading to mental health issues, increased anxiety, and a sense of isolation among victims.

Challenges in Addressing Online Harassment

Despite the growing awareness of online harassment, several challenges persist:

- **Lack of Legal Protections:** In many jurisdictions, laws addressing online harassment are inadequate. This gap allows perpetrators to act with impunity.

- **Platform Policies:** Social media platforms often have inconsistent policies regarding hate speech and harassment. The enforcement of these policies can be lax, leading to a culture of tolerance for abusive behavior.

- **Victim Blaming:** Victims of online harassment may face stigma and blame, discouraging them from reporting incidents or seeking help.

Strategies for Overcoming Online Harassment

To combat online harassment and hate speech effectively, several strategies can be employed:

1. **Empowering Individuals:** Educating LGBTQ individuals about their rights and available resources is essential. This includes knowledge of how to report harassment on various platforms and understanding the legal protections that may apply.

2. **Building Community Support:** Creating safe online spaces where LGBTQ individuals can share experiences and support one another is crucial. Online forums, social media groups, and community organizations can serve as vital support networks.

3. **Advocacy for Stronger Policies:** Engaging in advocacy to push for stronger anti-harassment policies on social media platforms can lead to more robust protections. This includes lobbying for clearer definitions of hate speech and more transparent reporting processes.

4. **Leveraging Technology:** Utilizing technology to filter and block harmful content can empower users. Many platforms now offer tools that allow users to control who can interact with them and what kind of content they see.

5. **Promoting Positive Narratives:** Countering hate speech with positive representations of LGBTQ individuals and communities can help shift public perception. Campaigns that highlight the contributions and experiences of LGBTQ individuals can foster empathy and understanding.

Case Studies and Examples

Several organizations and initiatives have successfully addressed online harassment:

- **The Trevor Project:** This organization provides crisis intervention and suicide prevention services to LGBTQ youth. They also advocate for safer online spaces and offer resources for dealing with online harassment.

- **GLAAD's Social Media Safety:** GLAAD has developed guidelines for LGBTQ individuals on how to navigate social media safely, including tips on reporting harassment and protecting personal information.

- **Cyber Civil Rights Initiative:** This initiative focuses on combating online harassment through legal advocacy and public awareness campaigns, aiming to create a safer online environment for all marginalized groups.

Conclusion

Overcoming online harassment and hate speech requires a multifaceted approach that combines individual empowerment, community support, policy advocacy, and positive narrative building. As LGBTQ activists continue to navigate the complexities of digital spaces, it is imperative to foster a culture of respect and inclusivity online. By addressing the challenges head-on and implementing effective strategies, the LGBTQ community can create safer environments that allow for authentic expression and engagement in the fight for equality.

The power of digital activism in promoting LGBTQ rights

In the contemporary landscape of social justice movements, digital activism has emerged as a transformative force, particularly in the realm of LGBTQ rights. The proliferation of social media platforms has created unprecedented opportunities for advocacy, community building, and awareness-raising. This section explores the theoretical foundations of digital activism, the challenges it faces, and real-world examples that illustrate its impact on the LGBTQ rights movement.

Theoretical Foundations of Digital Activism

Digital activism can be understood through various theoretical lenses, including networked social movements, the public sphere, and participatory culture. According to [?], networked social movements leverage digital technologies to facilitate decentralized and participatory forms of activism. This model contrasts with traditional hierarchical structures, allowing for more fluid and adaptive responses to social issues.

The concept of the public sphere, as articulated by [?], emphasizes the importance of open discourse in shaping public opinion. Digital platforms enable marginalized voices to enter the public sphere, challenging dominant narratives and fostering dialogue around LGBTQ rights. Furthermore, participatory culture, as described by [?], encourages individuals to engage actively in the creation and dissemination of content, empowering them to advocate for social change.

Challenges of Digital Activism

Despite its potential, digital activism is not without challenges. One significant issue is the digital divide, which refers to the disparities in access to technology and the internet. According to [?], socio-economic factors, geography, and education contribute to unequal access, leaving some LGBTQ individuals and communities marginalized in the digital space. This divide can hinder the effectiveness of online campaigns and limit the reach of advocacy efforts.

Moreover, digital activism is susceptible to backlash and online harassment. The phenomenon of trolling, particularly against LGBTQ activists, can create a hostile environment that discourages participation. [?] highlights the need for robust online safety measures and community guidelines to protect activists from harassment and to foster a supportive online environment.

Examples of Digital Activism in LGBTQ Rights

Several notable campaigns exemplify the power of digital activism in promoting LGBTQ rights. One such campaign is the #LoveIsLove movement, which gained momentum following the U.S. Supreme Court's decision to legalize same-sex marriage in 2015. The hashtag became a rallying cry for supporters of LGBTQ rights, transcending national borders and inspiring similar movements worldwide. The campaign utilized social media platforms to share personal stories, advocate for equality, and mobilize supporters, demonstrating the capacity of digital activism to effect change on a global scale.

Another impactful example is the #TransRightsAreHumanRights campaign, which emerged in response to the increasing violence and discrimination faced by transgender individuals. This campaign harnessed the power of social media to raise awareness about trans issues, advocate for policy changes, and highlight the stories of marginalized transgender individuals. By amplifying these voices, the campaign fostered a sense of community and solidarity, encouraging individuals to share their experiences and engage in advocacy.

The Role of Hashtags and Viral Campaigns

Hashtags play a crucial role in digital activism, serving as tools for organization, visibility, and solidarity. The use of hashtags such as #BlackTransLivesMatter and #QueerAndTransPeopleOfColor has brought attention to the intersectionality of

LGBTQ issues, highlighting the unique challenges faced by individuals at the intersection of multiple marginalized identities. These campaigns not only raise awareness but also mobilize support for specific initiatives and policy changes.

Viral campaigns, such as the Ice Bucket Challenge, have also demonstrated the potential of digital activism to raise funds and awareness for LGBTQ-related causes. Although initially focused on ALS research, the challenge's widespread participation showcased the power of social media to engage individuals in philanthropic efforts, inspiring similar initiatives aimed at supporting LGBTQ organizations and causes.

Conclusion

In conclusion, digital activism represents a powerful tool for promoting LGBTQ rights in the modern era. By leveraging the theoretical foundations of networked social movements, the public sphere, and participatory culture, activists can create inclusive spaces for dialogue and advocacy. However, the challenges of the digital divide and online harassment must be addressed to ensure equitable participation in these movements. Through real-world examples and the strategic use of hashtags and viral campaigns, digital activism continues to shape the landscape of LGBTQ rights, fostering community, raising awareness, and advocating for change on a global scale.

The Future of LGBTQ Rights in Uganda

Recent Developments and Changes

Evolving societal attitudes towards LGBTQ issues

The landscape of societal attitudes towards LGBTQ issues in Uganda has undergone significant transformations over the years. This evolution can be attributed to a complex interplay of cultural, religious, and political factors, each contributing to the shifting perceptions of LGBTQ individuals within Ugandan society.

Historically, Uganda has been characterized by a conservative stance towards homosexuality, deeply rooted in colonial laws and traditional beliefs. The infamous Anti-Homosexuality Act of 2014, which sought to impose severe penalties on LGBTQ individuals, exemplified the harsh realities faced by the community. However, as the global conversation surrounding LGBTQ rights has intensified, so too has the dialogue within Uganda, leading to gradual shifts in societal attitudes.

Cultural Context and Traditional Beliefs

In Uganda, cultural norms and traditional beliefs play a pivotal role in shaping societal attitudes towards LGBTQ individuals. The predominant narrative often aligns with conservative values, heavily influenced by religious teachings that view homosexuality as a sin. This cultural backdrop has historically contributed to widespread stigma and discrimination against LGBTQ individuals.

However, recent years have seen a subtle yet notable shift in the discourse surrounding these issues. Increased visibility of LGBTQ individuals and advocacy efforts have prompted some segments of society to question long-held beliefs. For instance, the rise of local LGBTQ organizations has fostered dialogue and awareness, challenging stereotypes and misconceptions.

The Role of Education and Awareness

Education serves as a powerful tool in transforming societal attitudes. As awareness campaigns gain traction, more Ugandans are exposed to the realities of LGBTQ lives. Initiatives aimed at educating the public about sexual orientation and gender identity have emerged, often spearheaded by grassroots organizations. These efforts aim to dismantle harmful stereotypes and promote understanding.

For example, community workshops and discussions have been organized to address misconceptions about LGBTQ individuals. By sharing personal stories and experiences, activists have humanized the LGBTQ struggle, fostering empathy and understanding among diverse audiences. As a result, some community members have begun to challenge the status quo, advocating for acceptance and inclusivity.

Influence of Global Movements

The global LGBTQ rights movement has also had a profound impact on societal attitudes in Uganda. International pressure, coupled with the rise of social media, has amplified the voices of LGBTQ activists, both locally and globally. This interconnectedness has facilitated the exchange of ideas and strategies, empowering Ugandan activists to advocate for their rights more effectively.

The visibility of international LGBTQ figures and their advocacy efforts has inspired many Ugandans to reconsider their perspectives. As global narratives shift towards acceptance and equality, local attitudes are gradually evolving. For instance, the participation of Ugandan activists in international conferences has provided a platform for sharing their experiences and challenges, garnering support from the global community.

Challenges and Resistance

Despite these positive developments, challenges remain. The backlash against LGBTQ rights in Uganda is often fierce, with conservative groups mobilizing against perceived threats to traditional values. This resistance manifests in various forms, including public protests and political campaigns aimed at preserving the status quo.

Moreover, the pervasive influence of religious institutions continues to shape societal attitudes. Many religious leaders maintain anti-LGBTQ stances, reinforcing negative perceptions within their congregations. This creates a challenging environment for activists striving for acceptance and equality.

A Glimpse into the Future

Looking ahead, the trajectory of societal attitudes towards LGBTQ issues in Uganda remains uncertain. While progress has been made, the fight for acceptance and equality is ongoing. Continued advocacy, education, and awareness efforts are essential in fostering a more inclusive society.

As younger generations become more exposed to diverse perspectives, there is hope for a cultural shift. The rise of social media as a platform for dialogue and advocacy presents an opportunity for LGBTQ individuals to share their stories and challenge prevailing narratives.

In conclusion, the evolving societal attitudes towards LGBTQ issues in Uganda reflect a complex interplay of cultural, educational, and global influences. While challenges persist, the gradual shift towards acceptance signals a hopeful future for LGBTQ individuals in the country. The ongoing efforts of activists and allies will be crucial in shaping a more inclusive society where everyone can live authentically, free from discrimination and prejudice.

Legal changes and reforms in LGBTQ rights

The landscape of LGBTQ rights in Uganda has been fraught with challenges, yet it has also witnessed significant legal changes and reforms over the years. These shifts reflect not only the struggles of activists like Frank Mugisha but also the broader societal transformations that have begun to take root in the country. This section delves into the key legal changes, the barriers that remain, and the ongoing efforts to reform laws affecting LGBTQ individuals.

Historical Context

Historically, Uganda has maintained some of the most stringent anti-LGBTQ laws in the world. The Penal Code Act of 1950 criminalized same-sex relations, imposing severe penalties, including life imprisonment. This legal framework created an environment of fear and persecution, where LGBTQ individuals faced harassment, violence, and discrimination. The infamous Anti-Homosexuality Bill of 2014, which sought to impose the death penalty for certain homosexual acts, exemplified the extreme measures taken against the LGBTQ community.

Recent Legal Developments

In recent years, there have been notable legal changes and reforms, albeit gradual and often met with resistance. The repeal of the Anti-Homosexuality Bill in 2014, following widespread international condemnation, marked a significant moment in Uganda's legal history. While the core criminalization of homosexuality remained intact, the rejection of the death penalty provision was a small victory for LGBTQ activists.

Furthermore, the increasing visibility of LGBTQ issues has prompted some legal scholars and human rights advocates to push for more comprehensive reforms. In 2019, a coalition of activists and lawyers submitted a petition to the Constitutional Court challenging the constitutionality of laws that criminalize homosexuality. This legal action reflects a growing recognition that the rights of LGBTQ individuals are human rights and must be protected under the law.

International Influence and Pressure

International human rights law plays a crucial role in advocating for legal reforms in Uganda. The Universal Declaration of Human Rights (UDHR) asserts that all individuals are entitled to fundamental freedoms, including the right to live free from discrimination based on sexual orientation. Activists have leveraged these international frameworks to pressure the Ugandan government to align its laws with global human rights standards.

Moreover, foreign governments and international organizations have exerted pressure on Uganda to improve its human rights record. The United Nations has repeatedly called for the decriminalization of homosexuality and the protection of LGBTQ rights. In response, the Ugandan government has occasionally softened its rhetoric, signaling a potential willingness to engage in dialogue about human rights issues.

Challenges to Legal Reforms

Despite these positive developments, numerous challenges persist in the quest for legal reforms. The deeply entrenched cultural and religious beliefs in Uganda often hinder progress. Many Ugandans view homosexuality as a Western import, leading to a backlash against LGBTQ rights. This cultural stigma is exacerbated by the influence of religious leaders who actively oppose any attempts to normalize LGBTQ identities.

Additionally, the legal system itself poses significant obstacles. Even with petitions for reform, the judiciary in Uganda has been known to be influenced by public opinion and political pressures, often leading to rulings that favor the status quo. The fear of backlash from conservative groups can deter judges from making progressive decisions.

Examples of Advocacy and Reform Efforts

Activists like Frank Mugisha have been at the forefront of advocating for legal changes. Through the organization Sexual Minorities Uganda (SMUG), Mugisha has worked tirelessly to challenge discriminatory laws and promote awareness of LGBTQ rights. The organization has engaged in strategic litigation, public education campaigns, and advocacy at both national and international levels.

One notable example is the collaboration between local activists and international human rights organizations. In 2020, a coalition of NGOs launched a campaign aimed at raising awareness about the plight of LGBTQ individuals in Uganda. This initiative included legal aid for victims of discrimination, public demonstrations, and outreach to lawmakers to advocate for legal reform.

Conclusion

The journey towards legal changes and reforms in LGBTQ rights in Uganda is ongoing and complex. While there have been significant strides, the path is fraught with challenges that require persistent advocacy and community support. The interplay between local activism and international pressure will be crucial in shaping the future of LGBTQ rights in Uganda. As activists continue to fight for justice, the hope remains that the legal landscape will evolve towards greater acceptance and protection for all individuals, regardless of their sexual orientation.

$$\text{Progress} = \text{Advocacy} + \text{International Pressure} - \text{Cultural Resistance} \qquad (38)$$

The impact of international pressure on Ugandan government

The intersection of international pressure and local governance presents a complex dynamic, particularly in the context of LGBTQ rights in Uganda. The Ugandan government has faced increasing scrutiny from global entities, including foreign governments, international human rights organizations, and advocacy groups, which has significantly influenced its policies and practices regarding LGBTQ individuals. This subsection explores the various dimensions of this pressure, the governmental responses, and the broader implications for the LGBTQ community in Uganda.

Theoretical Framework

To understand the impact of international pressure on the Ugandan government, we can employ the theory of *normative power*. According to Ian Manners, normative power is defined as the ability of an actor to shape what is considered "normal" in international relations through the promotion of values such as human rights, democracy, and the rule of law. This framework can be applied to analyze how international actors leverage their influence to advocate for LGBTQ rights, thereby challenging local norms and encouraging reform.

Mechanisms of International Pressure

International pressure manifests through various mechanisms, including:

- **Diplomatic Engagement:** Foreign governments often employ diplomatic channels to express their discontent with Uganda's treatment of LGBTQ individuals. This includes public statements, formal protests, and the use of bilateral discussions to raise concerns about human rights violations.

- **Economic Sanctions:** In some cases, nations have threatened or implemented economic sanctions against Uganda in response to anti-LGBTQ legislation. For instance, the U.S. government has previously withheld aid or imposed sanctions on Ugandan officials involved in human rights abuses.

- **International Treaties and Agreements:** Uganda's participation in international treaties, such as the International Covenant on Civil and Political Rights (ICCPR), creates a framework for accountability. When violations occur, international bodies can exert pressure by highlighting these discrepancies.

- **Public Advocacy Campaigns:** Global NGOs and activists often mobilize public opinion against oppressive regimes. Campaigns that highlight the plight of LGBTQ individuals in Uganda can lead to increased international scrutiny and pressure on the government.

Case Studies and Examples

One notable example of international pressure influencing Ugandan policy is the global outcry following the introduction of the Anti-Homosexuality Bill in 2014. This proposed legislation sought to impose severe penalties, including life imprisonment, for homosexual acts. In response to widespread condemnation from international leaders, human rights organizations, and even some foreign investors, the Ugandan government was compelled to withdraw the bill, at least temporarily. The backlash exemplified the effectiveness of coordinated international advocacy in challenging regressive policies.

Furthermore, the U.S. Secretary of State at the time, John Kerry, publicly criticized Uganda's human rights record, stating that the U.S. would reconsider its aid to the country if it continued to persecute LGBTQ individuals. Such statements from influential global leaders underscore the potential consequences of ignoring international human rights standards.

Challenges and Limitations

Despite the evident impact of international pressure, several challenges persist:

- **National Sovereignty:** The Ugandan government often frames international pressure as an infringement on its sovereignty. This narrative can galvanize nationalist sentiments and increase support for anti-LGBTQ policies among certain segments of the population.

- **Cultural Resistance:** Many Ugandans hold deep-seated beliefs regarding sexuality that conflict with international norms. This cultural resistance can undermine the effectiveness of international advocacy, as it may be perceived as Western imposition.

- **Political Will:** The Ugandan government's commitment to maintaining its stance against LGBTQ rights often outweighs the potential repercussions from the international community. Political leaders may prioritize maintaining power and appeasing conservative constituencies over addressing human rights concerns.

Conclusion

In conclusion, the impact of international pressure on the Ugandan government regarding LGBTQ rights is multifaceted and significant. While international advocacy has the potential to influence policy changes and improve conditions for LGBTQ individuals, it is met with formidable resistance rooted in nationalism, cultural beliefs, and political calculations. Moving forward, it is essential for international actors to adopt nuanced strategies that consider the local context while advocating for human rights. Only through sustained and sensitive engagement can the global community hope to foster a more inclusive environment for LGBTQ individuals in Uganda.

$$P_{\text{change}} = f(I, C, S) \quad (39)$$

Where P_{change} represents the probability of policy change, I is the intensity of international pressure, C is the level of cultural resistance, and S is the strength of political will. This equation illustrates the complex interplay of factors that influence the Ugandan government's response to international advocacy efforts.

Positive trends in acceptance and inclusivity

In recent years, Uganda has witnessed a gradual shift towards greater acceptance and inclusivity of LGBTQ individuals within its society. This transformation, while still fraught with challenges, reflects a growing recognition of human rights and dignity for all individuals, regardless of their sexual orientation or gender identity. This section explores the positive trends in acceptance and inclusivity, highlighting key developments, societal changes, and the impact of advocacy efforts.

One of the most significant indicators of this positive trend is the increasing visibility of LGBTQ individuals in Ugandan society. As activists like Frank Mugisha have taken to the forefront, their stories and experiences have resonated with a broader audience, challenging stereotypes and prejudices. The narrative surrounding LGBTQ identities is slowly shifting from one of secrecy and shame to one of pride and visibility. This visibility has been facilitated by various media platforms, including social media, which have provided a space for LGBTQ voices to be heard and celebrated.

$$\text{Visibility} \propto \text{Awareness} + \text{Acceptance} \quad (40)$$

In this equation, we can see that the visibility of LGBTQ individuals is directly proportional to the awareness and acceptance within society. As more people become informed about LGBTQ issues, misconceptions are challenged, paving the way for acceptance.

Educational initiatives have also played a crucial role in fostering acceptance. Schools and universities are increasingly incorporating discussions about sexual orientation and gender identity into their curricula. Programs aimed at educating students about diversity and inclusion are essential in shaping young minds to be more accepting of differences. For example, organizations like the Uganda Youth Coalition for Sexual and Reproductive Health and Rights have implemented workshops and seminars that focus on human rights education, emphasizing the importance of inclusivity.

Furthermore, there has been a notable increase in supportive allies within the community. Religious and cultural leaders, once staunch opponents of LGBTQ rights, are beginning to engage in dialogues that promote understanding and acceptance. This shift is crucial, as these leaders hold significant influence over public opinion. Initiatives that bring together religious leaders to discuss the importance of love and acceptance, regardless of sexual orientation, have begun to bear fruit. This gradual change in perspective is indicative of a broader trend towards inclusivity.

$$\text{Inclusivity} = \text{Dialogue} + \text{Education} + \text{Empathy} \tag{41}$$

The equation above illustrates that inclusivity is achieved through a combination of dialogue, education, and empathy. The more these elements are integrated into societal discussions, the more inclusive the environment becomes.

Moreover, the rise of LGBTQ advocacy groups has created a supportive network that empowers individuals to embrace their identities without fear. Organizations like Sexual Minorities Uganda (SMUG) and the Uganda Queer Community have been instrumental in providing safe spaces for LGBTQ individuals. These organizations not only offer support but also engage in advocacy that seeks to change discriminatory laws and practices. The establishment of pride events and awareness campaigns has further contributed to a sense of community and belonging among LGBTQ individuals.

The impact of international solidarity movements cannot be overlooked. Global campaigns advocating for LGBTQ rights have influenced local attitudes, as Ugandans are increasingly aware of international perspectives on human rights. The support from international organizations has provided both resources and a platform for local activists to amplify their voices. This global interconnectedness has fostered a sense of unity and shared purpose among LGBTQ activists in Uganda.

$$\text{International Support} \rightarrow \text{Local Empowerment} \tag{42}$$

This relationship highlights how international support can lead to local empowerment, encouraging activists to continue their fight for rights and recognition.

Despite these positive trends, it is essential to recognize that challenges remain. Societal attitudes are not monolithic; there are still significant pockets of resistance and prejudice. However, the momentum generated by these positive changes is a testament to the resilience of the LGBTQ community in Uganda. The journey towards acceptance and inclusivity is ongoing, and each step forward is a victory in itself.

In conclusion, the positive trends in acceptance and inclusivity for LGBTQ individuals in Uganda signify a hopeful shift in societal attitudes. Through visibility, education, dialogue, and international support, the landscape is slowly changing. While the path ahead may be fraught with challenges, the progress made thus far lays a strong foundation for continued advocacy and the eventual realization of equality for all individuals, regardless of their sexual orientation or gender identity. The work of activists like Frank Mugisha serves as a beacon of hope, inspiring future generations to carry the torch of acceptance and inclusivity forward.

The continued fight for comprehensive legal protections

The struggle for comprehensive legal protections for LGBTQ individuals in Uganda is a multifaceted battle, deeply rooted in the sociopolitical landscape of the country. Despite some positive shifts in societal attitudes towards LGBTQ rights, the legal framework remains largely oppressive. The continued fight for legal protections is not only essential for the safety and dignity of LGBTQ individuals but also for the advancement of human rights as a whole.

1. The Current Legal Landscape

In Uganda, homosexuality is criminalized under the Penal Code, specifically Section 145, which prohibits "carnal knowledge against the order of nature." This law has been a significant barrier to the recognition and protection of LGBTQ rights. The criminalization of same-sex relationships fosters an environment of fear and discrimination, where LGBTQ individuals are subjected to harassment, violence, and systemic discrimination.

The lack of legal recognition extends to various aspects of life, including employment, healthcare, and housing. For instance, LGBTQ individuals often face discrimination in the workplace, where they can be fired or denied employment based solely on their sexual orientation. This systemic inequality is further exacerbated by the influence of religious conservatism, which plays a pivotal role in shaping public opinion and policy against LGBTQ rights.

2. Advocacy for Legal Reform

Advocating for comprehensive legal protections requires a strategic approach that involves multiple stakeholders. LGBTQ activists in Uganda, alongside international human rights organizations, are working tirelessly to challenge the existing legal framework. This advocacy often takes the form of public campaigns, legal challenges, and lobbying efforts directed at policymakers.

One notable example of advocacy in action is the work of organizations like Sexual Minorities Uganda (SMUG), which has been at the forefront of fighting for the rights of LGBTQ individuals. SMUG has engaged in legal battles to challenge discriminatory laws and has sought to raise awareness of the human rights violations faced by LGBTQ individuals in Uganda. Their efforts have included filing petitions with the Constitutional Court and collaborating with international bodies to bring attention to these issues.

3. The Role of International Human Rights Law

International human rights law plays a crucial role in the fight for LGBTQ rights in Uganda. Instruments such as the Universal Declaration of Human Rights and the International Covenant on Civil and Political Rights provide a framework for advocating for the rights of all individuals, regardless of their sexual orientation.

Activists often invoke these international treaties to pressure the Ugandan government to align its laws with global human rights standards. The role of international organizations, such as the United Nations and various NGOs, is vital in providing support and resources for local activists. These organizations can amplify the voices of Ugandan LGBTQ individuals, helping to bring their struggles to a global audience.

4. Challenges to Legal Protections

Despite the concerted efforts of activists and international allies, the path to comprehensive legal protections remains fraught with challenges. The entrenched homophobia within Ugandan society, fueled by cultural and religious beliefs, poses significant obstacles to legal reform. Politicians often exploit anti-LGBTQ sentiment to garner support, leading to a hostile environment for advocacy.

Additionally, the fear of backlash can deter individuals from coming forward to advocate for their rights. Many LGBTQ activists face threats to their safety and well-being, making it difficult to sustain momentum in the fight for legal protections. The risk of persecution is a constant reality, and many activists have had to navigate a precarious balance between visibility and safety.

5. Building a Coalition for Change

To overcome these challenges, it is essential to build a broad coalition that includes allies from various sectors of society. Engaging with human rights organizations, legal experts, and sympathetic political figures can create a more robust support system for LGBTQ advocacy.

One effective strategy has been to engage in intersectional advocacy, addressing not only LGBTQ rights but also other human rights issues that affect marginalized communities in Uganda. By framing the fight for LGBTQ rights as part of a larger struggle for human rights, activists can appeal to a wider audience and garner broader support.

6. Conclusion: A Vision for the Future

The continued fight for comprehensive legal protections for LGBTQ individuals in Uganda is a testament to the resilience and determination of activists who refuse to be silenced. As societal attitudes continue to evolve, there is hope that legal reforms will follow suit.

The journey towards equality is long and fraught with challenges, but with sustained advocacy, international support, and a commitment to human rights, the vision of a more inclusive Uganda can become a reality. It is imperative that the fight for legal protections remains at the forefront of LGBTQ activism, ensuring that future generations can live freely and authentically without fear of persecution.

In conclusion, the ongoing battle for comprehensive legal protections is not merely a legal issue; it is a fight for dignity, respect, and the right to love. The voices of LGBTQ individuals in Uganda must be amplified, their stories must be told, and their rights must be recognized. Only then can true progress be achieved in the quest for equality and justice.

The Shifting Political and Social Landscape

Political environments and LGBTQ rights

The political environment in Uganda has been a complex tapestry woven with threads of tradition, colonial legacy, and contemporary global influences. Understanding LGBTQ rights within this context requires an examination of how political structures, ideologies, and power dynamics shape the lived experiences of LGBTQ individuals in Uganda.

Historically, Uganda's legal framework regarding homosexuality can be traced back to colonial laws that criminalized same-sex relationships. The legacy of these laws persists, with sections of the Penal Code, such as Section 145 and Section 146, which criminalize "carnal knowledge against the order of nature" and "gross indecency," respectively. The continued existence of these laws reflects a political environment that is deeply entrenched in conservative values and influenced by both local cultural norms and international pressures.

In recent years, the political landscape has been marked by a notable rise in anti-LGBTQ rhetoric, often fueled by politicians seeking to consolidate power and appeal to a conservative electorate. This political maneuvering is exemplified by the introduction of the Anti-Homosexuality Bill in 2009, which sought to impose severe penalties for homosexuality, including life imprisonment and even the death penalty for "aggravated homosexuality." Although the bill faced significant international backlash and was eventually withdrawn, it underscored the precarious position of LGBTQ individuals in Uganda and the extent to which political environments can directly impact their rights.

The interplay between politics and religion further complicates the situation. Uganda is a predominantly Christian nation, and religious leaders have been vocal in their opposition to LGBTQ rights. The alignment of political leaders with religious sentiments creates a formidable barrier to progress. Politicians often invoke religious beliefs to justify discriminatory practices, framing LGBTQ rights as a threat to traditional family values. This rhetoric resonates with many Ugandans, reinforcing societal stigma and discrimination against LGBTQ individuals.

Furthermore, the political environment in Uganda is characterized by a lack of accountability and transparency. The government often employs tactics of intimidation and violence against LGBTQ activists and organizations, stifling dissent and silencing voices advocating for change. Activists face harassment, arbitrary arrests, and even violence, creating a climate of fear that hinders advocacy efforts. The absence of legal protections for LGBTQ individuals exacerbates their vulnerability, as they lack recourse against discrimination and violence.

Despite these challenges, there are glimmers of hope within the political landscape. The resilience of LGBTQ activists and organizations demonstrates a growing movement advocating for rights and recognition. Grassroots campaigns and international solidarity have gained traction, pushing back against oppressive policies and fostering a sense of community among LGBTQ individuals. Activists have employed various strategies, including public protests, media campaigns, and legal challenges, to raise awareness and advocate for change.

One notable example is the work of organizations like Sexual Minorities

Uganda (SMUG), which has been at the forefront of advocating for LGBTQ rights. Through legal advocacy, public education, and community mobilization, SMUG has challenged discriminatory practices and worked to create safer spaces for LGBTQ individuals. Their efforts have not only highlighted the struggles faced by LGBTQ individuals but have also fostered a sense of solidarity and empowerment within the community.

In conclusion, the political environment in Uganda presents significant challenges for LGBTQ rights, shaped by historical legacies, religious conservatism, and a lack of accountability. However, the resilience of activists and the growing movement for change indicate that the fight for LGBTQ rights continues to evolve. As the political landscape shifts, it is crucial to remain vigilant and engaged, advocating for a future where all individuals, regardless of their sexual orientation or gender identity, can live freely and authentically.

The influence of religious conservatism on LGBTQ issues

In Uganda, religious conservatism plays a significant role in shaping societal attitudes towards LGBTQ individuals and issues. The intertwining of religious beliefs with cultural norms creates a complex landscape where faith informs public opinion and policy-making, often to the detriment of LGBTQ rights. This subsection explores the influence of religious conservatism on LGBTQ issues in Uganda, highlighting the theoretical frameworks, problems, and real-world examples that illustrate this dynamic.

Theoretical Frameworks

The relationship between religion and sexuality can be understood through various theoretical lenses, including Social Identity Theory and the Theory of Moral Foundations. Social Identity Theory posits that individuals derive a part of their self-concept from their membership in social groups, including religious affiliations. In Uganda, the dominant Christian identity often emphasizes heteronormativity, marginalizing those who deviate from traditional sexual norms. This creates an environment where LGBTQ individuals are seen as outsiders, leading to stigmatization and discrimination.

The Theory of Moral Foundations, developed by Jonathan Haidt, suggests that moral reasoning is influenced by innate psychological mechanisms shaped by cultural contexts. In conservative religious communities, moral foundations often prioritize loyalty, authority, and sanctity, which can lead to the demonization of LGBTQ identities as threats to societal cohesion and religious values. This moral framing reinforces negative stereotypes and justifies discriminatory practices against LGBTQ individuals.

Problems Arising from Religious Conservatism

The influence of religious conservatism on LGBTQ issues in Uganda manifests in several ways:

- **Legislation and Policy:** Religious groups have been instrumental in advocating for anti-LGBTQ legislation, such as the Anti-Homosexuality Act of 2014, which sought to impose harsh penalties on LGBTQ individuals. Although the bill was annulled on procedural grounds, the influence of religious conservatism remains a potent force in Ugandan politics, with calls for similar legislation continuing to emerge.

- **Social Stigmatization:** Religious teachings that condemn homosexuality contribute to widespread social stigmatization of LGBTQ individuals. This stigma not only affects personal relationships but also leads to systemic discrimination in various sectors, including healthcare, education, and employment. LGBTQ individuals often face rejection from their families and communities, exacerbating feelings of isolation and despair.

- **Violence and Harassment:** The rhetoric propagated by religious leaders often incites violence against LGBTQ individuals. Reports of harassment, physical assaults, and even mob justice against perceived homosexuals have been documented, fueled by the belief that such individuals are morally corrupt and deserving of punishment. This climate of fear stifles advocacy efforts and discourages individuals from living openly.

- **Mental Health Impacts:** The internalization of religiously-based homophobia can lead to significant mental health challenges for LGBTQ individuals, including anxiety, depression, and suicidal ideation. The pressure to conform to conservative religious values often results in a profound conflict between personal identity and societal expectations, leading to a crisis of self-acceptance.

Examples of Religious Influence

Several notable examples illustrate the profound impact of religious conservatism on LGBTQ issues in Uganda:

- **Pastor Martin Ssempa:** A prominent Ugandan pastor, Martin Ssempa, has gained notoriety for his vehement anti-LGBTQ stance, often using his platform to promote hate speech and misinformation about homosexuality. His campaigns have included public demonstrations and the distribution of materials that portray LGBTQ individuals as threats to family values and societal stability. Ssempa's influence exemplifies how religious leaders can mobilize public sentiment against marginalized groups.

- **The Role of the Church:** The Ugandan church, particularly evangelical and Pentecostal denominations, has been a vocal opponent of LGBTQ rights. Church leaders often preach against homosexuality, framing it as a sin that must be eradicated. This rhetoric not only shapes congregational attitudes but also resonates with broader societal beliefs, reinforcing the stigma faced by LGBTQ individuals.

- **International Influence:** The influence of American evangelical groups has also played a role in shaping anti-LGBTQ sentiments in Uganda. These groups have provided funding and support for local religious organizations that promote anti-LGBTQ agendas, creating a transnational network of conservative ideology that further entrenches discrimination.

Conclusion

The influence of religious conservatism on LGBTQ issues in Uganda is profound and multifaceted, shaping public attitudes, policy decisions, and the lived experiences of LGBTQ individuals. As religious beliefs continue to inform societal norms, the struggle for LGBTQ rights remains fraught with challenges. Understanding the interplay between faith and sexuality is crucial for advocates seeking to promote acceptance and inclusivity in a context where religious conservatism wields significant power.

In order to create a more equitable society, it is essential to engage with religious communities in dialogue, challenging harmful narratives while also finding common ground on values of love, compassion, and human dignity. Only through such efforts can the tide of discrimination be turned, paving the way for a future where all individuals, regardless of their sexual orientation, are treated with respect and equality.

Challenges in changing political attitudes towards LGBTQ rights

Changing political attitudes towards LGBTQ rights in Uganda presents a multifaceted challenge that is deeply intertwined with cultural, religious, and socio-political dynamics. The resistance to LGBTQ rights is not merely a reflection of individual prejudices but is often rooted in broader societal norms and political strategies that prioritize traditional values over human rights. This subsection will explore the theoretical frameworks that explain these challenges, the specific problems faced by advocates, and relevant examples that illustrate the complexity of the situation.

Theoretical Frameworks

To understand the challenges in changing political attitudes, we can apply several theoretical perspectives, including Social Identity Theory and the Theory of Planned Behavior.

Social Identity Theory posits that individuals derive a sense of identity and self-esteem from their group memberships. In Uganda, where cultural identity is often closely linked to heteronormative values, any deviation from these norms can lead to social ostracism. As such, politicians may align themselves with anti-LGBTQ sentiments to secure their standing within their communities, fearing backlash if they support LGBTQ rights. The equation can be represented as:

$$\text{Social Identity} = f(\text{In-group identity}, \text{Out-group perception}) \quad (43)$$

Here, the function f demonstrates that the stronger the in-group identity (traditional values), the more negative the perception of the out-group (LGBTQ individuals).

The Theory of Planned Behavior suggests that attitudes towards a behavior (in this case, supporting LGBTQ rights) are influenced by subjective norms and perceived behavioral control. In Uganda, the subjective norm heavily favors conservative views, making it difficult for politicians to advocate for LGBTQ rights without facing significant social and political repercussions. The relationship can be expressed as:

$$\text{Behavioral Intention} = \text{Attitude} + \text{Subjective Norm} + \text{Perceived Behavioral Control} \quad (44)$$

This equation illustrates that even if an individual holds a positive attitude towards LGBTQ rights, the prevailing subjective norms can diminish their intention to act.

Specific Problems

The challenges faced by LGBTQ activists in Uganda can be categorized into several key areas:

1. **Political Repression:** The Ugandan government has a history of criminalizing homosexuality, with laws that not only punish same-sex relationships but also stigmatize LGBTQ individuals. The infamous Anti-Homosexuality Act of 2014, although annulled, set a precedent for political repression that continues to influence political attitudes. Politicians often exploit anti-LGBTQ rhetoric to galvanize support and distract from pressing socio-economic issues.

2. **Religious Influence:** Uganda is a deeply religious country, with a significant portion of the population adhering to conservative Christian values. Religious leaders often play a pivotal role in shaping public opinion against LGBTQ rights, framing these issues as moral crises. This influence creates a hostile environment for political change, as politicians may fear losing electoral support if they oppose the religious establishment.

3. **Cultural Norms and Stigma:** The cultural narrative surrounding LGBTQ identities in Uganda is predominantly negative, characterized by stereotypes and misconceptions. Such stigma not only affects public opinion but also discourages politicians from advocating for change. The fear of being labeled as "un-Ugandan" or "immoral" can stifle political discourse surrounding LGBTQ rights.

4. **Lack of Political Will:** Many politicians in Uganda prioritize their political survival over human rights advocacy. The perception that supporting LGBTQ rights could lead to electoral losses inhibits political engagement with these issues. This lack of political will is compounded by the absence of a strong, organized LGBTQ voting bloc, which diminishes the incentive for politicians to champion LGBTQ rights.

Examples and Case Studies

Several examples illustrate the challenges faced in changing political attitudes towards LGBTQ rights in Uganda:

- **David Bahati's Anti-Homosexuality Bill:** The introduction of this bill in 2009, which sought to impose the death penalty for certain homosexual acts, exemplifies how political figures can leverage anti-LGBTQ sentiments to gain popularity. The bill garnered widespread international condemnation, yet it was supported by many Ugandan politicians who viewed it as a means to rally conservative voters.

- **The Role of Religious Leaders**: Prominent religious figures, such as Pastor Martin Ssempa, have been vocal opponents of LGBTQ rights, using their platforms to spread misinformation and incite violence against LGBTQ individuals. Their influence over public opinion creates a significant barrier for politicians who might otherwise support LGBTQ rights.

- **The Impact of International Pressure:** While international advocacy for LGBTQ rights has increased, it often faces backlash in Uganda. Politicians may use foreign criticism as a rallying point to reinforce nationalist sentiments, framing LGBTQ rights as a Western imposition. This dynamic complicates efforts to shift political attitudes, as it can entrench resistance rather than promote dialogue.

In conclusion, the challenges in changing political attitudes towards LGBTQ rights in Uganda are deeply rooted in a complex interplay of social identity, cultural norms, and political repression. Understanding these dynamics is crucial for activists and allies seeking to foster meaningful change. By addressing the underlying theories, specific problems, and illustrative examples, we can better navigate the path toward a more inclusive political landscape in Uganda.

The role of public opinion in shaping policy decisions

Public opinion plays a pivotal role in the formulation and implementation of policies, particularly concerning sensitive issues such as LGBTQ rights in Uganda. The interplay between societal attitudes and legislative frameworks is complex and multifaceted, often influenced by cultural, religious, and political factors. Understanding this relationship is crucial for activists and policymakers alike.

Theoretical Frameworks

Theories of public opinion can be categorized into several frameworks that explain how opinions are formed, expressed, and translated into policy. One prominent theory is the **Agenda-Setting Theory**, which posits that media and public discourse can shape what issues are considered important by the public and policymakers. According to McCombs and Shaw (1972), the media doesn't tell people what to think, but rather what to think about. This is particularly relevant in the context of LGBTQ rights, where media representation can significantly influence societal perceptions.

Another important framework is the **Spiral of Silence Theory**, proposed by Elisabeth Noelle-Neumann. This theory suggests that individuals may withhold their opinions if they perceive themselves to be in the minority, which can lead to a skewed representation of public sentiment. In Uganda, where LGBTQ individuals often face severe discrimination and violence, many may choose to remain silent, thus perpetuating the cycle of oppression.

Public Opinion and Policy Formation

Public opinion can shape policy decisions through various mechanisms, including electoral pressures, advocacy campaigns, and social movements. In democratic societies, elected officials are often responsive to their constituents' views, as public approval can significantly impact their chances of re-election. For instance, when public opinion shifts towards greater acceptance of LGBTQ rights, politicians may feel compelled to advocate for legal protections and reforms to align with their constituents' values.

In Uganda, however, the political landscape is more complicated. The government has often leveraged negative public sentiment towards LGBTQ individuals to consolidate power, framing homosexuality as a Western import contrary to traditional Ugandan values. This manipulation of public opinion has resulted in policies that criminalize same-sex relationships, exemplified by the Anti-Homosexuality Act of 2014, which drew widespread international condemnation but was supported by segments of the Ugandan populace.

Case Studies and Examples

Several case studies illustrate the impact of public opinion on LGBTQ policy in Uganda. One notable example is the influence of religious organizations, particularly Evangelical churches, which have played a significant role in shaping public attitudes. These organizations often propagate anti-LGBTQ rhetoric, framing homosexuality as a moral failing. Their influence can be seen in the public support for anti-LGBTQ legislation, which often aligns with the teachings of these religious institutions.

Conversely, there have been instances where shifts in public opinion have led to positive changes. For example, the international visibility of LGBTQ issues, bolstered by social media campaigns and advocacy from global organizations, has begun to challenge the narrative within Uganda. Activists have utilized platforms like Twitter and Facebook to share personal stories and foster dialogue, creating a counter-narrative that emphasizes human rights and dignity for all individuals, regardless of sexual orientation.

Challenges and Barriers

Despite the potential for public opinion to effect change, several challenges hinder progress towards LGBTQ rights in Uganda. The pervasive stigma surrounding homosexuality often leads to fear and social ostracism for those who speak out. This fear is compounded by the threat of violence and legal repercussions, which can deter individuals from participating in advocacy efforts or expressing their views publicly.

Furthermore, the entrenched power of conservative groups, including religious institutions and political leaders, creates a formidable barrier to changing public opinion. These groups often dominate the discourse, framing LGBTQ rights as a threat to societal values, which can stifle more progressive voices and perpetuate discrimination.

Conclusion

In conclusion, public opinion is a powerful force in shaping policy decisions regarding LGBTQ rights in Uganda. While societal attitudes can pose significant challenges, they also hold the potential for transformative change. By fostering open dialogue, increasing visibility, and challenging discriminatory narratives, activists can work towards shifting public opinion in favor of inclusivity and acceptance. Ultimately, as public sentiment evolves, so too may the policies that govern the lives of LGBTQ individuals in Uganda, paving the way for a more just and equitable society.

Navigating societal divisions and tensions

Navigating societal divisions and tensions in Uganda regarding LGBTQ rights is akin to traversing a turbulent sea, where waves of cultural beliefs, religious conservatism, and political agendas collide with the aspirations for equality and acceptance. In this complex landscape, LGBTQ activists like Frank Mugisha face the daunting task of addressing not only the external challenges posed by societal norms but also the internal divisions within the LGBTQ community itself.

Cultural Beliefs and Normative Pressures

Uganda's cultural beliefs are deeply rooted in traditional values that often view homosexuality as taboo. This cultural backdrop creates a hostile environment for LGBTQ individuals, leading to widespread discrimination and violence. The pervasive belief that homosexuality is unnatural is often reinforced by religious teachings, particularly from evangelical and conservative factions. For instance, the anti-LGBTQ rhetoric espoused by influential religious leaders has significant sway over public opinion, making it difficult for activists to advocate for change.

The impact of these cultural beliefs can be illustrated through the case of the 2014 Anti-Homosexuality Act, which, despite being struck down by the Constitutional Court, demonstrated the extent to which societal attitudes can influence legislation. The act was fueled by a moral panic that portrayed LGBTQ individuals as threats to the fabric of Ugandan society. Activists had to navigate these cultural waters carefully, employing strategies that resonate with the values of the broader population while advocating for human rights.

Religious Conservatism and Its Influence

The role of religion in shaping societal attitudes towards LGBTQ issues cannot be overstated. In Uganda, many religious institutions actively promote anti-LGBTQ sentiments, framing homosexuality as a sin. This religious conservatism exacerbates societal divisions, creating an environment where LGBTQ individuals are often ostracized.

For example, during public debates on LGBTQ rights, religious leaders frequently invoke scripture to justify discrimination, further polarizing the discourse. Activists, therefore, must find ways to engage with religious communities, encouraging dialogue that emphasizes compassion and understanding. Initiatives that promote interfaith discussions can serve as platforms for bridging divides, allowing for a re-examination of religious texts through a lens of love and acceptance.

Political Dynamics and Divisions

The political landscape in Uganda presents additional challenges, as politicians often exploit societal divisions for electoral gain. The use of anti-LGBTQ legislation as a rallying point can galvanize support among conservative constituents. This political maneuvering complicates advocacy efforts, as activists must contend with leaders who prioritize their political survival over the rights of marginalized communities.

One notable example is the 2017 parliamentary discussions surrounding the reintroduction of anti-LGBTQ legislation. Politicians leveraged public sentiment against LGBTQ individuals to bolster their platforms, creating a climate of fear and hostility. To counteract this, activists have focused on building coalitions with progressive political figures and leveraging international human rights frameworks to advocate for change.

Internal Divisions within the LGBTQ Community

While external societal tensions pose significant challenges, internal divisions within the LGBTQ community can also hinder progress. Differences in identity, race, class, and gender expression can lead to fragmentation, making it difficult to present a united front. For instance, the experiences of queer individuals may differ vastly from those of transgender individuals, leading to divergent priorities and strategies within the movement.

To navigate these internal tensions, it is essential to foster inclusivity and solidarity among diverse groups within the LGBTQ community. This can be achieved through community-building initiatives that emphasize shared goals and collective action. Workshops and training sessions that address intersectionality can help activists understand and appreciate the varied experiences within the community, ultimately strengthening their advocacy efforts.

Strategies for Bridging Divides

To effectively navigate societal divisions and tensions, activists must employ multifaceted strategies:

- **Education and Awareness:** Initiatives aimed at educating the public about LGBTQ issues can help dispel myths and reduce stigma. Collaborating with local universities and schools to incorporate LGBTQ topics into curricula can foster a more informed and accepting society.

- **Community Engagement:** Creating spaces for dialogue between LGBTQ individuals and the broader community can facilitate understanding. Community forums that invite participation from various stakeholders, including religious leaders, can help bridge gaps and promote empathy.

- **Advocacy through Art and Culture:** Utilizing art and culture as tools for advocacy can resonate deeply with Ugandan society. By showcasing LGBTQ stories through theater, music, and visual arts, activists can humanize their struggles and foster connections with wider audiences.

- **Building Alliances:** Forming alliances with other marginalized groups can amplify voices and create a stronger front against discrimination. Collaborating with women's rights organizations, for instance, can highlight the intersectionality of oppression and foster solidarity.

- **Leveraging International Support:** Engaging with international human rights organizations can provide crucial support and resources. By highlighting Uganda's human rights obligations on global platforms, activists can apply pressure on local leaders to foster change.

Conclusion

Navigating societal divisions and tensions in Uganda is a complex endeavor that requires resilience, creativity, and strategic engagement. By addressing cultural beliefs, religious conservatism, political dynamics, and internal community divisions, LGBTQ activists can work towards a more inclusive society. The journey may be fraught with challenges, but through collective action and unwavering commitment, progress is possible. As Frank Mugisha and his fellow activists continue to advocate for LGBTQ rights, they embody the spirit of perseverance and hope, inspiring future generations to join the fight for equality and justice.

Challenges and Opportunities Ahead

Addressing the ongoing threats and challenges to LGBTQ rights

The struggle for LGBTQ rights in Uganda is fraught with ongoing threats and challenges that stem from a complex interplay of cultural, political, and social factors. Despite the remarkable strides made by activists like Frank Mugisha, the fight for equality remains an uphill battle, marred by systemic discrimination and societal backlash.

1. The Cultural Context

In Uganda, deeply rooted cultural norms and traditional beliefs often dictate attitudes towards LGBTQ individuals. The prevailing view is that homosexuality is a Western import, leading to a pervasive sense of otherness among LGBTQ individuals. This perception fosters an environment where discrimination is not only socially acceptable but also legally sanctioned. The Ugandan Penal Code criminalizes same-sex relationships, imposing harsh penalties that perpetuate fear and silence within the community.

$$\text{Discrimination} = \text{Cultural Beliefs} + \text{Legal Framework} + \text{Social Norms} \quad (45)$$

CHALLENGES AND OPPORTUNITIES AHEAD

This equation illustrates how the combination of cultural beliefs, legal frameworks, and social norms creates a formidable barrier to the acceptance of LGBTQ rights. Activists face the daunting task of challenging these entrenched beliefs while advocating for legal reforms.

2. Political Landscape

The political landscape in Uganda poses significant challenges to the advancement of LGBTQ rights. The government has historically leveraged anti-LGBTQ sentiment to galvanize support, often using the community as a scapegoat for broader societal issues. Politicians frequently resort to inflammatory rhetoric, portraying LGBTQ individuals as threats to national security and moral integrity. This political exploitation not only endangers the lives of LGBTQ individuals but also undermines the efforts of activists striving for change.

$$\text{Political Exploitation} = \text{Rhetoric} + \text{Scapegoating} + \text{Fear-Mongering} \quad (46)$$

The equation above highlights the mechanisms through which political exploitation occurs, demonstrating how rhetoric, scapegoating, and fear-mongering contribute to a hostile environment for LGBTQ rights.

3. Societal Backlash

The societal backlash against LGBTQ individuals in Uganda manifests in various forms, including violence, harassment, and discrimination. Reports of mob violence against perceived LGBTQ individuals are not uncommon, with many victims suffering serious injuries or even death. This climate of fear discourages individuals from openly identifying as LGBTQ, leading to a culture of secrecy and shame.

$$\text{Societal Backlash} = \text{Violence} + \text{Harassment} + \text{Discrimination} \quad (47)$$

The societal backlash equation encapsulates the multifaceted nature of the threats faced by LGBTQ individuals, emphasizing the urgent need for protective measures and community support.

4. Mental Health Implications

The ongoing threats to LGBTQ rights in Uganda have profound implications for mental health. The constant fear of violence and discrimination can lead to anxiety, depression, and other mental health issues. Many LGBTQ individuals report feeling isolated and unsupported, further exacerbating their struggles.

$$\text{Mental Health Impact} = \text{Fear} + \text{Isolation} + \text{Discrimination} \qquad (48)$$

This equation illustrates the direct correlation between the ongoing threats to LGBTQ rights and the mental health challenges faced by individuals within the community.

5. Resistance and Resilience

Despite these challenges, the LGBTQ community in Uganda continues to demonstrate remarkable resilience and resistance. Activists are employing innovative strategies to combat discrimination and raise awareness. For instance, grassroots organizations are increasingly utilizing social media to amplify their voices and mobilize support, creating a sense of community and solidarity among LGBTQ individuals.

$$\text{Resistance} = \text{Community Mobilization} + \text{Awareness Campaigns} + \text{Support Networks} \qquad (49)$$

This equation highlights the proactive measures being taken by activists to counteract the threats they face, emphasizing the importance of community mobilization, awareness campaigns, and support networks in the fight for LGBTQ rights.

In conclusion, addressing the ongoing threats and challenges to LGBTQ rights in Uganda requires a multifaceted approach that encompasses cultural, political, and social dimensions. Activists like Frank Mugisha serve as beacons of hope, inspiring a new generation of advocates to continue the fight for equality. The journey is fraught with obstacles, but the resilience of the LGBTQ community is a testament to the enduring spirit of activism in the face of adversity. The path forward demands unwavering solidarity, strategic advocacy, and a commitment to dismantling the barriers that hinder progress.

Building alliances and coalitions for change

The journey toward achieving LGBTQ rights in Uganda is not a solitary endeavor; it requires the collective strength of diverse voices united for a common cause. Building alliances and coalitions is essential for fostering change, as it amplifies the impact of advocacy efforts and creates a broader support network. This section explores the theoretical underpinnings of coalition-building, the challenges faced in the Ugandan context, and successful examples of collaborative efforts that have made a difference.

Theoretical Framework of Coalition-Building

Coalition-building can be understood through various theoretical lenses, including social movement theory and intersectionality. Social movement theory emphasizes the importance of collective action and the mobilization of resources to challenge systemic injustices. According to Tilly and Tarrow (2015), social movements are driven by grievances that compel individuals to unite and advocate for change. In the context of LGBTQ rights, the shared experiences of discrimination and marginalization serve as powerful motivators for coalition-building.

Intersectionality, a concept coined by Kimberlé Crenshaw (1989), further enriches our understanding of coalition dynamics. It posits that individuals possess multiple, intersecting identities that influence their experiences of oppression and privilege. By recognizing the diverse identities within the LGBTQ community—such as race, gender, and socioeconomic status—coalitions can develop more inclusive and effective strategies for advocacy. This approach not only fosters solidarity among LGBTQ individuals but also encourages allies from various backgrounds to join the fight for equality.

Challenges in Coalition-Building

Despite the potential benefits of alliances, several challenges can hinder the formation and sustainability of coalitions in Uganda. One significant barrier is the pervasive stigma surrounding LGBTQ identities, which can lead to mistrust among potential allies. Many individuals may fear backlash from their communities or face personal repercussions for associating with LGBTQ causes. This fear can create a reluctance to engage in coalition-building efforts, limiting the diversity of voices in advocacy.

Additionally, cultural and political contexts in Uganda often prioritize heteronormative values, further complicating coalition dynamics. Religious institutions, for instance, wield considerable influence and frequently oppose LGBTQ rights, framing advocacy efforts as a threat to traditional family values. This opposition can alienate potential allies who may be sympathetic to LGBTQ causes but are hesitant to publicly support them due to fear of ostracism or backlash from their communities.

Examples of Successful Coalitions

Despite these challenges, several successful coalitions have emerged in Uganda, demonstrating the power of collective action. One notable example is the formation of the *Coalition of African Lesbians (CAL)*, which unites LGBTQ activists from across the continent to address shared challenges and advocate for rights at both national and regional levels. CAL's collaborative approach has enabled members to share resources, strategies, and experiences, fostering a sense of solidarity that transcends national borders.

Another example is the *Uganda LGBTQ Coalition*, which brings together various LGBTQ organizations and allies to coordinate advocacy efforts and amplify their collective voice. This coalition has played a pivotal role in organizing public demonstrations, engaging with policymakers, and raising awareness about LGBTQ issues in Uganda. By pooling resources and expertise, coalition members have been able to navigate the complex political landscape more effectively than they could individually.

Strategies for Effective Coalition-Building

To build effective alliances and coalitions for change, several strategies can be employed:

1. **Establishing Common Goals:** Coalition members must identify shared objectives that resonate with all participants. This involves open dialogue and negotiation to ensure that diverse perspectives are acknowledged and integrated into the coalition's mission.

2. **Fostering Trust and Communication:** Building trust among coalition members is crucial for collaboration. Regular communication, transparency, and inclusive decision-making processes can help cultivate a sense of belonging and shared purpose.

3. **Engaging Allies:** Expanding the coalition to include allies from various sectors—such as healthcare, education, and legal advocacy—can strengthen the movement. Allies can leverage their platforms and resources to amplify LGBTQ voices and advocate for policy changes.

4. **Utilizing Digital Platforms:** In an increasingly digital world, social media and online networks can serve as powerful tools for coalition-building. These platforms enable activists to connect, share information, and mobilize support for campaigns, transcending geographical barriers.

5. **Training and Capacity Building:** Providing training and resources to coalition members can enhance their advocacy skills and empower them to take on leadership roles within the movement. This investment in capacity building fosters sustainability and resilience within the coalition.

Conclusion

Building alliances and coalitions for change is a vital component of the fight for LGBTQ rights in Uganda. By leveraging the collective power of diverse voices, activists can challenge systemic injustices and advocate for meaningful change. Despite the challenges posed by stigma and cultural opposition, successful examples of coalition-building demonstrate the potential for solidarity and collaboration to drive progress. As the movement continues to evolve, fostering inclusive alliances will be essential for sustaining momentum and achieving lasting change in the pursuit of LGBTQ rights.

The importance of engaging with youth and future generations

Engaging with youth and future generations is paramount in the fight for LGBTQ rights, particularly in a context like Uganda where societal attitudes are often steeped in conservatism and discrimination. The youth represent not only the future of the LGBTQ movement but also a critical demographic capable of driving change through their energy, creativity, and adaptability. This section delves into the theoretical underpinnings, practical challenges, and real-world examples that highlight the significance of youth engagement in advocacy efforts.

Theoretical Foundations

The importance of youth engagement can be understood through several theoretical frameworks. One such framework is the **Social Change Theory**, which posits that social movements are driven by collective action and participation from various societal segments. Youth, with their unique perspectives and experiences, can significantly contribute to the narrative and strategies employed in advocacy work.

Moreover, the **Youth Empowerment Theory** emphasizes the need to equip young individuals with the tools, knowledge, and confidence necessary to advocate for their rights and the rights of others. This empowerment is crucial in fostering a sense of ownership and responsibility among youth, enabling them to become effective advocates for change.

Challenges in Engaging Youth

Despite the clear benefits of engaging youth, several challenges persist. One significant issue is the pervasive **homophobia** and **transphobia** embedded within many educational and social institutions. Young LGBTQ individuals often face bullying, ostracization, and violence, which can deter them from participating in advocacy initiatives.

Furthermore, societal norms and expectations can stifle youth voices, particularly in conservative cultures where discussing sexuality is taboo. This creates a barrier to open dialogue, making it difficult for young activists to express their identities and advocate for their rights.

Another challenge is the **digital divide**, where access to technology and the internet can be limited for many young people, particularly in rural areas. This divide restricts their ability to engage with broader movements and access vital resources that could aid their activism.

Strategies for Engagement

To effectively engage youth, it is essential to develop targeted strategies that resonate with their experiences and aspirations. Here are several approaches that have proven effective:

1. **Creating Safe Spaces**: Establishing safe, inclusive environments where young LGBTQ individuals can express themselves without fear of judgment or reprisal is fundamental. These spaces can be physical, such as community centers, or virtual, through online platforms that promote dialogue and connection.

2. **Educational Programs**: Implementing educational initiatives that focus on LGBTQ rights, history, and advocacy can empower youth with knowledge and skills. Workshops, seminars, and peer-led discussions can facilitate learning and encourage active participation in the movement.

3. **Mentorship Opportunities**: Pairing young activists with experienced mentors in the LGBTQ community can provide invaluable support and guidance. Mentorship fosters a sense of belonging and helps youth navigate the complexities of activism while building their confidence.

4. **Utilizing Social Media**: Social media platforms are powerful tools for youth engagement. They provide a space for young activists to share their stories, connect with peers, and mobilize support. Campaigns that encourage youth to use their voices online can amplify their impact and reach a broader audience.

5. **Incorporating Youth Perspectives**: It is crucial to actively listen to and incorporate the perspectives of young people in advocacy strategies. Engaging youth

in decision-making processes ensures that their voices are heard and that initiatives reflect their needs and aspirations.

Real-World Examples

Several organizations and initiatives have successfully engaged youth in LGBTQ advocacy, providing models for future efforts. One notable example is the **Youth Empowerment Project** in Uganda, which focuses on training young LGBTQ individuals in advocacy skills, leadership, and community organizing. Through workshops and mentorship programs, participants have been empowered to lead local initiatives and advocate for their rights.

Additionally, the **Queer Youth Network** has utilized social media to create a platform for young LGBTQ individuals to share their stories and connect with allies. Their campaigns have raised awareness about the challenges faced by LGBTQ youth and have mobilized support from both local and international communities.

Furthermore, the annual **Pride Youth Summit** serves as a gathering for young activists to share ideas, network, and collaborate on advocacy projects. This event not only fosters community but also provides a space for young people to learn from one another and develop their activism skills.

Conclusion

Engaging with youth and future generations is not just beneficial; it is essential for the sustainability and effectiveness of the LGBTQ rights movement in Uganda. By empowering young individuals, creating safe spaces, and utilizing innovative strategies, the movement can harness the passion and creativity of youth to drive meaningful change. As we look to the future, it is imperative that we invest in the next generation of advocates, ensuring that they have the tools and support necessary to continue the fight for equality and justice. In doing so, we not only honor the struggles of those who came before but also inspire a new wave of activism that champions love, acceptance, and human rights for all.

Nurturing LGBTQ-friendly spaces and communities

Creating and nurturing LGBTQ-friendly spaces and communities is essential for fostering acceptance, support, and resilience among LGBTQ individuals. These spaces serve as sanctuaries where individuals can express their identities freely, connect with others who share similar experiences, and mobilize for collective action.

Theoretical Framework

The concept of safe spaces is rooted in social identity theory, which posits that individuals derive part of their identity from the groups to which they belong. For LGBTQ individuals, the existence of supportive environments can enhance their sense of belonging and self-worth. According to [1], social identity can significantly influence one's self-esteem and overall mental health. Thus, nurturing LGBTQ-friendly spaces is not merely a matter of comfort; it is a critical component of well-being.

Identifying Problems

Despite the importance of these spaces, several challenges hinder their development:

- **Stigmatization:** Many LGBTQ individuals face stigma and discrimination, which can lead to isolation and a reluctance to seek out supportive communities. This stigma is often perpetuated by societal norms and cultural beliefs that marginalize LGBTQ identities.

- **Lack of Resources:** Many LGBTQ organizations operate with limited funding and resources, making it difficult to establish and maintain safe spaces. This scarcity can result in fewer opportunities for community engagement and support.

- **Safety Concerns:** In regions where LGBTQ rights are not protected, individuals may fear for their safety when accessing LGBTQ-friendly spaces. Instances of violence and harassment can deter participation and engagement in these communities.

Examples of Successful Initiatives

Despite these challenges, numerous initiatives have successfully nurtured LGBTQ-friendly spaces:

- **Community Centers:** Organizations such as the *LGBTQ Community Center* in New York City provide vital resources, including counseling, social activities, and educational programs. These centers foster a sense of belonging and empower individuals to engage with their communities.

- **Online Platforms:** In the digital age, online communities have emerged as essential safe spaces. Websites and social media platforms dedicated to

LGBTQ issues allow individuals to connect, share experiences, and mobilize for advocacy. For example, platforms like *Tumblr* and *Reddit* have been instrumental in creating virtual safe spaces for LGBTQ youth.

- **Support Groups:** Many organizations offer support groups tailored for specific demographics within the LGBTQ community. For instance, PFLAG provides support for parents and allies of LGBTQ individuals, fostering understanding and acceptance within families.

Strategies for Nurturing LGBTQ-Friendly Spaces

To effectively nurture LGBTQ-friendly spaces, several strategies can be employed:

- **Education and Awareness:** Raising awareness about LGBTQ issues within the broader community can help reduce stigma and promote acceptance. Workshops, seminars, and outreach programs can educate individuals about the importance of inclusivity and diversity.

- **Collaboration with Allies:** Building alliances with allies and advocacy groups can amplify efforts to create safe spaces. By collaborating with organizations that share similar goals, LGBTQ groups can pool resources and expand their reach.

- **Creating Inclusive Policies:** Establishing clear policies that promote inclusivity and protect against discrimination is vital for the sustainability of LGBTQ-friendly spaces. This includes implementing anti-discrimination policies in schools, workplaces, and community organizations.

- **Empowerment through Leadership:** Encouraging LGBTQ individuals to take on leadership roles within their communities fosters a sense of ownership and responsibility. Leadership training programs can equip individuals with the skills needed to advocate for their rights and the rights of others.

Conclusion

Nurturing LGBTQ-friendly spaces and communities is a fundamental aspect of promoting acceptance, resilience, and empowerment among LGBTQ individuals. By addressing the challenges they face and implementing effective strategies, we can create environments where everyone can thrive authentically. These spaces not only provide refuge but also serve as catalysts for broader societal change, fostering a culture of understanding and respect for all identities.

The role of education in promoting acceptance and understanding

Education serves as a powerful tool in shaping societal attitudes and fostering acceptance, particularly regarding marginalized communities such as the LGBTQ population. By integrating LGBTQ issues into educational curricula, schools can cultivate an environment of understanding and empathy, ultimately reducing discrimination and promoting equality. This section explores the theoretical frameworks that underpin the role of education in promoting acceptance, the challenges faced in implementing inclusive education, and successful examples that illustrate the positive impact of education on societal attitudes towards LGBTQ individuals.

Theoretical Frameworks

Several theoretical frameworks provide insight into how education can foster acceptance and understanding of LGBTQ issues. One prominent theory is the **Social Learning Theory**, proposed by Albert Bandura, which posits that individuals learn behaviors and attitudes through observation and imitation of others. In the context of LGBTQ education, when students observe positive representations of LGBTQ individuals and receive affirming messages about diversity, they are more likely to adopt inclusive attitudes.

Another relevant framework is the **Critical Pedagogy** approach, championed by Paulo Freire. This theory emphasizes the importance of dialogue and critical reflection in education, encouraging students to question societal norms and engage in discussions about power dynamics and injustices. By incorporating LGBTQ topics into the curriculum, educators can challenge heteronormative assumptions and promote critical consciousness among students.

Challenges in Implementing Inclusive Education

Despite the potential benefits of LGBTQ-inclusive education, several challenges hinder its implementation. One significant barrier is the **lack of training** for educators. Many teachers may feel uncomfortable discussing LGBTQ topics due to their own biases or a lack of knowledge. This discomfort can lead to avoidance of the subject altogether, perpetuating ignorance and stigma.

Additionally, **cultural and religious beliefs** often play a significant role in shaping attitudes toward LGBTQ issues. In many societies, traditional beliefs may conflict with the principles of inclusivity and acceptance, leading to resistance against LGBTQ-inclusive curricula. As a result, educators may face pushback from parents, community members, or school administrations when attempting to introduce LGBTQ topics into the classroom.

Successful Examples of LGBTQ Education

Despite these challenges, there are numerous examples of successful LGBTQ-inclusive education initiatives that have positively impacted societal attitudes. For instance, in the United States, the **Safe Schools Coalition** has worked to create supportive environments for LGBTQ students by providing training and resources for educators. Schools that have adopted the coalition's guidelines have reported a decrease in bullying and increased feelings of safety among LGBTQ students.

Another notable example is the **No Outsiders** project in the United Kingdom, which aims to promote diversity and inclusion in primary schools. By incorporating LGBTQ themes into storybooks and lesson plans, the program has successfully fostered understanding and acceptance among young children. Research evaluating the project has shown significant improvements in students' attitudes toward LGBTQ individuals, demonstrating the effectiveness of early intervention through education.

The Impact of Education on Societal Attitudes

The impact of education on societal attitudes towards LGBTQ individuals is profound. Studies have shown that individuals who receive LGBTQ-inclusive education are more likely to support LGBTQ rights and advocate for equality. For instance, a study conducted by the **Williams Institute** found that exposure to LGBTQ-inclusive curricula in schools correlated with increased support for same-sex marriage and anti-discrimination laws among students.

Furthermore, education plays a crucial role in combating stereotypes and misconceptions about LGBTQ individuals. By providing accurate information and diverse representations, educational institutions can dismantle harmful narratives that perpetuate discrimination. For example, incorporating LGBTQ history and contributions into social studies curricula can help students understand the rich tapestry of human experiences and the importance of inclusivity.

Conclusion

In conclusion, education is a vital component in promoting acceptance and understanding of LGBTQ issues. By integrating inclusive curricula, providing training for educators, and fostering supportive environments, schools can play a transformative role in shaping societal attitudes. While challenges remain, successful initiatives demonstrate that education can lead to significant changes in perceptions and behaviors towards LGBTQ individuals. As we envision a future where acceptance and understanding are the norms, the importance of education in this journey cannot be overstated. By empowering future generations through knowledge, we can cultivate a society that values diversity and champions equality for all.

Strategies for Continued Advocacy and Change

Policy advocacy and legal reform efforts

The path towards achieving meaningful change in LGBTQ rights in Uganda is intrinsically linked to effective policy advocacy and legal reform efforts. This section delves into the theoretical frameworks that underpin advocacy, the challenges faced, and the successful examples that illuminate the way forward.

Theoretical Frameworks of Advocacy

Policy advocacy is grounded in several theoretical frameworks that guide activists in their efforts to influence legislation and public policy. One prominent theory is the **Advocacy Coalition Framework (ACF)**, which posits that policy change occurs through the collaboration of various stakeholders who share a common belief system. This framework emphasizes the importance of coalitions formed by activists, legal experts, and sympathetic policymakers who work together to promote LGBTQ rights.

Another important theory is the **Social Movement Theory**, which explores how collective action can lead to social change. This theory highlights the role of grassroots movements in mobilizing communities and raising awareness about LGBTQ issues, thereby pressuring the government to enact legal reforms.

Challenges in Policy Advocacy

Despite the theoretical frameworks that guide advocacy efforts, LGBTQ activists in Uganda face significant challenges. One major obstacle is the entrenched **homophobia** within Ugandan society, which is often reinforced by cultural and religious beliefs. This societal stigma creates a hostile environment for advocates, making it difficult to garner public support for legal reforms.

Moreover, the **political landscape** in Uganda is fraught with resistance to LGBTQ rights. Politicians often exploit anti-LGBTQ sentiments to gain popularity, leading to the introduction of draconian laws. For instance, the proposed Anti-Homosexuality Bill of 2014 sought to impose severe penalties on LGBTQ individuals, including life imprisonment. Such political maneuvers not only hinder advocacy efforts but also create a climate of fear among activists.

Examples of Successful Advocacy and Legal Reform

Despite these challenges, there have been notable successes in policy advocacy and legal reform efforts aimed at promoting LGBTQ rights in Uganda. One significant example is the collaboration between local NGOs and international human rights organizations. Through these partnerships, activists have been able to leverage international pressure to advocate for legal protections.

A prime instance of this is the **"Free to Be" campaign**, which aimed to raise awareness about LGBTQ rights and mobilize support for legal reform. The campaign utilized various strategies, including public demonstrations, social media outreach, and community engagement, to challenge the prevailing narratives around LGBTQ individuals.

Another successful initiative is the establishment of legal aid clinics that provide support to LGBTQ individuals facing discrimination. These clinics not only offer legal assistance but also serve as educational platforms to inform individuals about their rights. By empowering the community with knowledge, activists are fostering a culture of resistance against discriminatory practices.

The Role of International Support

International support plays a crucial role in bolstering local advocacy efforts. Collaborations with global LGBTQ organizations have proven effective in amplifying the voices of Ugandan activists. For example, organizations such as **Human Rights Watch** and **Amnesty International** have provided critical resources and platforms for local activists to share their experiences on international stages.

Moreover, international human rights treaties, such as the **Universal Declaration of Human Rights**, serve as foundational documents that activists can reference in their advocacy efforts. These treaties provide a legal basis for demanding equal rights and protections for LGBTQ individuals, thereby strengthening the case for legal reform.

Conclusion

In conclusion, policy advocacy and legal reform efforts are essential components of the struggle for LGBTQ rights in Uganda. While challenges such as societal stigma and political resistance persist, the theoretical frameworks of advocacy, successful campaigns, and international support provide a pathway for progress. By continuing to build coalitions, engage with policymakers, and mobilize public support, activists can work towards a more inclusive legal framework that recognizes and protects the rights of LGBTQ individuals in Uganda. The journey may be fraught with obstacles, but the resilience and determination of activists pave the way for a brighter future.

Strengthening LGBTQ organizations and networks

The landscape of LGBTQ advocacy in Uganda is marked by both resilience and challenges. Strengthening LGBTQ organizations and networks is essential for fostering a united front against discrimination and promoting the rights of LGBTQ individuals. This subsection explores the theoretical frameworks, existing problems, and practical examples of how to enhance the effectiveness of LGBTQ organizations in Uganda.

Theoretical Frameworks

To understand the importance of strengthening LGBTQ organizations, we can draw upon several theoretical frameworks:

- **Social Capital Theory:** This theory posits that social networks have value and can facilitate collective action. For LGBTQ organizations, building social capital through connections with allies, activists, and community members can enhance their capacity to advocate for change. The equation representing social capital can be expressed as:

$$SC = \sum_{i=1}^{n}(C_i + R_i + N_i) \qquad (50)$$

where SC is social capital, C_i represents the connections, R_i represents the resources, and N_i represents the networks of each individual i.

- **Intersectionality:** This framework emphasizes the interconnected nature of social categorizations such as race, class, and gender. LGBTQ organizations must adopt an intersectional approach to address the unique challenges faced by individuals at the intersections of multiple identities. This is crucial

STRATEGIES FOR CONTINUED ADVOCACY AND CHANGE   289

for creating inclusive spaces that cater to the diverse needs of the LGBTQ community.

- **Collective Efficacy:** This concept refers to a community's ability to work together effectively to achieve common goals. Strengthening LGBTQ organizations can enhance collective efficacy, enabling members to mobilize resources, share knowledge, and strategize for advocacy efforts.

Existing Problems

Despite the critical role LGBTQ organizations play, several challenges hinder their effectiveness:

- **Limited Resources:** Many LGBTQ organizations operate on shoestring budgets, relying heavily on donations and volunteer work. This financial instability limits their capacity to implement programs, conduct outreach, and sustain advocacy efforts.

- **Governmental Repression:** The Ugandan government has historically targeted LGBTQ organizations, leading to closures, arrests, and harassment. This repression creates an environment of fear that stifles organizational growth and collaboration.

- **Fragmentation:** The LGBTQ movement in Uganda is often fragmented, with various groups focusing on specific issues, such as health, legal rights, or social acceptance. This fragmentation can lead to competition for limited resources rather than collaboration, weakening the overall movement.

- **Cultural Stigmatization:** Cultural attitudes towards homosexuality in Uganda remain largely negative, which can deter individuals from openly engaging with LGBTQ organizations. This stigmatization can also lead to a lack of public support and funding.

Practical Examples

To address these challenges and strengthen LGBTQ organizations, several strategies can be employed:

- **Capacity Building:** Training programs focusing on leadership, advocacy, and organizational management can empower LGBTQ activists. For example, workshops led by experienced activists can provide valuable skills in fundraising, project management, and media engagement.

- **Coalition Building:** Encouraging collaboration among LGBTQ organizations can foster a sense of unity and shared purpose. Initiatives like the *Coalition of African Lesbians* exemplify how collective action can amplify voices and resources, leading to more significant impact.

- **Community Engagement:** Building strong relationships with local communities can enhance visibility and support for LGBTQ organizations. Outreach programs that educate the public about LGBTQ issues can help combat stigma and foster acceptance.

- **Leveraging Technology:** Utilizing social media and digital platforms can facilitate networking and resource sharing among LGBTQ organizations. For instance, platforms like *Facebook* and *Twitter* have been instrumental in mobilizing support for LGBTQ rights and raising awareness about issues faced by the community.

- **International Partnerships:** Forming alliances with international LGBTQ organizations can provide critical resources and support. Collaborations with groups such as *Human Rights Watch* and *ILGA* (International Lesbian, Gay, Bisexual, Trans and Intersex Association) can enhance advocacy efforts and provide access to funding and legal expertise.

Conclusion

Strengthening LGBTQ organizations and networks in Uganda is a multifaceted endeavor that requires addressing theoretical frameworks, existing problems, and practical strategies. By enhancing social capital, adopting an intersectional approach, and fostering collective efficacy, LGBTQ organizations can create a more robust and united movement. Through capacity building, coalition building, community engagement, leveraging technology, and forming international partnerships, the LGBTQ community can better advocate for their rights and create a more inclusive society. The journey towards equality is ongoing, but with strengthened organizations, there is hope for a brighter future for LGBTQ individuals in Uganda.

Engaging with political leaders and influencers

Engaging with political leaders and influencers is a crucial strategy in the fight for LGBTQ rights in Uganda. This engagement not only helps to raise awareness about the challenges faced by the LGBTQ community but also fosters the

STRATEGIES FOR CONTINUED ADVOCACY AND CHANGE

potential for meaningful legislative changes and social acceptance. The process of engaging with these key stakeholders involves a multifaceted approach that includes building relationships, advocating for policy changes, and leveraging the influence of prominent figures to amplify the message of equality and justice.

Understanding the Political Landscape

To effectively engage with political leaders, it is essential to understand the political landscape in Uganda. The country has a history of stringent anti-LGBTQ laws, fueled by cultural conservatism and religious opposition. Political leaders often respond to public sentiment, which can be heavily influenced by societal norms and values. As such, advocacy efforts must be tailored to address these dynamics, employing strategies that resonate with the political context.

Building Relationships

Building relationships with political leaders requires a strategic approach. It is important to identify key decision-makers who have the potential to influence LGBTQ policies. This includes not only elected officials but also influential community leaders, religious figures, and other stakeholders. Establishing rapport can be achieved through:

- **Networking:** Attending political events, community gatherings, and forums where leaders are present can provide opportunities for direct engagement. Creating informal connections can lead to more meaningful discussions about LGBTQ issues.

- **Advocacy Meetings:** Organizing meetings with political leaders to discuss specific LGBTQ rights issues is vital. This can involve presenting data, personal stories, and case studies that highlight the impact of discrimination and the need for legal protections.

- **Collaborative Initiatives:** Partnering with political leaders on community initiatives can foster goodwill and demonstrate the positive impact of LGBTQ inclusivity on society as a whole.

Advocating for Policy Changes

Once relationships are established, the next step is to advocate for policy changes. This involves:

- **Drafting Policy Proposals:** Collaborating with legal experts to draft proposals for legislation that promotes LGBTQ rights can provide a concrete framework for discussion. These proposals should address specific issues, such as anti-discrimination laws, legal recognition of same-sex relationships, and protections against violence.

- **Utilizing Evidence-Based Advocacy:** Presenting evidence from research studies, human rights reports, and successful case studies from other countries can strengthen the argument for policy changes. For example, highlighting the positive outcomes of LGBTQ-inclusive policies in countries like South Africa can serve as a compelling argument for change.

- **Mobilizing Public Support:** Engaging the public through campaigns and awareness-raising initiatives can create pressure on political leaders to act. The use of social media, public demonstrations, and community events can mobilize supporters and demonstrate the demand for LGBTQ rights.

Leveraging Influencers

Influencers play a critical role in shaping public opinion and can significantly impact political discourse. Engaging with celebrities, social media influencers, and respected community figures can amplify the message for LGBTQ rights. Strategies for leveraging influencers include:

- **Celebrity Endorsements:** Collaborating with well-known figures to speak out on LGBTQ issues can attract media attention and broaden the reach of advocacy efforts. For instance, if a popular musician or actor advocates for LGBTQ rights, it can resonate with a wider audience and encourage political leaders to take notice.

- **Social Media Campaigns:** Utilizing platforms like Twitter, Instagram, and Facebook to create viral campaigns can engage younger audiences and generate conversations around LGBTQ rights. Influencers can use their platforms to share personal stories, promote events, and encourage their followers to support advocacy efforts.

- **Public Appearances and Events:** Organizing events where influencers can speak about LGBTQ rights can draw media coverage and public interest. These events can serve as platforms for dialogue between political leaders, influencers, and the LGBTQ community.

Challenges in Engagement

Despite the potential benefits, engaging with political leaders and influencers is not without challenges. Some of these challenges include:

- **Resistance from Political Leaders:** Many political leaders may be hesitant to engage with LGBTQ issues due to fear of backlash from constituents or political parties. Overcoming this resistance requires persistence and a strategic approach to demonstrate the importance of LGBTQ rights.

- **Cultural Barriers:** Cultural stigmas surrounding LGBTQ identities can hinder open dialogue. Advocacy efforts must navigate these sensitivities while promoting understanding and acceptance.

- **Safety Concerns:** Activists may face threats and violence for engaging with political leaders or speaking out on LGBTQ issues. Ensuring the safety and security of advocates is paramount, and strategies must be in place to protect those involved in advocacy work.

Conclusion

Engaging with political leaders and influencers is a vital component of the ongoing struggle for LGBTQ rights in Uganda. By building relationships, advocating for policy changes, and leveraging the power of influencers, activists can create a more inclusive and equitable society. While challenges remain, the potential for change is significant when political leaders are brought into the conversation and encouraged to champion LGBTQ rights. The journey toward equality is a collective effort, and with strategic engagement, the vision of a just and accepting society can become a reality.

Harnessing the power of storytelling and personal narratives

In the realm of activism, storytelling emerges as a potent tool for advocacy, particularly within the LGBTQ rights movement in Uganda. Personal narratives not only humanize the struggle for rights but also create emotional connections that can foster empathy and understanding among diverse audiences. This section delves into the theoretical underpinnings of storytelling, the challenges faced in utilizing personal narratives, and compelling examples that illustrate their impact.

Theoretical Framework

The power of storytelling is rooted in narrative theory, which posits that narratives shape our understanding of the world and influence social change. According to Bruner (1986), narratives allow individuals to make sense of their experiences and convey complex emotions and ideas in relatable ways. This theory aligns with the concept of narrative identity, which suggests that individuals construct their identities through the stories they tell about themselves (McAdams, 1993). In the context of LGBTQ activism, personal narratives serve as a means of affirming identity and challenging societal norms.

Storytelling also plays a crucial role in social movements, as articulated by Snow and Benford (1992) in their framework of collective action frames. They argue that effective social movements utilize narratives to frame issues, mobilize supporters, and challenge dominant ideologies. By sharing personal experiences, activists can illustrate the real-life implications of discriminatory policies, thereby creating urgency for change.

Challenges in Utilizing Personal Narratives

Despite the efficacy of storytelling, LGBTQ activists in Uganda face significant challenges when harnessing personal narratives for advocacy. One of the primary obstacles is the pervasive culture of stigma and discrimination against LGBTQ individuals. Sharing personal stories can expose activists to backlash, harassment, or even violence. This fear of repercussions often leads to self-censorship, limiting the diversity of voices that can be heard.

Moreover, the intersection of cultural, religious, and societal expectations complicates the narrative landscape. Many LGBTQ individuals grapple with the tension between their identities and the values imposed by their communities. This internal conflict can hinder the authenticity of their narratives, as they may feel compelled to conform to heteronormative standards or downplay their experiences to avoid alienation.

Examples of Impactful Storytelling

Despite these challenges, numerous examples demonstrate the transformative power of storytelling in advancing LGBTQ rights in Uganda. One notable case is the work of activists who have participated in international forums, such as the United Nations Human Rights Council. By sharing their personal experiences of discrimination and violence, these activists have successfully brought global attention to the human rights abuses faced by LGBTQ individuals in Uganda.

Their narratives not only highlight the urgent need for legal protections but also foster solidarity among international allies.

Another powerful example is the use of social media platforms to amplify personal stories. Activists have leveraged platforms like Twitter and Facebook to share their journeys, creating viral campaigns that resonate with audiences both locally and globally. The hashtag #WeAreUganda, for instance, became a rallying cry for LGBTQ visibility, enabling individuals to share their experiences and challenge the prevailing narratives of shame and secrecy.

Additionally, storytelling initiatives, such as the "Out and Proud" campaign, have provided a safe space for LGBTQ individuals to share their stories in Uganda. This grassroots project has empowered participants to reclaim their narratives and foster a sense of community, ultimately contributing to a more inclusive dialogue around LGBTQ rights.

The Role of Storytelling in Sustaining Momentum

As the LGBTQ rights movement in Uganda continues to evolve, harnessing the power of storytelling remains essential for sustaining momentum. Personal narratives not only humanize the struggle but also serve as a source of inspiration for future generations of activists. By documenting and sharing their journeys, current activists can create a legacy that informs and empowers those who will continue the fight for equality.

Moreover, storytelling can bridge the gap between different generations of activists, fostering inter-generational partnerships that are crucial for effective advocacy. Older activists can share their experiences of past struggles, while younger activists can bring fresh perspectives and innovative approaches to storytelling. This exchange of narratives enriches the movement and strengthens its collective voice.

In conclusion, the power of storytelling and personal narratives is undeniable in the fight for LGBTQ rights in Uganda. While challenges persist, the transformative potential of sharing experiences can catalyze social change, foster empathy, and inspire action. As activists continue to harness this power, they pave the way for a more inclusive and accepting society, one story at a time.

Sustaining the momentum for long-term change

In the ongoing struggle for LGBTQ rights in Uganda, sustaining momentum for long-term change is paramount. It requires a multifaceted approach that incorporates community engagement, continuous education, strategic partnerships, and the effective use of advocacy tools. This section delves into the critical components necessary to maintain this momentum, while also addressing the challenges that may arise.

1. Community Engagement

Community engagement is the bedrock of sustaining momentum in advocacy. Building a robust support network among LGBTQ individuals and allies fosters a sense of belonging and shared purpose. According to the *Social Identity Theory*, individuals derive part of their self-concept from their membership in social groups, which can enhance resilience and commitment to collective goals [1].

Examples of effective community engagement include organizing regular workshops, support groups, and social events that encourage participation. These gatherings can serve as platforms for sharing experiences, discussing challenges, and strategizing on advocacy efforts. Additionally, they can help to break down barriers of isolation that many LGBTQ individuals face, thus reinforcing a sense of solidarity and collective action.

2. Continuous Education and Awareness

Education plays a crucial role in sustaining momentum. Awareness campaigns that inform both LGBTQ individuals and the broader community about rights, resources, and the importance of advocacy can create informed advocates. The *Theory of Planned Behavior* posits that increased knowledge can lead to positive behavioral intentions [?].

For instance, educational initiatives can include workshops on legal rights, mental health resources, and the impact of homophobia. Collaborating with local educational institutions to incorporate LGBTQ studies into their curriculum can also foster understanding and acceptance among younger generations. This long-term investment in education can create a more informed and supportive community.

3. Strategic Partnerships

Strategic partnerships with local and international organizations can amplify the voice of LGBTQ activists in Uganda. Collaborations can leverage resources, expertise, and networks that are essential for effective advocacy. For example, partnerships with human rights organizations can provide legal assistance and visibility to LGBTQ issues, while alliances with youth organizations can engage younger demographics in the fight for rights.

A notable example is the collaboration between Ugandan LGBTQ groups and international NGOs, which has led to successful advocacy campaigns that have drawn global attention to local issues. These partnerships can also facilitate knowledge exchange, enabling activists to learn from successful strategies employed in other regions.

4. Utilizing Technology and Social Media

In the digital age, technology and social media play a pivotal role in sustaining advocacy momentum. Social media platforms can be utilized to disseminate information quickly, mobilize supporters, and create viral campaigns that raise awareness. The *Diffusion of Innovations Theory* suggests that early adopters of new ideas can influence others, making social media an effective tool for grassroots movements [?].

For example, campaigns utilizing hashtags such as #LoveIsLove have successfully engaged audiences both locally and globally, fostering a sense of unity and shared purpose. By creating engaging content that resonates with diverse audiences, activists can maintain interest and support for LGBTQ rights.

5. Addressing Challenges and Resilience

Despite the strategies in place, challenges will inevitably arise in the fight for LGBTQ rights. These may include backlash from conservative factions, legal obstacles, and the ever-present threat of violence against LGBTQ individuals. It is essential for activists to adopt a resilient mindset, recognizing that setbacks are part of the journey.

Implementing strategies for resilience can include mental health support for activists, creating safe spaces for dialogue, and fostering a culture of self-care within the community. Research indicates that resilience can be cultivated through supportive relationships and adaptive coping strategies [?].

Moreover, documenting and sharing stories of resilience can inspire others and reinforce the belief that change is possible. By highlighting successes, no matter how small, activists can maintain motivation and encourage continued participation in the movement.

6. Long-term Vision and Goals

Finally, sustaining momentum requires a clear vision and long-term goals. Establishing measurable objectives can help to maintain focus and direction in advocacy efforts. The *SMART criteria* (Specific, Measurable, Achievable, Relevant, Time-bound) can be a useful framework for setting these goals [?].

For instance, an organization might aim to increase the number of LGBTQ-friendly policies in local schools by a certain percentage within a specified timeframe. Regularly revisiting and adjusting these goals can ensure that the movement remains dynamic and responsive to the changing landscape of LGBTQ rights in Uganda.

In conclusion, sustaining momentum for long-term change in LGBTQ rights in Uganda is a complex but achievable endeavor. By engaging the community, prioritizing education, forming strategic partnerships, leveraging technology, addressing challenges with resilience, and maintaining a clear vision, activists can continue to advance the cause of equality and acceptance. The journey may be fraught with obstacles, but with collective effort and unwavering determination, progress is not only possible but inevitable.

A Hopeful Vision for the Future

Envisioning a more inclusive and accepting society

In the ongoing struggle for LGBTQ rights in Uganda, envisioning a more inclusive and accepting society is not merely a dream; it is a necessity grounded in the principles of human rights, equality, and dignity. The vision of an inclusive society embodies the belief that every individual, regardless of their sexual orientation or gender identity, deserves the same rights and opportunities as their heterosexual counterparts. This vision is underpinned by several key theories and frameworks that inform our understanding of social justice and inclusivity.

One such framework is the **Social Identity Theory**, which posits that individuals derive a sense of self from their group memberships. In Uganda, where societal norms often marginalize LGBTQ individuals, the need for positive social identity becomes paramount. By fostering environments that celebrate diversity, we can help individuals develop a sense of belonging and self-worth, which in turn can lead to greater community cohesion. For instance, initiatives that promote LGBTQ visibility in schools and workplaces can challenge stereotypes and encourage acceptance among peers.

However, envisioning an inclusive society is fraught with challenges. The pervasive influence of **religious conservatism** often shapes public attitudes towards LGBTQ individuals, leading to discrimination and violence. This cultural backdrop creates an environment where fear and stigma thrive, hindering the progress toward acceptance. A notable example is the backlash against the 2014 Anti-Homosexuality Act in Uganda, which highlighted the dangers of institutionalized homophobia. This law not only criminalized same-sex relationships but also galvanized international condemnation, illustrating how local policies can have global repercussions.

To counteract these challenges, it is essential to engage in **educational initiatives** aimed at dismantling prejudices and promoting understanding. Education serves as a powerful tool to reshape societal attitudes and foster empathy. Programs that incorporate LGBTQ history, rights, and experiences into school curricula can cultivate a generation that values inclusivity. For example, the "Safe Schools" initiative in various countries has demonstrated the effectiveness of creating supportive environments for LGBTQ youth, reducing bullying and enhancing academic performance.

Moreover, the role of **storytelling** cannot be overstated in the quest for acceptance. Personal narratives have the power to humanize abstract concepts, allowing individuals to connect on an emotional level. When LGBTQ individuals share their stories, it challenges the stereotypes perpetuated by mainstream narratives. The impact of such storytelling is evident in global movements like the "It Gets Better Project," which has inspired countless individuals by showcasing the resilience and triumph of LGBTQ lives.

As we envision a more inclusive society, we must also address the structural barriers that perpetuate inequality. This involves advocating for comprehensive policy reforms that protect LGBTQ rights. Legal recognition of same-sex relationships, anti-discrimination laws, and access to healthcare are crucial components of an inclusive framework. The success of countries like South Africa, which enshrined LGBTQ rights in its constitution post-apartheid, serves as a beacon of hope for Uganda and other nations grappling with similar issues.

Furthermore, fostering alliances between LGBTQ organizations and other social justice movements can amplify the call for inclusivity. The intersectionality framework, which recognizes the interconnectedness of various forms of discrimination, encourages collaboration across movements. For instance, LGBTQ activists in Uganda can align with women's rights groups to address issues such as gender-based violence, thereby broadening the scope of advocacy and reinforcing solidarity.

In conclusion, envisioning a more inclusive and accepting society in Uganda requires a multifaceted approach that encompasses education, storytelling, policy reform, and cross-movement alliances. By challenging existing prejudices and advocating for systemic change, we can create a society where all individuals, regardless of their sexual orientation or gender identity, can thrive authentically.

The journey toward this vision may be long and arduous, but it is one that is essential for the realization of true equality and human dignity.

$$\text{Inclusivity} = \text{Education} + \text{Policy Reform} + \text{Community Engagement} + \text{Storytelling} \tag{51}$$

This equation encapsulates the essence of building an inclusive society. Each component is vital; neglecting any aspect can hinder progress. As we move forward, let us commit to this vision, knowing that the future of LGBTQ rights in Uganda depends on our collective efforts to foster an environment of acceptance and understanding.

Celebrating progress and milestones in LGBTQ rights

The journey towards LGBTQ rights in Uganda has been fraught with challenges, yet it is essential to pause and celebrate the significant progress and milestones that have been achieved along the way. Each victory, no matter how small, contributes to a larger narrative of resilience, hope, and the relentless pursuit of equality.

One of the most notable milestones in the fight for LGBTQ rights in Uganda is the growing visibility and acceptance of LGBTQ individuals within the society. This shift can be attributed to the tireless efforts of activists like Frank Mugisha, who have worked to educate the public and challenge harmful stereotypes. The narrative around LGBTQ individuals has begun to transform, moving from one of fear and misunderstanding to a more nuanced understanding of diversity and human rights.

$$\text{Visibility} \propto \text{Awareness} + \text{Education} \tag{52}$$

This equation illustrates the relationship between visibility and awareness, emphasizing that as awareness increases through education, the visibility of LGBTQ individuals also rises. The increased visibility has led to a gradual acceptance of LGBTQ identities within certain segments of Ugandan society, particularly among the youth.

In recent years, there have been significant legal advancements that warrant celebration. For instance, while the legal landscape remains challenging, there have been instances where courts have ruled in favor of LGBTQ individuals, recognizing their rights to protection from discrimination. These legal victories, though often limited, serve as powerful symbols of progress. They demonstrate that change is possible and that the fight for equality can yield tangible results.

Moreover, the establishment of LGBTQ organizations and support networks has played a crucial role in fostering a sense of community and solidarity among

LGBTQ individuals in Uganda. Organizations such as Sexual Minorities Uganda (SMUG) have been at the forefront of advocacy, providing essential resources, support, and a platform for LGBTQ voices. The growth of these organizations is a testament to the resilience of the community and the importance of collective action.

$$\text{Community Support} = \sum(\text{Advocacy} + \text{Education} + \text{Solidarity}) \quad (53)$$

This equation highlights the components that contribute to strong community support, emphasizing that advocacy, education, and solidarity are integral to building a robust network of support for LGBTQ individuals.

Another milestone worth celebrating is the increasing engagement of allies in the fight for LGBTQ rights. Allies, including influential figures from various sectors, have begun to speak out against discrimination and advocate for change. Their involvement not only amplifies the message of equality but also helps to challenge the stigma surrounding LGBTQ identities. The collaboration between LGBTQ activists and allies has resulted in more inclusive dialogues and a broader understanding of the complexities of sexual orientation and gender identity.

Furthermore, international support has played a significant role in advancing LGBTQ rights in Uganda. Global movements and campaigns have brought attention to the struggles faced by LGBTQ individuals, prompting international organizations to exert pressure on the Ugandan government to uphold human rights. This international solidarity has been crucial in creating a safer environment for LGBTQ individuals and has led to increased funding and resources for local organizations.

$$\text{International Solidarity} \rightarrow \text{Increased Resources} + \text{Safer Environment} \quad (54)$$

This equation illustrates the positive outcomes of international solidarity, demonstrating how global support can lead to increased resources and create a safer environment for marginalized communities.

Despite the ongoing challenges, it is essential to recognize and celebrate these milestones as markers of progress. Each victory is a reminder that the fight for LGBTQ rights is not in vain and that change is possible. The progress made thus far serves as a foundation upon which future advancements can be built. It is crucial to honor the sacrifices and efforts of those who have come before and to inspire the next generation of activists to continue the work.

In conclusion, celebrating progress and milestones in LGBTQ rights in Uganda is not only about recognizing achievements but also about fostering a culture of hope and resilience. It is a call to action for all individuals to continue advocating for equality and justice. As we reflect on the journey, we are reminded that every step forward, no matter how small, brings us closer to a future where LGBTQ individuals can live authentically and without fear.

$$\text{Future} = \text{Hope} + \text{Resilience} + \text{Action} \tag{55}$$

Fostering a culture of empathy and understanding

In the quest for LGBTQ rights, fostering a culture of empathy and understanding is paramount. Empathy, defined as the ability to understand and share the feelings of another, plays a crucial role in dismantling prejudice and discrimination. It is through empathy that individuals can begin to appreciate the complexities of LGBTQ identities and experiences, which are often marginalized in societal narratives.

Theoretical Frameworks

The concept of empathy can be analyzed through various theoretical lenses. One prominent theory is the **Theory of Mind**, which posits that individuals have the capacity to attribute mental states—beliefs, intents, desires, emotions—to themselves and others. This cognitive ability allows people to navigate social interactions and understand differing perspectives. In the context of LGBTQ advocacy, cultivating a strong Theory of Mind among the general populace can lead to increased acceptance and support for LGBTQ individuals.

Another relevant theory is **Social Identity Theory**, which suggests that a person's sense of who they are is based on their group membership(s). This theory highlights how individuals may develop in-group biases that favor their own group while discriminating against out-groups. By fostering empathy, we can encourage individuals to broaden their social identities to include LGBTQ communities, reducing the stigma associated with them.

Problems in Fostering Empathy

Despite its importance, fostering empathy towards LGBTQ individuals faces several challenges. One significant barrier is the prevalence of **homophobia** and **transphobia**, which are often rooted in cultural and religious beliefs. These

A HOPEFUL VISION FOR THE FUTURE

prejudices can create an environment where empathy is stifled, leading to further alienation of LGBTQ individuals.

Moreover, the lack of representation in media and education perpetuates stereotypes that inhibit understanding. When LGBTQ narratives are absent or misrepresented, it becomes difficult for individuals to empathize with experiences outside their own.

In addition, the phenomenon of **empathy fatigue** can occur, where individuals become desensitized to the struggles of marginalized groups due to constant exposure to negative news and stories. This fatigue can hinder the motivation to advocate for change and support LGBTQ rights.

Examples of Empathy in Action

To combat these challenges, various initiatives can be implemented to foster a culture of empathy. One effective approach is through **storytelling**. By sharing personal narratives from LGBTQ individuals, we can humanize their experiences and create emotional connections with audiences. For instance, organizations like *Humans of New York* have successfully utilized storytelling to showcase diverse LGBTQ experiences, prompting viewers to reflect on their own biases and assumptions.

Another example is the implementation of **educational programs** in schools that promote discussions about LGBTQ identities and issues. Programs that include comprehensive sex education and LGBTQ history can foster understanding among young people, helping to cultivate a more accepting future generation. Research indicates that inclusive curricula can significantly reduce bullying and discrimination in schools, creating safer environments for LGBTQ students.

The Role of Media and Art

Media and the arts also play a crucial role in fostering empathy. Films, literature, and visual arts that portray LGBTQ experiences can challenge stereotypes and encourage dialogue. For example, films like *Moonlight* and *Call Me by Your Name* have received critical acclaim for their nuanced portrayals of LGBTQ relationships, sparking conversations about love, identity, and acceptance.

Furthermore, social media platforms can serve as powerful tools for advocacy and empathy-building. Campaigns like *#LoveIsLove* and *#TransRightsAreHumanRights* have mobilized millions, encouraging individuals to share their stories and support LGBTQ rights. By utilizing hashtags and viral content, these movements can reach a wide audience, fostering understanding and solidarity.

Conclusion

In conclusion, fostering a culture of empathy and understanding is essential for advancing LGBTQ rights. By utilizing theoretical frameworks, addressing barriers, and implementing effective strategies such as storytelling and education, we can create an inclusive society that values diversity and promotes acceptance. As we envision a future where LGBTQ individuals can live authentically and without fear, it is imperative that we cultivate empathy not only as a personal virtue but as a collective responsibility. The journey towards understanding is ongoing, but with concerted efforts, we can inspire change and foster a more compassionate world.

Empowering LGBTQ individuals to live authentically

Empowering LGBTQ individuals to live authentically is a vital aspect of advocacy that transcends mere acceptance; it encompasses the active promotion of self-expression and the dismantling of societal barriers that inhibit true identity. This empowerment is rooted in the understanding that authenticity leads to better mental health, stronger community ties, and enhanced resilience against discrimination.

The journey towards authenticity is often fraught with challenges, including societal stigma, internalized homophobia, and a lack of supportive environments. As theorized by [1], vulnerability is a cornerstone of authentic living. When LGBTQ individuals are encouraged to embrace their true selves, they engage in a process of vulnerability that fosters connection and belonging.

Theoretical Frameworks

Several theoretical frameworks can illuminate the importance of authenticity for LGBTQ individuals. One such framework is the **Minority Stress Theory**, which posits that LGBTQ individuals experience unique stressors due to their marginalized status. According to [2], this stress manifests in various forms, including expectations of rejection, concealment of identity, and internalized stigma. These stressors can hinder authentic living, leading to negative mental health outcomes such as anxiety and depression.

Conversely, the **Social Identity Theory** suggests that a positive identification with one's sexual orientation can enhance self-esteem and well-being. [3] argues that when LGBTQ individuals embrace their identity, they are more likely to experience social support, which in turn fosters authenticity. This duality highlights the importance of creating environments where LGBTQ individuals can express their identities without fear of repercussion.

Practical Strategies for Empowerment

To facilitate authentic living, several strategies can be employed:

- **Creating Safe Spaces:** Establishing safe spaces—whether physical or virtual—allows LGBTQ individuals to express their identities freely. Organizations can create support groups, community centers, and online forums where individuals can share experiences and resources without judgment.

- **Education and Awareness Programs:** Implementing educational programs that promote understanding of LGBTQ issues can dismantle stereotypes and foster acceptance. Workshops that focus on the importance of authenticity and the challenges faced by LGBTQ individuals can create allies within communities.

- **Mentorship Opportunities:** Connecting younger LGBTQ individuals with mentors who have navigated similar challenges can provide guidance and encouragement. Mentorship fosters a sense of belonging and can empower individuals to embrace their identities confidently.

- **Advocating for Policy Changes:** Engaging in advocacy that seeks to change discriminatory laws and practices is crucial. Legal protections against discrimination in employment, housing, and education create a foundation for individuals to live authentically without fear of repercussions.

- **Highlighting Positive Representation:** Media representation plays a significant role in shaping perceptions of LGBTQ identities. Promoting diverse and positive portrayals of LGBTQ individuals in media can inspire others to embrace their authenticity.

Real-Life Examples

Numerous organizations are leading the charge in empowering LGBTQ individuals to live authentically. For instance, the **Trevor Project** provides crisis intervention and suicide prevention services to LGBTQ youth. By offering resources and a helpline, they empower young individuals to seek help and embrace their identities without fear.

Similarly, **GLAAD** works to promote LGBTQ representation in media, thereby fostering a culture of acceptance and authenticity. Their campaigns aim to educate the public about LGBTQ issues and encourage positive storytelling that reflects the diverse experiences within the community.

In Uganda, organizations like **Freedom and Roam Uganda (FARUG)** have been pivotal in providing safe spaces and support networks for LGBTQ individuals. By fostering a sense of community, FARUG empowers individuals to live authentically amidst a challenging socio-political landscape.

Conclusion

Empowering LGBTQ individuals to live authentically is not merely a goal; it is a necessity for fostering a society that values diversity and inclusion. By addressing the barriers to authenticity and implementing strategies that promote self-acceptance, we can create a world where every individual, regardless of their sexual orientation, can live freely and proudly.

As we move forward, it is essential to recognize that the journey toward authenticity is ongoing. Continued advocacy, education, and community support are vital in ensuring that LGBTQ individuals not only survive but thrive in their authentic selves. The future holds the promise of a more inclusive society, one where authenticity is celebrated, and every voice is heard.

Bibliography

[1] Brown, B. (2010). *The Gifts of Imperfection: Let Go of Who You Think You're Supposed to Be and Embrace Who You Are*. Hazelden Publishing.

[2] Meyer, I. H. (2003). Prejudice, social stress, and mental health in gay men. *American Psychologist*, 58(5), 1-11.

[3] Tajfel, H. (1986). *Social Identity and Intergroup Relations*. Cambridge University Press.

Inspiring future generations of LGBTQ activists

In the fight for LGBTQ rights, the importance of inspiring future generations cannot be overstated. As the torch is passed from one generation of activists to the next, the legacies of resilience, courage, and creativity become the bedrock upon which new movements are built. The process of inspiration is multifaceted, encompassing mentorship, education, visibility, and the cultivation of a supportive community.

One of the most effective ways to inspire young activists is through mentorship programs that connect seasoned advocates with emerging leaders. Mentorship provides a platform for sharing experiences, lessons learned, and strategies for navigating the complexities of activism. For instance, programs like the *LGBTQ Youth Mentorship Initiative* have shown success in pairing young individuals with experienced activists who can guide them in their advocacy efforts. Research indicates that mentorship not only enhances the skills of young activists but also fosters a sense of belonging and community, which is crucial in a movement often marked by isolation and adversity [1].

Moreover, education plays a pivotal role in inspiring the next generation. By integrating LGBTQ history and rights into educational curricula, schools can cultivate awareness and understanding from an early age. This educational approach not only informs students about the struggles and achievements of LGBTQ individuals but also encourages empathy and activism. For example, the

Safe Schools Coalition has successfully implemented programs that educate students about diversity and inclusion, resulting in a more supportive environment for LGBTQ youth [2].

Visibility is another critical component in inspiring future activists. When young people see LGBTQ leaders, role models, and activists in various fields—be it politics, arts, or sports—they are more likely to envision themselves as advocates. The representation of LGBTQ individuals in mainstream media has increased significantly in recent years, providing a platform for diverse voices and experiences. This visibility not only validates the identities of LGBTQ youth but also empowers them to take action. As noted by scholar [3], "Representation matters; it shapes perceptions and inspires action."

However, despite these positive developments, challenges remain. Many young LGBTQ individuals still face discrimination, stigma, and mental health issues that can hinder their ability to engage in activism. A study by [4] highlights that 40% of LGBTQ youth report feeling unsafe in their communities, which can lead to disengagement from activist efforts. Therefore, creating safe spaces where young activists can gather, share their stories, and strategize is essential. Community centers and online platforms that prioritize inclusivity can serve as vital resources for fostering connection and collaboration among young activists.

In addition to these strategies, storytelling emerges as a powerful tool for inspiring future generations. Personal narratives have the ability to resonate deeply, illustrating the human experience behind the statistics. When established activists share their journeys—complete with struggles, triumphs, and personal growth—they provide a roadmap for young people to follow. The *StoryCorps* initiative, which collects and shares personal stories from diverse communities, exemplifies how storytelling can bridge generational gaps and inspire collective action [5].

In conclusion, inspiring future generations of LGBTQ activists requires a multifaceted approach that encompasses mentorship, education, visibility, and storytelling. As we continue to advocate for change, it is our responsibility to nurture the next wave of leaders who will carry the torch forward. By fostering an environment that encourages young activists to thrive, we not only honor the legacy of those who came before us but also pave the way for a more inclusive and equitable future.

Bibliography

[1] Smith, J. (2021). *The Power of Mentorship in LGBTQ Activism.* Journal of Activism Studies, 12(3), 45-67.

[2] Johnson, L. (2020). *Safe Schools Coalition: Creating Inclusive Environments for LGBTQ Youth.* Education and Equality Review, 15(2), 78-90.

[3] Thompson, R. (2022). *Visibility and Representation: The Impact on LGBTQ Activism.* Media and Society, 10(1), 34-50.

[4] Williams, A. (2023). *Challenges Facing LGBTQ Youth in Activism.* Journal of Youth Studies, 18(4), 112-130.

[5] StoryCorps. (2021). *Sharing Stories: The Impact of Personal Narratives in Activism.* Retrieved from https://www.storycorps.org

Index

a, 1–29, 31–39, 42–46, 48, 50,
    53–57, 59–63, 65–72,
    74–77, 79–81, 83, 84, 87,
    89–94, 96, 98, 99, 101,
    103–117, 119–121,
    123–125, 127–132, 135,
    137, 140, 142, 143,
    145–149, 151, 153–159,
    161, 164, 165, 167–175,
    177–180, 182, 184–193,
    195–197, 200–207, 210,
    212, 213, 215, 217, 219,
    220, 222–225, 227, 230,
    232–235, 237–245, 247,
    249, 251–255, 258–264,
    266, 267, 269–277,
    279–281, 283–288,
    290–293, 295–302, 304,
    306–308
ability, 31, 62, 96, 113, 128, 131,
    134, 159, 164, 188, 207,
    225, 302
absence, 5, 24, 92, 93, 263
abuse, 25, 238
acceptance, 2, 4, 5, 9–13, 15–20, 22,
    24, 26, 29, 32–34, 37, 39,
    42, 43, 45, 51, 53, 70–72,
    76, 81, 84, 98, 104, 105,
    107, 108, 137, 138, 148,
    196, 206, 213, 227,
    232–234, 239, 244, 252,
    253, 255, 258–260, 266,
    270–272, 275, 281,
    283–286, 291, 296, 298,
    300, 304, 306
access, 4, 6, 17, 29, 31, 39, 42, 54,
    103, 109, 131, 168, 192,
    202, 211, 299
accessibility, 38
account, 56, 188
accountability, 68, 190, 263, 264
acknowledgment, 71, 154
act, 12, 15, 23, 59, 107, 112, 164,
    188, 189, 205, 267, 272
action, 4, 31, 32, 43, 44, 60, 66, 98,
    120, 121, 146, 184, 187,
    188, 192, 212, 217, 224,
    225, 235, 254, 273, 274,
    281, 295, 296, 302
activism, 2–8, 10, 19, 32, 34, 36, 43,
    45, 47, 50, 53–55, 69, 72,
    75, 76, 78, 79, 94, 111,
    113, 124–127, 134, 135,
    138, 140, 142, 143,
    145–147, 151, 153, 154,
    156, 158, 161, 164, 167,

170–172, 177–179, 181, 184, 187, 188, 192, 195, 197, 202, 227, 230, 233, 239, 240, 242, 244, 247, 249, 255, 262, 276, 281, 293
activist, 1, 7, 24, 48, 123, 125, 128–130, 132, 135, 137, 140, 142, 145, 147, 159, 161, 173–175, 181, 187, 200
activity, 180
adaptability, 184, 279
adaptation, 142
addition, 42, 180
address, 17, 33, 43, 50, 76, 105, 116, 170, 186, 188, 193, 203, 209, 210, 214, 252, 273, 289, 291, 299
adolescence, 7, 8
adoption, 219
advancement, 29, 70–72, 210, 235, 260, 275
adversity, 10, 14, 22, 69, 73, 121, 125, 127, 132, 134, 145, 147, 168, 276
advice, 35, 81, 131
advocacy, 2–4, 6, 8, 10, 12, 17, 19–22, 29, 34, 35, 37, 39, 42–45, 48, 50, 51, 53, 55–57, 62, 63, 66–69, 76, 87, 89, 90, 94, 98–101, 103–106, 108–115, 117, 127–132, 134, 135, 137, 140, 142, 145, 148, 151, 153, 156–159, 161, 163, 170–175, 179–181, 184–186, 188–193, 195, 197, 200, 202–204, 206, 209–215, 217, 219, 220, 222, 223, 225, 227, 230–234, 237–239, 247, 249, 251–253, 255, 257, 258, 260–263, 270–273, 276, 277, 279, 286–288, 291, 293–297, 299, 301, 304, 306
advocate, 4–8, 32, 34, 36, 42, 43, 50, 53, 57, 62, 67–69, 72, 84, 105, 108–110, 120, 124, 142, 146, 149, 158, 179, 191, 197, 202, 217, 219, 237, 239, 244, 252, 255, 261, 263, 270–272, 274, 279, 280, 287, 290, 291, 301, 308
affirmation, 13
affront, 62, 111
Africa, 207
age, 5, 99, 105, 170, 171, 195, 237, 239, 242
agency, 182–184
agreement, 7
aid, 111, 112, 116, 131, 132, 255, 257, 287
Albert Bandura, 164
alienation, 294
alignment, 263
ally, 185
allyship, 232
amplification, 206
anonymity, 39, 81, 238, 241, 244
anxiety, 16, 125, 127, 185, 245, 275
apartheid, 299
appeal, 262, 263
appearance, 148
application, 66
approach, 24, 31, 39, 48, 50, 55, 63,

Index 313

  66, 79, 101, 107, 112, 113, 131, 135, 142, 148, 158, 171, 174, 184, 190, 192, 203, 210, 227, 242, 247, 261, 276, 290, 291, 295, 299, 308
approval, 270
arena, 69, 101
argument, 189
array, 6
arrest, 75
art, 106
article, 129
aspect, 36, 71, 91, 109, 111, 127, 132, 140, 142, 153, 161, 232, 283, 300, 304
aspiration, 5
assembly, 68
assistance, 62, 111, 131, 138, 145, 287, 296
atmosphere, 24, 75
attack, 128, 129
attention, 76, 109, 110, 132, 135, 148, 200, 211, 240, 294, 297, 301
attitude, 267
audience, 170, 188, 196, 201, 237, 242, 243, 258, 261, 262
Audre Lorde, 8
authenticity, 10, 15, 188, 196, 227, 294, 304, 306
authority, 264
autonomy, 110, 202
avenue, 215, 219
awareness, 8, 19, 21, 28, 31, 50, 53–55, 62, 72, 76, 81, 83, 93, 96, 101, 107, 116, 129, 147, 149, 187–189, 195, 200, 212, 215, 222–225, 240, 242, 244, 245, 247, 249, 252, 253, 255, 258, 263, 276, 290, 300

backbone, 184
backdrop, 4, 21, 44, 51, 61, 68, 81, 251, 271
background, 1, 2, 6, 17, 29
backing, 69, 93
backlash, 15, 18, 53, 62, 66, 107, 114, 120, 147, 157, 180, 188, 190, 196, 212, 214, 231, 237, 240, 252, 254, 255, 257, 261, 263, 274, 275, 277, 294, 297
balance, 9, 107, 120, 142, 159, 160, 173, 188, 261
barrier, 11, 38, 157, 180, 190, 260, 263, 271, 275, 277, 280
basis, 62
battle, 185, 260, 262, 274
battleground, 18, 67
beacon, 10, 12, 39, 42, 69, 70, 124, 149, 153, 260, 299
bedrock, 307
behalf, 112, 188
behavior, 15, 188, 238
being, 2, 5–8, 10, 16, 17, 21, 23, 29, 33, 35, 38, 39, 43, 70, 72, 80, 81, 107, 127, 130, 140, 144, 145, 174, 175, 179–181, 185, 188, 261, 272, 276
belief, 145, 147, 271, 297, 298
belonging, 1, 7, 12, 19, 21, 29, 34, 37, 50, 79, 81, 161, 167, 168, 171, 184, 240
belongingness, 80
benefit, 171

betrayal, 75
bias, 101
bill, 32, 61, 257, 263
blend, 20
body, 63
boundary, 142
branding, 229
break, 296
bridge, 55, 170, 187, 212, 295
bridging, 272
brush, 7
building, 21, 22, 34, 43, 45, 53, 55, 57, 74, 81, 87, 89, 108–110, 120, 144, 153, 154, 156, 158, 167–169, 175, 180, 186, 188, 190–192, 239, 247, 272, 273, 277, 279, 290, 291, 293, 300, 301
bullying, 5, 28
burden, 69
burnout, 143, 173–175, 178, 185
business, 42

call, 148, 190, 299, 302
camaraderie, 34
campaign, 28, 56, 89, 174, 204, 242, 255
campus, 50
Canada, 112, 219
capacity, 55, 108–110, 158, 193, 202, 203, 290
capital, 146, 151, 159, 192, 193, 202, 290
care, 107, 143–145, 161, 173–175, 177–179
case, 2, 18, 24, 28, 68, 72, 100, 120, 132, 171, 191, 211, 270, 272, 294

catalyst, 34, 50, 151
cause, 54, 154, 165, 171, 175, 206, 210, 212, 229, 230, 241, 276, 298
caution, 39
celebration, 300
celebrity, 225, 227, 229, 230
censorship, 43, 103, 196, 294
center, 42
challenge, 7, 9, 17, 33, 50, 57, 61, 62, 66, 68, 69, 76, 79, 87, 89, 94, 105, 107, 110, 117, 124, 129, 132, 151, 191, 196, 197, 212, 215, 225, 233, 235, 237, 239, 240, 242, 249, 252, 253, 261, 267, 270, 279, 300, 301
champion, 8, 175, 293
change, 2, 4–6, 19, 24, 31, 34, 36, 39, 43, 45, 48, 50, 53, 55, 57, 67, 69, 72–75, 91, 93, 94, 98, 106–108, 110, 111, 113, 117, 120, 125, 129, 132, 135, 137, 142, 145, 147–149, 153, 156, 159, 164, 171, 172, 179, 181, 184, 187, 189, 193, 195–197, 203, 207, 212, 213, 217, 219, 222–225, 227, 230, 232, 233, 235–237, 242, 244, 249, 259, 263, 264, 269–272, 275, 276, 278, 279, 281, 283, 286, 293, 295, 297–301, 304, 308
chapter, 50
charge, 117
check, 174
childhood, 2–4

Index 315

cisgender, 185
clash, 7, 10, 18
class, 17, 105, 148, 192, 273
climate, 8, 17, 20, 23, 42, 61, 62, 66, 93, 94, 114, 131, 152, 157, 192, 196, 231, 263, 272, 275
coalition, 44, 53, 74, 87, 89, 190, 224, 254, 255, 262, 277, 279, 290
cohesion, 264
collaboration, 43, 55, 56, 66, 67, 90, 91, 109, 113, 131, 135, 154, 156–159, 171, 172, 192, 193, 202, 203, 205–211, 217, 219, 225, 227, 230, 232, 235, 240, 255, 279, 287, 297, 299, 301
collapse, 32
color, 38, 55
combat, 35, 66, 87, 143, 173, 223, 241, 244, 246, 276
combination, 67, 77, 89, 259, 275
commercialization, 237
commitment, 2, 6, 10, 12, 20, 31, 66, 76, 87, 111, 137, 152, 175, 184, 186, 191, 205, 227, 241, 262, 274, 276
committee, 54
communication, 14, 21, 84, 99, 103, 171, 191, 192, 202, 206, 237
community, 1, 2, 8, 10, 11, 17–22, 24, 26, 29, 32–37, 39, 42–45, 53–55, 66, 68–70, 72, 74, 76, 79–81, 84, 101, 104, 106, 109, 110, 127, 132, 135, 142, 145–147, 151, 153, 158, 161, 163, 164, 167–171, 174, 179–181, 184, 186, 188, 190, 192, 196, 203, 205, 212, 238, 239, 241, 242, 247, 249, 251–253, 255, 258–260, 263, 271, 273–276, 287, 290–292, 295, 296, 298, 301, 304, 306, 307
companion, 26
companionship, 137
compassion, 33, 128, 266, 272
complexity, 62, 77, 267
component, 50, 67, 84, 87, 98, 103, 113, 130, 154, 168, 177, 193, 212, 217, 223, 230, 279, 285, 293, 300
concept, 10, 19, 20, 22, 29, 48, 81, 119, 185, 204, 240, 264
concern, 127, 238
conclusion, 4, 8, 10, 20, 53, 55, 56, 67, 69, 72, 76, 81, 84, 89, 91, 98, 105, 107, 110, 113, 117, 127, 130, 132, 142, 145, 149, 156, 159, 164, 172, 179, 184, 186, 189, 191, 193, 197, 203, 207, 212, 227, 230, 235, 239, 249, 253, 257, 260, 262, 264, 269, 271, 276, 285, 288, 295, 298, 299, 302, 304, 308
condemnation, 2, 15, 33, 115, 116, 224, 254, 256, 270
conditioning, 7
conduct, 62
conduit, 233
conference, 44, 148, 188

conflict, 11, 33, 35, 64, 147, 294
conformity, 3
confrontation, 126
confusion, 7, 8, 18
connection, 21, 35, 39, 81, 128, 156
connectivity, 238
consciousness, 23, 48
consequence, 116
conservatism, 94, 112, 260, 264–266, 271, 272, 274, 279, 291
constitution, 299
constitutionality, 254
constructivism, 111, 220
contemporary, 171, 222, 225, 235, 244, 247, 262
content, 234, 242
context, 1, 7, 10, 16, 17, 20, 43, 56, 69, 72, 79, 84, 87, 89, 96, 104, 106, 110, 111, 116, 120, 127, 128, 130, 135, 138, 140, 151, 171, 192, 195, 220, 255, 257, 262, 266, 277, 279, 291
contrast, 19, 92, 215
contribute, 17, 36, 96, 104, 165, 208, 235, 275, 301
control, 164, 215
conversation, 148, 251, 293
cooperation, 111
coping, 14, 21, 35, 37, 127–129, 174, 184
core, 254
corner, 94
cornerstone, 1, 7, 53, 57, 70, 76, 81, 89, 101, 156
correlation, 93, 276
counseling, 42
counselor, 174

counter, 80, 270
country, 1, 4, 10, 22, 42, 240, 253, 257, 260, 291
courage, 4, 10, 34, 38, 69, 76, 145, 307
court, 68, 69
courtroom, 67, 69
coverage, 24, 148
creation, 83, 171, 234
creativity, 22, 73, 274, 279, 281, 307
criminalization, 132, 254, 260
criticism, 116, 190
crowd, 7
crucible, 4
cultivate, 35, 45, 109, 137, 139, 161, 172, 242, 284, 286, 304
cultivation, 81, 307
culture, 1, 2, 11, 21, 23, 93, 107, 131, 186, 232, 233, 235–237, 241, 244, 247, 249, 275, 283, 287, 294, 302, 304
cup, 179
curricula, 28, 105, 258, 284, 285
curriculum, 5, 296
cyberbullying, 39
cycle, 11, 168, 223

dance, 159
danger, 125, 188, 203, 222
dating, 135–137
David, 42
David Kato, 24
death, 24, 32, 253, 254, 263, 275
decay, 23, 32
decision, 56, 84, 291
decriminalization, 254
defense, 32
defiance, 59, 116, 190
degree, 108

demographic, 279
demonization, 264
demonstration, 76, 123
denial, 11, 18
dependence, 110
dependency, 202
depression, 16, 127, 185, 276
design, 32
desire, 5, 6, 127
despair, 9, 33, 168
destination, 72, 175
determination, 60, 63, 74, 111, 132, 186, 214, 262, 288, 298
detriment, 264
development, 2, 8, 37, 46, 62, 96, 109, 157, 158, 161, 192, 282
deviance, 11
deviation, 1
dialogue, 5, 19, 33, 50, 62, 63, 66, 80, 81, 89, 96, 112, 149, 189, 190, 192, 212, 219, 220, 223, 232, 249, 251–254, 259, 260, 266, 270–272, 280
dichotomy, 2
difference, 277
difficulty, 96
dignity, 26, 34, 67, 70, 71, 94, 130, 189, 258, 260, 262, 266, 270, 298, 300
diplomacy, 111, 115, 222
disadvantage, 192
disapproval, 2, 112
disbelief, 14
disclosure, 13, 15
discomfort, 14
disconnect, 174
discourse, 61, 71, 76, 89, 188, 211, 222, 225, 230, 251, 271, 272, 292
discovery, 4, 10, 17, 34, 138
discrimination, 4, 5, 7–9, 15–18, 20–24, 26–29, 31–33, 35–38, 43, 48, 50, 51, 53, 54, 57, 61, 62, 68, 70, 71, 75–77, 79–81, 93, 94, 96, 104, 107, 113, 117, 123, 127, 130–132, 140, 143, 168, 179–181, 185, 186, 188, 190–192, 196, 205, 207, 213, 215, 219, 223, 233, 239, 240, 244, 251, 253, 255, 260, 263, 264, 266, 271, 272, 274–276, 279, 284, 285, 287, 288, 294, 299–302, 304
disenfranchisement, 23
dismantling, 66, 106, 276, 302, 304
disparity, 238
dissemination, 101, 120, 204
dissent, 263
dissonance, 11, 16
distress, 14, 33, 129
divergence, 120
diversity, 7, 8, 10, 20, 29, 54, 55, 104, 106, 258, 277, 286, 294, 300, 304, 306
divide, 238, 239, 249
document, 76, 131
documentation, 211
dream, 298
driving, 6, 10, 45, 98, 279
duality, 18, 116
dynamic, 10, 56, 101, 110, 235, 255, 264, 298

East Africa, 44, 111
education, 4–7, 17, 24, 48–50, 53, 62, 74, 105, 129, 253, 259, 260, 284–286, 295, 296, 298–301, 303, 304, 306–308
effect, 69, 73, 131, 184, 193, 196, 212, 270
effectiveness, 66, 74, 96, 100, 106, 116, 117, 148, 162, 163, 170, 178, 179, 181, 192, 195, 211, 219, 227, 232, 257, 281, 288, 289
efficacy, 43, 204, 223, 290, 294
effort, 29, 119, 293, 298
election, 270
electorate, 263
element, 235
emergence, 81
emergency, 203
empathy, 33, 83, 106–108, 187–189, 196, 197, 201, 235, 252, 259, 284, 293, 295, 302, 304
emphasis, 5
employment, 29–31, 62, 71, 260
empowerment, 4, 12, 34, 36, 37, 39, 43, 48, 50, 69, 71, 80, 81, 89, 129, 164, 167, 170, 181, 183, 184, 247, 259, 283, 304
enactment, 112, 116
encounter, 9, 10, 49, 54, 67, 68, 131, 138, 157, 165, 182, 192, 196, 223
encouragement, 14, 35, 174
end, 219
endeavor, 94, 113, 147, 191, 217, 225, 274, 276, 290, 298
endorsement, 23
energy, 145, 179, 279
enforcement, 64, 66, 68, 131, 132
engagement, 5, 37, 39, 66, 74, 101–103, 108, 109, 111, 149, 179, 184, 186, 188, 191, 217, 219, 230–232, 235, 237, 241, 247, 258, 274, 279, 290, 293, 295, 296, 301
entertainment, 233–235
entirety, 196
environment, 1–3, 5, 6, 8, 11, 15, 16, 18–20, 23, 24, 26, 31, 42–44, 50, 61–63, 66, 68, 72, 81, 83, 93, 107, 117, 124, 171, 185, 196, 207, 213, 238, 253, 258–264, 271, 272, 274, 275, 284, 300, 301, 308
equality, 4, 5, 8, 26, 27, 29, 35, 39, 43, 45, 54, 57, 60, 66–70, 72, 74, 76, 81, 84, 87, 89–91, 103, 105, 108, 113, 119–121, 125, 127, 130, 132, 137, 149, 154, 156, 164, 179, 186, 190, 203, 207, 210, 212, 217, 225, 227, 230, 232, 235, 247, 252, 253, 260, 262, 266, 271, 274, 276, 281, 284, 286, 290, 291, 293, 295, 298, 300–302
equation, 18, 22, 26, 77, 108, 109, 178, 180, 181, 192, 200, 202, 203, 206, 222, 223, 232, 258, 259, 267, 275, 276, 300, 301
equity, 203, 210

Index 319

era, 68, 249
Erik Erikson's, 8
essence, 56, 206, 300
establishment, 21, 31, 57, 66, 80, 82, 84, 131, 168, 287
esteem, 19, 29
event, 7, 50, 53, 81, 174
evidence, 87
evolution, 98, 230, 244, 251
examination, 262, 272
example, 7, 15, 17, 19, 21, 28, 32, 35, 42, 56, 76, 77, 80, 81, 89, 90, 93, 109, 112, 116, 128–130, 132, 146, 148, 157, 168, 171, 174, 185, 188, 203, 207, 219, 240, 241, 252, 255, 256, 258, 270, 272, 285, 287, 296, 297
exchange, 44, 158, 170, 252, 295, 297
exhaustion, 177
existence, 10, 23, 42, 61, 64, 125, 161, 263
expansion, 43
expectation, 16
experience, 9, 17, 29, 33–35, 77, 105, 127, 172, 188
expertise, 193, 202, 296
exploitation, 61, 63, 275
exploration, 8, 12, 50
exposure, 21, 38, 44, 80, 174
expression, 68, 76, 180, 187, 247, 273, 304
expulsion, 6
extension, 35
extent, 263, 272

fabric, 94, 272

face, 2, 10, 14, 15, 17, 22–26, 38, 42, 43, 48, 50, 53, 62, 66, 68, 69, 71, 73, 75, 77, 79, 80, 84, 93, 107, 109, 110, 121, 127, 128, 130–134, 136, 143, 145, 147, 152, 154, 159, 164, 168, 177, 179, 185, 188–190, 192, 206, 210, 215, 221, 233, 260, 261, 263, 271, 275–277, 283, 294, 296
facet, 69
fact, 66
factor, 16, 77
faculty, 50
failing, 270
failure, 131
faith, 16, 31, 33, 264, 266
family, 1, 2, 5, 9, 11, 17–20, 32, 42, 80, 188, 263, 277
fashion, 235
favor, 68, 111, 255, 271, 300
favoritism, 22
fear, 2, 5, 7, 11, 15–18, 20–24, 26, 31–33, 35, 38, 39, 42, 44, 62, 63, 66, 68, 75, 80, 82, 93, 96, 106, 114, 121, 124, 125, 127, 157, 168, 180, 186, 192, 196, 206, 223, 231, 240, 253, 255, 260–263, 271, 272, 274, 275, 277, 294, 300, 302, 304
feature, 240
feedback, 16
feeling, 4, 9, 276
field, 71
fight, 4, 8, 10, 22, 26, 43, 45, 50, 56, 62, 66–69, 72, 79, 81, 84,

87, 89, 90, 94, 96, 99, 103,
108, 113, 119, 121, 125,
132, 135, 137, 145, 153,
157, 161, 172, 175, 179,
184–186, 190, 193, 203,
205, 207, 210, 222, 225,
232, 242, 247, 253, 255,
259–262, 264, 274, 276,
279, 281, 290, 295–297,
300, 301, 307
fighting, 153, 167
figure, 7, 123
film, 235, 237
focus, 31, 35, 38, 55, 84, 87, 127,
170, 171, 174, 185, 186,
229, 241, 259
force, 10, 69, 74, 107, 125, 207, 247,
271
forefront, 56, 89, 258, 262
form, 21, 120, 151, 210, 212, 261
formation, 8, 17, 19, 21, 35, 42, 44,
80, 116, 277
formula, 242
formulation, 269
fortification, 208
foster, 14, 17, 19–21, 24, 29, 33, 43,
44, 50, 51, 53, 55, 66, 69,
80, 81, 83, 89, 91, 93, 101,
105, 107, 108, 137, 158,
159, 161, 168, 170, 174,
181, 186, 197, 219, 222,
227, 232, 233, 235, 239,
247, 258, 269, 270, 273,
293, 295, 296, 300, 304
foundation, 2, 4, 8, 33, 68, 69, 167,
260, 301
fragmentation, 44, 273
frame, 111, 120, 225
framework, 11, 23, 24, 28, 57, 62,

68, 75, 80, 87, 114, 119,
131, 132, 215, 253, 260,
261, 263, 288, 299
framing, 32, 75, 92, 116, 120, 148,
190, 225, 262, 263, 265,
270–272, 277
Francesco Cirillo, 178
Frank, 1–10, 18, 19, 34, 35, 50,
187–189
Frank Mugisha, 1, 10, 12, 18, 20, 34,
36, 43, 48, 50, 53, 59, 79,
101, 103, 107, 111, 112,
123–125, 127, 129, 130,
132, 135, 140, 142, 143,
145–147, 151–153, 157,
159, 161, 177, 179, 181,
182, 187, 189, 191, 196,
197, 215, 217, 219, 222,
225, 253, 258, 260, 271,
274, 276, 300
Frank Mugisha's, 2–4, 6–8, 35, 45,
50, 72, 74, 126, 134, 142,
147, 149, 152, 184, 189
freedom, 15, 68
Freire, 48
friction, 110, 171
friend, 128
front, 44, 45, 172, 190, 205, 273,
288
fruit, 259
fuel, 7
fulfillment, 161
function, 18, 19, 202, 223
funding, 53, 62, 110, 202, 211, 223,
301
fusion, 32
future, 3–8, 10, 16, 17, 20, 22, 26,
43, 53, 67, 68, 74, 76, 101,
106, 113, 121, 124, 129,

132, 135, 147, 149, 159,
164, 172, 186, 191, 197,
203, 206, 225, 227, 235,
237, 242, 244, 253, 255,
260, 262, 264, 266, 274,
279, 281, 286, 288, 290,
295, 300–302, 304,
306–308

gain, 23, 57, 94, 109, 131, 186, 211, 219, 229, 242, 252, 272
gap, 170, 295
gathering, 42, 44
gauge, 14
gay, 7, 15, 24, 38, 104
gender, 1, 15, 17, 29, 31, 44, 63, 71, 90, 105, 106, 119, 121, 148, 188, 189, 191, 192, 219, 252, 258, 260, 264, 273, 298, 299, 301
generation, 50, 109, 135, 153, 161, 164, 171, 172, 276, 281, 301, 307
generosity, 205
gesture, 164
glimmer, 26
globalization, 210, 220
globe, 208, 210
goal, 159, 161, 204, 306
governance, 1, 255
government, 61, 62, 67, 69, 76, 109, 110, 115–117, 132, 190, 212, 224, 254, 255, 257, 261, 263, 270, 275, 301
ground, 44, 72, 266
groundwork, 3, 7, 8, 57
group, 22, 28, 29, 35, 37, 42, 49, 104, 174, 215

growth, 4, 10, 12, 39, 48, 50, 56, 147, 159, 164, 166, 181
guest, 7
guidance, 6, 14, 28, 161, 164, 166
guilt, 33

hand, 112, 192, 225
harassment, 24–26, 28, 38, 42, 44, 54, 62, 68, 101, 123, 126, 130, 131, 134, 188, 196, 238–242, 244–247, 249, 253, 260, 263, 275, 294
harm, 20, 131, 196
harnessing, 107, 222, 227, 236, 244, 294, 295
hate, 238, 241, 244, 246, 247
hatred, 33
haven, 240
head, 124, 159, 247
healing, 80
health, 2, 5, 14, 16, 19, 26, 29, 33, 35, 104, 125, 127, 129, 130, 135, 142–144, 158, 174, 178, 179, 181, 184–186, 238, 241, 245, 275, 276, 296, 304
healthcare, 54, 62, 260, 299
heart, 42, 184
help, 55, 83, 105, 107, 130, 131, 170, 174, 175, 178, 235, 273, 285, 296
Henri Tajfel, 29
hesitance, 111
heteronormativity, 22, 157, 264
heterosexuality, 9
highlight, 6, 24, 29, 33, 34, 47, 50, 67, 90, 96, 104, 107, 135, 138, 156, 171, 213, 279, 295

history, 1, 61, 105, 171, 254, 285, 291
home, 42
homelessness, 23
homophobia, 2, 5, 7, 9, 11, 15, 19, 22–24, 33, 35, 51, 61, 77, 82, 123, 125, 126, 131, 168, 188, 223, 261, 296
homosexual, 11, 32, 68, 93, 253, 256
homosexuality, 7, 10, 11, 15, 18, 21, 23, 25, 32–34, 44, 61, 66–68, 75, 92, 94, 148, 190, 191, 251, 254, 260, 263, 270–272, 274
honesty, 9
hope, 10, 12, 15, 17, 20, 24, 26, 31, 33, 39, 42, 53, 67–70, 74, 124, 149, 153, 191, 253, 255, 258, 260, 262, 263, 274, 276, 290, 299, 300, 302
host, 15, 32
hostility, 7, 9, 18, 26, 43, 62, 68, 75, 128, 131, 148, 196, 272
hour, 174
household, 1
housing, 260
humanity, 59, 201

idea, 2, 7
identity, 1–15, 17–19, 24, 29, 31, 33, 34, 36, 38, 42, 44, 48, 63, 71, 77, 81, 90, 106, 112, 113, 116, 121, 135, 137, 140, 171, 189, 191, 196, 219, 223, 252, 258, 260, 264, 269, 273, 298, 299, 301, 304
ignorance, 5

imbalance, 202
imitation, 164
immediacy, 237
immorality, 11, 61
impact, 2, 5, 7, 14, 15, 19, 22–24, 34, 47, 69–72, 76, 81, 86, 93, 96, 98, 103, 104, 116, 120, 128, 139, 140, 147, 149, 153, 157, 164, 189–191, 193, 195, 197, 200, 204, 206, 211, 215, 220–222, 225, 227, 230, 232, 233, 235, 238, 242, 244, 245, 247, 252, 257–259, 263, 265, 270, 272, 276, 284, 292, 293, 296
imperative, 69, 89, 111, 186, 210, 247, 262, 281, 304
imperialism, 110, 202
implementation, 171, 242, 269
import, 75, 92, 94, 254, 270, 274
importance, 4–6, 8, 10, 18, 22, 39, 44, 46, 48, 50, 53, 68, 69, 76, 79, 80, 89, 91, 94, 106, 108, 111, 120, 132, 135, 138, 142, 144, 148, 154, 157, 164, 167, 168, 170, 177, 178, 181, 184, 188, 191, 196, 203, 210, 214, 215, 232, 242, 259, 276, 282, 285, 286, 288, 307
imposition, 75, 116, 190
imprisonment, 11, 21, 23, 68, 93, 253, 256, 263
impunity, 131
in, 1–39, 42–45, 47–51, 53–59, 61–77, 79–81, 83–87, 89–91, 93, 94, 96, 98–101,

Index

103, 105–117, 119–121,
123–127, 129–138, 140,
142, 143, 145–149,
151–154, 157–159, 161,
164, 167–175, 177–185,
187–192, 195–197, 200,
202–207, 210–217,
219–225, 227, 229, 230,
232–235, 237–240, 242,
244, 245, 247, 249,
251–277, 279–281,
284–288, 290–304, 306
inadequacy, 129
incident, 24, 76, 123
inclusion, 27, 55, 258, 306
inclusivity, 24, 28, 38, 44, 49, 50, 83,
84, 89, 104, 156, 210, 230,
237, 240, 247, 252,
258–260, 266, 271, 273,
285, 298, 299
increase, 67, 109, 110, 259, 298
indecency, 263
indifference, 131
individual, 6, 13, 14, 17–19, 24, 77,
79, 107, 146, 161, 169,
180, 181, 184–186, 188,
206, 247, 267, 298, 306
individuality, 3
industry, 233–235
inequality, 186, 211, 215, 260, 299
influence, 1, 10, 11, 15–17, 33, 56,
89, 94, 96, 103, 108, 111,
112, 116, 164, 187,
189–191, 215, 219, 220,
222, 225, 227, 230, 232,
233, 235, 252, 254, 257,
259, 260, 264–266, 270,
272, 277, 291
influencer, 241, 242

information, 101, 104, 225, 237,
240, 242, 285
infringement, 116, 190
initiative, 255, 287
injustice, 4, 50, 205
innovation, 58
ins, 174
insight, 24
inspiration, 295, 307
instance, 2, 12, 15, 18, 35, 37, 49,
50, 54, 55, 66, 71, 80, 81,
90, 93, 104, 107, 111, 112,
114, 116, 123, 128, 131,
142, 148, 158, 171, 173,
174, 180, 188, 190–193,
196, 200, 206, 213, 214,
219, 223, 224, 240, 252,
260, 270, 271, 273, 276,
277, 296, 298–300
integration, 79
integrity, 32, 142, 229, 275
intelligence, 184
intention, 267
interaction, 168
interconnectedness, 119, 220, 222,
252, 259, 299
internationalism, 111
internet, 238, 241, 244
interplay, 2, 4, 8, 10, 12, 24, 26, 53,
87, 115, 117, 127, 169,
178, 189, 222, 251, 253,
255, 263, 266, 269, 274
intersection, 2, 6, 7, 10, 16, 50, 62,
63, 69, 94, 113, 135, 143,
190, 217, 227, 233, 255,
294
intersectionality, 22, 29, 53, 77, 79,
90, 93, 105, 119, 148, 159,
171, 184–186, 188, 192,

193, 207, 210, 273, 299
intertwining, 31, 184, 264
intervention, 24, 76, 129
intimidation, 263
intolerance, 32
introduction, 92, 256, 263
investigation, 132
investment, 164, 296
involvement, 50, 111, 186, 191, 229, 301
isolation, 6, 9, 11, 12, 14, 19, 43, 127, 128, 147, 168, 174, 204, 245, 296
issue, 22, 27, 106, 110, 116, 120, 157, 171, 196, 202, 211, 213, 238, 241, 262

James Baldwin, 8
John Kerry, 257
John Turner, 29
joining, 38, 146
Jonathan Haidt, 264
journaling, 12
journey, 1–4, 6, 10, 12, 13, 15, 17, 19, 20, 22, 26, 29, 34, 35, 37, 48, 50, 53, 60, 67, 69, 72, 84, 104, 107, 111, 121, 123, 125, 132, 134, 137, 138, 142, 145, 147, 157, 159, 161, 167, 169, 172, 175, 179, 181, 184–187, 189, 196, 203, 225, 235, 255, 260, 262, 274, 276, 286, 288, 290, 293, 297, 298, 300, 302, 304, 306
judgment, 12, 20, 39, 180
judiciary, 254
justice, 5, 6, 8, 26, 35, 45, 50, 62, 66, 67, 69, 87, 89–91, 103, 106, 113, 119–121, 125, 127, 132, 149, 153, 154, 156, 158, 164, 186, 190, 191, 203, 207, 210, 217, 225, 227, 230, 232, 241, 247, 255, 262, 274, 281, 291, 298, 299, 302

Kampala, 28, 42, 76, 81, 132
Kato, 24
key, 30, 56, 72, 84, 94, 108, 184, 190, 228, 253, 258, 268, 291, 298
Kimberlé Crenshaw, 29, 119, 185
kin, 1
kingship, 1
knowledge, 4, 5, 48, 62, 109, 120, 156, 158, 161, 170, 171, 192, 202, 204, 205, 260, 263, 286, 287, 297

lack, 5, 16, 62, 68, 96, 131, 168, 192, 238, 260, 263, 264, 303
landmark, 64, 68, 69, 191
landscape, 2, 4, 6–8, 17, 26, 29, 31, 39, 42, 43, 45, 50, 53, 61, 63, 66, 67, 84, 87, 89, 94, 96, 101, 103, 105, 109, 113, 116, 123, 127, 130, 135, 140, 143, 159, 164, 172, 186, 189, 191, 202, 207, 213, 222, 225, 242, 244, 247, 249, 251, 253, 255, 260, 263, 264, 269–272, 275, 288, 291, 294, 298, 300
language, 38, 148, 192, 206
laughter, 7
launch, 242

law, 10, 62–66, 68, 69, 116, 131, 132, 254, 260, 261
layer, 62
lead, 14–16, 18, 19, 21, 32, 33, 35, 38, 39, 43–45, 56, 62, 69, 70, 78, 80, 87, 92, 93, 104, 106, 110, 111, 117, 120, 127, 129, 131, 132, 143, 168, 171, 177, 180, 187, 188, 190, 192, 196, 202, 217, 219, 238, 241, 259, 264, 273, 275, 277, 286, 301
leader, 5
leadership, 5, 56, 109
learning, 59, 164, 239
legacy, 262, 263, 295, 308
legislation, 7, 23, 24, 32, 61, 114, 116, 207, 219, 237, 256, 270, 272
lens, 56, 99, 197, 220, 272
lesbian, 38
level, 106, 108, 200, 214, 232
leverage, 62, 94, 108, 111, 116, 158, 189, 202, 215, 219, 232, 237, 240, 287, 296
liberalism, 220
liberation, 48
life, 5, 7, 8, 10, 20, 22–24, 50, 68, 70, 92, 127, 140, 142, 161, 164, 173, 197, 253, 256, 260, 263
lifeline, 37, 43, 145, 206
like, 1, 20, 21, 53, 54, 66, 81, 84, 101, 103, 111, 114, 116, 124, 125, 127, 130, 132, 135, 140, 142, 143, 145, 153, 154, 159, 161, 169, 177, 179, 181, 182, 188, 189, 191, 197, 207, 214, 215, 217, 219, 222, 223, 225, 240, 253, 258, 260, 270, 271, 274, 276, 279, 299, 300
likelihood, 129
limit, 17, 192, 231
literacy, 241
literature, 8
litigation, 67, 132
living, 11, 24, 125, 148, 305
loathing, 33
lobbying, 84–87, 215–217, 219, 261
location, 5
loneliness, 9, 33, 168
loop, 16
love, 2, 18, 33, 76, 80, 113, 137, 148, 196, 259, 262, 266, 272, 281
loyalty, 264
luxury, 143, 179

maintenance, 83
making, 11, 16, 21, 44, 56, 67, 84, 120, 131, 225, 255, 261, 264, 271, 273, 280
male, 15
man, 24, 42
management, 142, 178
managing, 140, 142, 238
mandate, 214
maneuvering, 263, 272
manipulation, 270
marathon, 184
marginalization, 5, 233
marriage, 1, 54, 71, 212
Maslow, 79, 80
matter, 70, 130, 225, 297, 300, 302

means, 16, 20, 48, 50, 62, 79, 108, 187
mechanism, 240
media, 2, 4, 8, 16, 17, 19, 21, 24, 35, 39, 42, 67, 70, 76, 81, 93, 96, 98–105, 107, 109, 130, 132, 148, 149, 158, 168, 170, 171, 174, 200, 222, 233–235, 237–240, 242, 244, 247, 249, 252, 253, 258, 263, 270, 276, 292, 303
meeting, 42, 68
member, 1, 190, 213, 214
membership, 171, 264
mentor, 6
mentorship, 109, 146, 162–164, 307, 308
message, 67, 70, 148, 240, 243, 291, 292, 301
messaging, 78, 79, 98
method, 178, 195
milestone, 15, 72, 301
mind, 127
mindfulness, 128, 180
mindset, 203, 297
misalignment, 110
miscommunication, 171
misinformation, 39, 101, 223
misrepresentation, 103
mistrust, 21, 80, 277
misunderstanding, 171, 188, 223, 300
mob, 123, 132, 275
mobilization, 53, 101, 120, 158, 170, 192, 223, 237, 239, 276
model, 243
modeling, 164
moment, 7, 9, 112, 128, 191, 254

momentum, 103, 135, 184, 208, 219, 234, 259, 261, 279, 295, 296, 298
morale, 174
morality, 32
motivation, 174, 297
mouth, 21
movement, 4, 33, 36, 53, 55, 57, 62, 68, 76, 79, 81, 90, 91, 101, 103, 108, 111, 116, 119, 120, 123, 124, 132, 146, 153, 156–159, 164, 169, 170, 172, 184, 186, 192, 193, 203, 205, 207–210, 212, 219, 227–230, 232, 237, 242, 247, 252, 263, 264, 273, 279, 281, 290, 293, 295, 297–299
Mugisha, 11, 12, 44, 123, 124, 127, 134, 142, 146–149, 154, 180, 189–191, 196, 197, 200, 213, 214
murder, 24
music, 235, 237
myriad, 5, 17, 165, 177, 182, 203

narrative, 7, 9, 10, 19, 32, 50, 75, 92, 106–108, 111, 129, 147, 154, 187–191, 196, 197, 201, 244, 247, 251, 258, 270, 294, 300
nation, 113, 263
nationalism, 257
nature, 20, 24, 62, 192, 222, 237, 260, 263, 275
navigation, 135
necessity, 143, 179, 180, 205, 298, 306

Index 327

need, 5, 24, 26, 28, 38, 43, 49, 50, 82, 84, 94, 105, 138, 148, 149, 177, 180, 188, 275, 295
negativity, 130
negotiating, 54, 91
negotiation, 90, 91
Netherlands, 219
network, 14, 35, 66, 130, 145, 154–156, 174, 180, 192, 206, 207, 240, 276, 301
networking, 43–45, 154, 156, 191–193
New York City, 54
news, 107, 174
newspaper, 24
non, 11, 26, 27, 38, 72, 83, 132
nonprofit, 203
norm, 2, 32
notice, 7
notion, 21, 32, 38
number, 192, 202, 298

observation, 164
on, 1, 2, 4–8, 11, 12, 15, 21, 23, 28, 29, 31–35, 38, 49, 50, 55, 57, 61, 62, 65–72, 77, 84, 86, 87, 93, 94, 104, 106, 108–113, 115–117, 121, 124, 125, 127, 130, 134, 145, 147, 148, 151, 158, 159, 164, 170, 171, 174, 185–193, 200, 202, 210–212, 214, 215, 217, 219–222, 224, 225, 229, 235, 240, 241, 247, 249, 251, 252, 254, 257, 259–261, 264–266, 270, 272, 284, 296, 300–302

one, 1, 13–15, 18, 24, 50, 77, 81, 104, 140, 145, 147, 159, 161, 164, 168, 183, 187, 189, 192, 258, 295, 300, 306, 307
openness, 43, 188
opinion, 65, 89, 93, 101, 103, 106–108, 115, 116, 191, 230, 232, 240, 255, 259, 260, 264, 269–271, 292
opportunity, 16, 191, 237, 242, 253
opposition, 93, 263, 277, 279, 291
oppression, 5, 17, 50, 59, 75, 77, 80, 119, 186
order, 62, 260, 263, 266
organization, 120, 214, 298
organizing, 21, 53, 55, 72, 76, 109, 158, 174, 296
orientation, 1, 9, 11, 13, 14, 17, 24, 29, 31, 33, 34, 44, 63, 71, 90, 106, 121, 127, 148, 171, 188, 189, 191, 219, 252, 255, 258–261, 264, 266, 270, 298, 299, 301, 306
ostracism, 11, 16, 18, 62, 66, 75, 157, 223, 271, 277
ostracization, 2, 23
other, 17, 34, 43, 67, 90, 124, 142, 146, 186, 190, 192, 219, 225, 262, 276, 291, 297, 299
otherness, 274
out, 2, 4, 6, 10, 13, 15, 18, 20–22, 28, 127, 138, 174, 271, 301
outcome, 109
outcry, 256
outlet, 12
outrage, 224

outreach, 62, 255
outside, 303
overshadowing, 230
oversimplification, 106
overwhelm, 174

panic, 272
parade, 54
paradox, 111
part, 8, 24, 90, 190, 262, 264, 297
participation, 38, 148, 188, 200, 241, 249, 252, 296, 297
partnership, 55, 66, 90, 108, 157, 171, 203, 241
passion, 4, 6, 8, 145, 175, 179, 181, 281
past, 172, 208, 295
path, 8, 10, 12, 39, 67, 74, 125, 137, 186, 197, 213, 255, 260, 261, 269, 276, 286
pathway, 5, 7, 48, 288
pattern, 124
Paulo Freire's, 48
pedagogy, 48
peer, 28, 35, 146, 174
penalty, 32, 253, 254, 263
people, 55, 104, 202, 258
percentage, 298
perception, 10, 69, 75, 111, 197, 225, 233, 274
performance, 5, 29
peril, 123, 125
persecution, 21, 82, 124, 203, 253, 261, 262
perseverance, 274
persist, 26, 57, 81, 96, 101, 114, 120, 147, 189, 193, 207, 212, 214, 223, 245, 253, 254, 257, 288, 295

persistence, 214
person, 39, 168
perspective, 8, 94, 170, 178, 259
petition, 254
phenomenon, 22, 33, 227
philanthropic, 249
picture, 9
Pierre Bourdieu, 151
pillar, 43
place, 42, 297
planning, 54, 217, 225
platform, 5, 21, 37, 53, 54, 57, 59, 76, 109, 110, 112, 128, 184, 189, 225, 240, 242, 252, 253, 259
play, 20, 28, 56, 63, 65, 67, 83, 93, 105, 107, 111, 113, 121, 129, 132, 151, 161, 170, 230, 234, 240, 244, 251, 285, 289, 292
playing, 71
plight, 116, 132, 135, 200, 255
point, 132, 272
police, 68, 76, 131, 132
policy, 67, 84, 87, 101, 112, 116, 191, 197, 217, 219, 247, 256, 257, 260, 264, 266, 270, 271, 286–288, 291, 293, 299
pop, 235–237
populace, 270
population, 56, 237, 240, 272, 284
position, 61, 263
post, 299
potential, 6, 7, 13–15, 38, 44, 49, 56, 62, 66, 73, 75, 80, 81, 90, 99, 101–103, 106, 107, 110, 112, 113, 116, 128, 132, 147, 156, 157, 163,

171, 188, 190, 193, 202,
212, 215, 217, 221, 222,
230–234, 236, 238, 244,
249, 254, 257, 270, 271,
277, 279, 291, 293, 295
poverty, 148
power, 35, 42, 43, 50, 56, 91, 94,
101, 106, 107, 120, 121,
134, 145, 146, 154, 156,
169, 172, 187, 191, 196,
197, 201, 202, 205, 212,
215, 217, 219, 224, 229,
230, 235, 239, 242, 244,
249, 262, 263, 266, 270,
271, 279, 293–295
practice, 128, 195
precedent, 68
prejudice, 22, 87, 89, 253, 259, 302
presence, 1, 148
preservation, 9, 43
pressure, 15, 16, 65, 67, 89, 93,
108–110, 112, 115–117,
132, 190, 196, 220–222,
224, 252, 254–257, 261,
287, 301
prevalence, 104, 238, 241
prevention, 242
pride, 21, 53, 54, 171, 258
principle, 189
privacy, 38
privilege, 119, 185
problem, 56
process, 8, 10, 12, 13, 15, 19, 48, 84,
90, 129, 152, 164, 174,
180, 183, 291, 307
procreation, 1
professional, 29, 38, 48, 66, 129,
130, 140–142, 145, 146,
154–157, 159–161, 174,
175
progress, 31, 57, 89, 96, 104, 106,
120, 127, 184, 186, 190,
213, 223, 244, 253, 254,
260, 262, 263, 270, 273,
274, 276, 279, 288, 298,
300–302
proliferation, 247
prominence, 222
promise, 22, 306
promotion, 17, 24, 32, 111, 304
prosecution, 132
protection, 62, 130–132, 254, 255,
260, 300
protest, 76
provision, 68, 254
psychology, 188
public, 16, 19, 24, 62, 65, 67, 69, 75,
76, 84, 89, 93, 96, 101,
103, 106–108, 115, 116,
123, 142, 147–149, 191,
197, 225, 230, 233, 235,
237, 240, 249, 252, 255,
259–261, 263, 264, 266,
270–272, 288, 291, 292,
300
purpose, 171, 175, 212, 259
pursuit, 6, 48, 50, 61, 67, 125, 207,
279, 300

quality, 192, 202
queer, 273
quest, 7, 66, 91, 93, 94, 111, 138,
254, 262, 302
question, 251
quo, 69, 124, 132, 151, 252, 255
quorum, 68

race, 17, 105, 119, 148, 188, 192,

273
racism, 77
radio, 101
raising, 48, 55, 76, 93, 107, 147, 189, 222, 223, 240, 247, 249, 255
rally, 61
rallying, 132, 272
range, 42, 53
rapport, 291
re, 131, 270, 272
reach, 121, 148, 170, 225, 227, 235, 240, 242
reaction, 18, 50
reality, 6, 9, 60, 84, 123, 130, 261, 262, 293
realization, 7, 260, 300
realm, 29, 43, 55, 99, 106, 151, 156, 161, 170, 179, 187, 195, 203, 227, 230, 247, 293
reasoning, 264
recognition, 61, 66, 67, 70–72, 94, 130, 146, 151–153, 167, 168, 208, 254, 258–260, 263, 299
record, 76, 111, 254, 257
recourse, 62, 131, 263
reflection, 12, 24, 31, 142, 175, 178, 181, 182, 184, 267
reform, 24, 62, 63, 67, 190, 253–255, 261, 286–288, 299
refuge, 8, 42, 43, 80, 134, 283
reinforcement, 19, 106
reintroduction, 272
rejection, 2, 9, 11, 12, 14–16, 18, 19, 33, 37, 42, 62, 80, 168, 179, 254

relationship, 6, 87, 203, 259, 264, 269, 300
relevance, 120
reliance, 116
religion, 1, 17, 31–33, 263, 264, 272
relocation, 203
reluctance, 11, 29, 93, 157, 168, 231, 277
reminder, 22, 301
repeal, 191, 254
repercussion, 42
report, 123, 127, 131, 132, 241, 276
reporting, 202
representation, 4, 5, 16, 17, 19, 69, 70, 105, 131, 132, 233–235, 237, 303
representative, 79
repression, 23, 53, 75, 76, 93, 269
reprisal, 66
reputation, 16
research, 49, 211, 219, 249
resilience, 2, 4, 10, 12, 14, 15, 20, 22, 26, 36–39, 43, 45, 53, 58, 59, 63, 68, 69, 73, 74, 76, 79, 81, 84, 87, 111, 117, 124, 127–130, 132, 134, 135, 145–147, 153, 167, 169, 173, 184, 191, 196, 214, 217, 223, 225, 241, 260, 262–264, 274, 276, 281, 283, 288, 297, 298, 300, 302, 304, 307
resistance, 61, 63, 64, 66, 67, 81, 94, 110, 111, 116, 117, 132, 202, 214, 222, 252, 254, 257, 259, 267, 276, 287, 288
resolution, 191, 200, 219
resolve, 8, 146

resonance, 111
resource, 55, 63, 108, 192, 204–206, 210, 212, 223
respect, 56, 70, 71, 94, 109, 202, 203, 247, 262, 266, 283
response, 18, 116, 124, 148, 224, 254, 256
responsibility, 4, 304, 308
rest, 173, 178
result, 9, 25, 66, 75, 131, 252
retreat, 116
retribution, 18
rhetoric, 15, 23, 32, 61, 67, 92, 94, 96, 111, 254, 263, 270, 271, 275
right, 68, 75, 94, 130, 145, 262
rise, 39, 93, 158, 234, 252, 253, 263
risk, 21, 26, 44, 66, 75, 106, 127, 175, 188, 196, 229, 261
roadmap, 225
role, 2–4, 6, 8, 15, 16, 19, 20, 28, 31, 33, 34, 48, 53, 63, 65–67, 69, 70, 83, 93, 105, 107, 109, 111–113, 115, 117, 121, 132, 138, 146, 148, 151, 153, 161, 164, 170, 179, 185, 188, 191, 200, 206, 210, 220, 222, 223, 230, 233, 234, 240, 244, 251, 258, 260, 261, 264, 269, 270, 272, 284–286, 289, 292, 301, 302
room, 1
root, 17, 253
rule, 94
ruling, 68, 69

s, 1–15, 18, 19, 24, 32, 34, 35, 45, 48, 50, 72, 74, 76, 79, 80, 111, 112, 115, 116, 123, 126, 127, 131, 134, 140, 142, 147, 149, 152, 164, 175, 180, 183, 184, 187–190, 196, 200, 213, 214, 219, 224, 249, 254, 257, 263, 271, 299
safety, 24, 26, 35, 42, 53, 66, 80, 81, 107, 123, 124, 126, 130, 132, 147, 148, 188, 196, 203, 241, 260, 261
San Francisco, 54
sanctity, 264
sanctuary, 36
saying, 179
scale, 215, 217, 222, 249
scapegoat, 275
scapegoating, 275
scarcity, 168
school, 7, 28
schooling, 5
scope, 158, 299
scripture, 272
scrutiny, 76, 132, 142, 190, 255
sea, 271
secrecy, 23, 62, 258, 275
secret, 16
section, 15, 17, 22, 24, 29, 32, 34, 45, 57, 75, 87, 89, 94, 96, 101, 111, 113, 115, 128, 130, 132, 135, 138, 151, 154, 157, 159, 164, 167, 181, 189, 191, 195, 208, 225, 227, 237, 242, 247, 253, 258, 276, 279, 284, 286, 293, 296
sector, 157
security, 29, 62, 130–132, 275
self, 2–4, 7–13, 15, 17, 19, 22, 29,

33, 34, 37, 42, 43, 107,
128, 138, 143–145, 161,
173–175, 177–179, 181,
182, 184, 187, 196, 264,
294, 304, 306
seminar, 50
sensationalist, 24
sense, 1, 2, 4, 6–8, 10–12, 16, 19, 21,
22, 29, 34, 37, 44, 50, 69,
79–81, 108, 112, 158, 159,
161, 164, 167, 168, 170,
171, 174, 175, 182, 184,
201, 212, 240, 242, 245,
259, 263, 274, 276, 296
sentiment, 94, 261, 270–272, 275,
291
set, 8, 68, 135, 174
setting, 159, 161, 175
severity, 22
sex, 7, 23, 32, 62, 66, 68, 71, 75, 114,
131, 132, 242, 253, 260,
263, 270, 274, 299
sexuality, 1, 4, 13, 15, 18, 119, 188,
264, 266, 280
shame, 2, 7, 11, 33, 35, 258, 275
shaping, 2, 4–6, 10, 15, 20, 31, 36,
50, 79, 101, 106, 135, 154,
189, 206, 220, 223, 230,
233, 240, 244, 251, 253,
255, 258, 260, 264, 266,
270–272, 284, 286, 292
share, 21, 35, 36, 38, 39, 42, 50, 53,
66, 79, 81, 106, 112, 134,
147, 149, 156, 158, 168,
170, 174, 184, 187–189,
196, 197, 212, 237, 240,
253, 270, 281, 295, 302
sharing, 38, 43, 55, 107, 108, 120,
129, 146, 154, 156,
187–189, 192, 193, 196,
203–206, 252, 294–297
shield, 70
shift, 63, 93, 107, 225, 234, 244,
251–253, 258–260, 300
side, 161
siege, 113
significance, 34, 43, 55, 75, 138, 151,
170, 181, 195, 230, 237,
279
silence, 11, 123, 274
sin, 251, 272
situation, 56, 263, 267
SMUG, 21
society, 1–3, 5, 7, 10, 11, 15, 17, 18,
22, 24, 27, 29, 33, 34, 50,
53, 56, 60, 69, 79–82, 89,
93, 94, 105, 107, 108, 110,
124, 125, 142, 157, 159,
168, 186, 197, 202, 225,
232, 235, 237, 239, 242,
251, 253, 258, 261, 262,
266, 271, 272, 274, 286,
290, 293, 295, 298–300,
304, 306
socio, 5, 22, 29, 38, 94, 148, 171,
267
solace, 6, 8, 20, 43
solidarity, 2, 4, 18, 21, 22, 35–37,
39, 42–45, 53, 69, 79, 81,
84, 108, 111, 117,
119–121, 135, 147, 148,
158, 159, 164, 168, 170,
186, 188, 192, 203, 212,
223–225, 227, 240, 242,
259, 263, 273, 276, 279,
295, 296, 299, 301
source, 2, 18, 295
South Africa, 299

Index

sovereignty, 116, 190, 214
space, 4, 12, 22, 35, 43, 53, 81, 130, 146, 174, 237, 239, 258
speaker, 7
speaking, 107, 147–149
spectrum, 17, 19, 38
speech, 129, 200, 238, 241, 244, 246, 247
sphere, 249
spirit, 125, 274, 276
spotlight, 117
spread, 242, 244
sprint, 184
stage, 8, 109, 189, 200, 219
stance, 10, 111, 115, 212, 251
stand, 76, 219
standing, 5, 132
state, 26, 117, 175
statement, 59, 127
status, 5, 17, 29, 69, 124, 132, 151, 252, 255
step, 13, 39, 53, 127, 174, 186, 260, 291, 302
stereotype, 104
stigma, 5, 21, 23, 26, 29, 33, 35, 36, 43–45, 51, 68, 79, 80, 83, 94, 96, 104, 120, 127, 131, 132, 157, 207, 223, 240, 251, 254, 263, 270, 277, 279, 288, 294, 301
stigmatization, 1, 61, 264
story, 7, 10, 42, 50, 74, 134, 187–189, 201, 295
storytelling, 87, 106–108, 188, 189, 195–197, 201, 233, 235, 293–295, 299, 304, 308
strain, 62
strategy, 14, 43, 66, 75, 84, 101, 106, 108, 110, 129, 131, 189, 240, 262, 290
streaming, 234
strength, 19, 22, 26, 35, 39, 57, 79, 121, 125, 172, 186, 200, 207, 232, 276
stress, 127, 175, 179–181, 185
structure, 1, 38
struggle, 2, 4, 5, 7, 10, 15, 20, 24, 35, 38, 57, 63, 69, 70, 76, 80, 84, 87, 90, 93, 94, 98, 107, 111, 113, 117, 128, 130, 149, 168, 184, 190, 196, 211, 212, 217, 222, 230, 252, 260, 262, 266, 274, 288, 293, 295, 298
student, 5, 50
study, 72
subsection, 13, 20, 27, 43, 61, 68, 99, 119, 125, 140, 145, 215, 220, 222, 225, 230, 255, 264, 267, 288
success, 5, 7, 132, 161, 299
suggestion, 177
suit, 262
sum, 180
summary, 2, 50, 63, 94, 96, 146
summit, 148
support, 1, 2, 8, 14, 15, 17–22, 24, 28, 32, 33, 35–39, 42, 43, 45–47, 49–51, 57, 61, 62, 69, 72, 76, 79–81, 83, 87, 92–94, 96, 99, 101, 110–113, 116, 117, 127, 130–132, 135, 138, 142, 145, 146, 149, 158, 161, 164–169, 174, 175, 179–181, 186, 188, 191, 200, 202, 206, 207, 211, 219, 223, 240–242, 247,

252, 255, 259–262, 270, 272, 275–277, 281, 287, 288, 296, 301, 306
surrounding, 5, 11, 15, 21, 35, 44, 68, 75, 83, 104, 129, 157, 219, 251, 258, 270, 272, 277, 301
surveillance, 43
survival, 272
sustainability, 173, 181, 277, 281
sustenance, 145
sway, 271
sword, 4
system, 5, 6, 45, 46, 67, 68, 254, 262

table, 171
tabloid, 24
taboo, 61, 190, 271, 280
tapestry, 1, 3, 262, 285
target, 116
task, 89, 271, 275
teacher, 6
technicality, 23, 61, 116
technique, 178
technology, 171, 222, 290, 298
television, 101, 235
tension, 2, 6, 90, 120, 171, 294
term, 116, 178, 179, 184, 295, 296, 298
testament, 22, 111, 125, 172, 186, 260, 262, 276
the Middle East, 207
the United States, 112, 116
theory, 8, 17, 29, 53, 77, 106, 119, 120, 159, 161, 164, 170, 171, 187, 192, 197, 201, 204, 215, 219, 220
therapist, 174
therapy, 129

thinking, 5, 48
thirst, 5
threat, 2, 7, 20, 42, 53, 66, 113, 125, 188, 263, 271, 277, 297
tide, 266
time, 7, 69, 127, 158, 173, 178, 189, 191, 237, 257, 295
timeframe, 298
today, 75
toll, 5, 125, 127, 174, 185, 238
tool, 4, 7, 12, 23, 35, 45, 48, 91, 96, 99, 106, 108, 117, 170, 182, 187, 225, 237, 249, 252, 284, 293
torch, 149, 260, 307, 308
traction, 242, 252, 263
tradition, 262
training, 42, 66, 109, 158, 170, 273, 285
trajectory, 253
trans, 171
transformation, 7, 55, 258
transgender, 38, 55, 104, 273
transnationalism, 119
transparency, 263
transphobia, 131
transportation, 106
treatment, 5, 132
trend, 227, 258, 259
trepidation, 9
trust, 80, 84, 131, 192
truth, 15
turmoil, 10, 18
turn, 16, 128

U.S., 93, 116, 257
Uganda, 1–12, 15–18, 20–24, 26, 27, 29–34, 36, 42–44, 48–51, 53, 55–59, 61–63,

Index 335

66–69, 72–76, 79–81,
83–87, 89–92, 94, 96,
106–109, 111–114, 116,
117, 123–127, 130–133,
135, 140, 146–149,
151–153, 157, 159,
167–169, 177, 184,
187–191, 196, 197, 200,
203, 207, 211, 213,
219–224, 237–240, 242,
251–255, 257–272,
274–277, 279, 281,
286–288, 290, 291,
293–296, 298–302
Ugandan, 89, 251, 261
uncertainty, 24
underpinning, 96
understanding, 1–3, 5–8, 15, 20, 33,
50, 51, 53, 55, 66, 77, 79,
81, 83, 84, 87, 91, 93, 94,
96, 104–106, 110, 112,
119, 129, 137, 142, 156,
168, 171, 186–190, 192,
196, 201, 217, 232, 235,
237, 242, 244, 252, 259,
272, 283–286, 293, 296,
298, 300–304
unit, 1, 18
unity, 55, 81, 172, 210, 259
university, 6
upbringing, 1
urgency, 8, 16, 29, 112
use, 15, 21, 101, 106, 132, 148, 149,
234, 244, 249, 272, 296
utilization, 99

vacuum, 17, 119
validation, 128, 174
value, 170
variety, 190, 223
vehicle, 235
viability, 42
victim, 132
victory, 68, 69, 254, 260, 300, 301
view, 15, 51, 61, 62, 75, 116, 171,
190, 251, 254, 271, 274
vigor, 172
violence, 8, 20, 21, 23–26, 35, 38,
44, 54, 62, 68, 71, 75, 76,
80, 81, 93, 107, 114, 120,
123, 124, 126, 127,
130–132, 157, 180, 185,
188, 191, 196, 207, 213,
219, 223, 237, 244, 253,
260, 263, 271, 275, 294,
297, 299
virtue, 56, 304
visa, 116
visibility, 10, 19–22, 29, 53, 55, 56,
67, 69, 70, 75, 76, 93, 117,
153, 154, 188, 191, 197,
202, 211, 225, 227, 230,
232, 237, 239, 251, 252,
254, 258, 260, 261, 270,
271, 296, 300, 307, 308
vision, 6, 35, 60, 69, 84, 121, 147,
206, 262, 293, 298, 300
voice, 5, 35, 50, 109, 146, 149, 244,
295, 296, 306
void, 5
voter, 87
vulnerability, 107, 263

warrant, 300
wave, 7, 281, 308
way, 20, 53, 106, 124, 189, 232, 235,
242, 258, 266, 271, 286,
288, 295, 300, 308

wealth, 202
weaving, 106
web, 15, 206
weight, 143, 178, 179
well, 7, 10, 16, 17, 29, 33, 35, 39, 43, 56, 57, 70, 72, 80, 81, 107, 113, 130, 144, 145, 174, 175, 179–181, 185, 206, 240, 261
wellness, 143, 145
whole, 29, 260
will, 13, 20, 32, 57, 66, 76, 79, 81, 89, 91, 94, 96, 101, 103, 108, 121, 125, 130, 135, 145, 154, 156, 169, 181, 186, 193, 205, 215, 217, 227, 230, 242, 244, 253, 255, 262, 267, 279, 295, 297, 308
willingness, 116, 254
wisdom, 172

word, 21
work, 2, 4, 6–8, 45, 48, 53, 62, 66, 110, 127, 130, 132, 142, 149, 151, 156, 161, 173–175, 178–180, 202–204, 213, 214, 219, 240, 260, 271, 274, 288, 294, 301
workforce, 31
workplace, 31, 260
world, 3, 8, 9, 16, 71, 94, 111, 120, 121, 125, 145, 170, 177, 189, 192, 193, 207, 210, 212, 222, 225, 247, 249, 253, 264, 279, 304, 306
worth, 2, 182, 301
writing, 49

youth, 4, 6, 164, 165, 169, 170, 172, 279–281, 296, 300
Yoweri Museveni, 23, 61